The Chinese Grammar Wiki

BOOK:

Intermediate (B1)

The Chinese Grammar Wiki BOOK:

Intermediate (B1)

Editor-in-Chief John Pasden

Foreword by Dr. David Moser

SHANGHAI

Published by AllSet Learning, Shanghai, China.

For information about educational or bulk purchases, please contact AllSet Learning at sales@allsetlearning.com.

1st print edition, 2018.

Paperback ISBN: 978-1-941875-35-3
eBook ISBN: 978-1-941875-36-0
ASID: 20181208T230043

For my parents, who taught me
the power of knowledge
and the value of persistence.

And for all the learners struggling
on the "Intermediate Plateau."
Have faith you're progressing,
and just keep pushing forward.

Table of Contents

B1 Grammar Points: Grammatical Structures

Complements

Foreword

Learning Chinese used to be a frustratingly "front-loaded" endeavor. One had to first learn pinyin, the four tones, how to write thousands of characters with the correct stroke order, how to use the 214 radicals to look up unfamiliar characters in a dictionary, and, of course, how to limn the mysterious principles of Chinese grammar. This process entailed inordinate sacrifices of eyesight, friends, and years of precious life spent "learning to learn Chinese," before the hapless student could be weaned from a diet of pre-digested pabulum and delve into the messy, glorious world of real texts.

The Chinese Grammar Wiki is on the cutting edge of a growing arsenal of digital and web resources that have made this front-loaded Sisyphean nightmare a thing of the past. This very cool tool, developed by John Pasden and the folks at AllSet Learning, is in accordance with the new "learning grammar as you go" principle of Chinese study in the digital age. Learners can now boldly embark on the ocean of Chinese very early on, with navigational tools like the Grammar Wiki to reduce the risk of getting lost at sea. For the intrepid, motivated learner, studying Chinese can now be an adventure, instead of a five-year stint in solitary confinement. And from the very outset, students can begin to move toward the goal that was formerly so elusive: the acquisition of 语感 (yǔgǎn), the "feeling for the language."

In my opinion, the Chinese Grammar Wiki has at least three very strong characteristics:

Modularity. This is a long-standing commonsense feature of website design, but it's absolutely crucial for a grammar tool like this. The Wiki has conveniently carved up Chinese grammar into useful modular chunks with the beginner in mind, so that searching for a structure or topic is intuitive, quick, and yields a clear explanation that enables the user to forge ahead, enlightened and empowered. The structure and site map is user-friendly at every level, which means that the Wiki can be easily "plugged in" to existing Chinese syllabi, or simply employed by the student independently to explore texts and materials outside of class.

Interlinking. The Wiki is structured so that alongside the grammar points on most pages there are helpful links to related or similar grammar points within the Wiki. For example, in exploring the grammatical points for 比 (bǐ) involving comparison, you will find explanations of the basic 比 (bǐ) structure, examples, and common errors, but in addition you will also see links to other "comparison" structures using 没有 (méiyǒu). This interlinking feature gives the user a fuller picture of various grammatical structures that serve similar functions in the language.

Universality. One of the strongest points of the Chinese Grammar Wiki is that the grammatical explanations have been tailored so as to contain the right amount of information, at the right level of specificity and complexity for the majority of learners. Designing a grammar resource with such wide applicability is not an easy task, requiring not only technical know-how and careful thinking, but also a strong intuitive sense of what the average student needs to know. Linguist Edward Sapir said "all grammars leak," and this mutable, watery quality of language means that no grammatical framework is going to contain only tidy, airtight rules that cover every situation. In explanations, there is always a tradeoff between succinct simplicity and the real-life complexity, and the Wiki does an admirable job of striking a satisfying balance between these two yin-yang poles.

Being digital in nature, the Chinese Grammar Wiki is very much a work in progress, and the designers always welcome input and suggestions. Product development is always an interactive process, and the more people use the resource, the more useful it will become. I encourage Chinese students at all levels – and even Chinese teachers – to check it out and discover what the reference tools of the 21st century will look like.

No matter what well-meaning pedagogical Pollyannas might tell you, Chinese is still "damn hard." Thankfully, there now are digital resources like the Chinese Grammar Wiki, which goes a long way to making the struggle easier.

David Moser
Academic Director, CET Beijing Chinese Studies
Beijing Capital Normal University

Introduction

The **Chinese Grammar Wiki** began life as an Excel spreadsheet full of grammar points organized by difficulty level. This list was needed to track the progress of AllSet Learning's clients and to design personalized grammar practice where it was most needed. But as the lists continued to grow and evolve, it quickly became apparent that it made sense to put the grammar points online, so that the newest version would always be front and center. For ease of editing, what could be better than a wiki? And if AllSet Learning teachers were to have access, why not open up access to *all learners*? The Chinese Grammar Wiki was developed internally for about a year before becoming public in January of 2012. Since then, it has grown tremendously, both in content and in traffic.

Probably the most important feature of the Chinese Grammar Wiki, which has always been kept at the forefront of its development, is its focus on learner level. An absolute beginner can't absorb a multitude of uses for every grammar point she encounters, and she shouldn't be expected to. And she certainly shouldn't be given frustratingly difficult example sentences when trying to grasp the most basic grammar concepts. That's why example sentences on the Chinese Grammar Wiki are plentiful, but relentlessly edited to be level-appropriate. And for the learners that can't get enough, relevant articles of all levels are always just a link away. Although the wiki aims to be 100% comprehensive, it's no coincidence that there are fewer A1 grammar points than A2 grammar points, and fewer A2 grammar points than B1 grammar points. Considerable thought and care has gone into curating and pruning the lists of grammar points.

The Chinese Grammar Wiki is not a Chinese course. Rather, it is a companion resource that can complement any Chinese class. Don't expect to read it from start to finish, or to go through the grammar point lists from top to bottom. But do expect to come back often. And expect to get sucked into the curiously logical world of Chinese grammar.

John Pasden
Editor-in-Chief and CEO
AllSet Learning, Shanghai, China

Adjectives with "-ji le" (B1)

Just as 死了 (sǐle) can be used to intensify negative adjectives, 极了 (jíle) is a somewhat less common way to intensify both positive and negative adjectives. It is used in spoken, colloquial Chinese. 极 (jí) means "extreme" or "utmost."

Structure

This structure is technically a kind of degree complement[1] and one of the few that you can use after the adjective and without adding a 得 (de). Remember to add the 了 (le), since it would be incorrect without it.

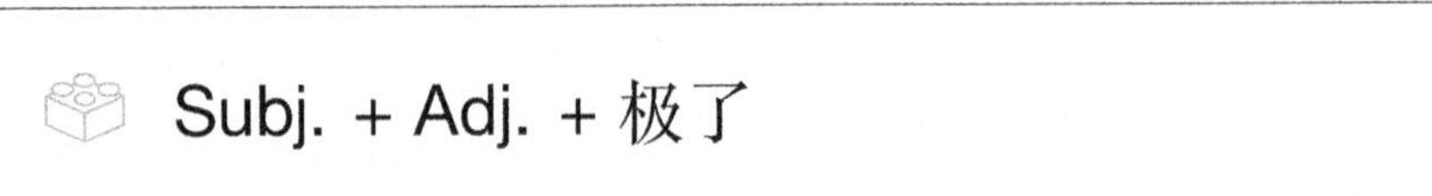

Examples

Some examples with a positive connotation:

- 这个主意好 极了 。
  Zhège zhǔyi hǎo jíle.
  This idea is perfect.
- 味道好 极了 ！
  Wèidào hǎo jíle!
  The taste is perfect!
- 他的英文棒 极了 。
  Tā de Yīngwén bàng jíle.
  His English is perfect.
- 婚礼热闹 极了 。
  Hūnlǐ rènao jíle.
  The wedding was very lively.
- 一点声音都没有，安静 极了 。
  Yīdiǎn shēngyīn dōu méiyǒu, ānjìng jíle.
  There is no sound at all. It's extremely quiet.

Some examples with a negative connotation:

1. Degree complement (B1), page 206

- 昨天的派对无聊 极了 ！
  Zuótiān de pàiduì wúliáo jíle!
  Yesterday's party was so boring!
- 他那么生气，我们都害怕 极了 。
  Tā nàme shēngqì, wǒmen dōu hàipà jíle.
  He was so angry. We were all so scared.
- 高考那天，我紧张 极了 。
  Gāokǎo nà tiān, wǒ jǐnzhāng jíle.
  I was super nervous the day I took the college entrance examination.
- 这件事让我们都尴尬 极了 。
  Zhè jiàn shì ràng wǒmen dōu gāngà jíle.
  This incident made us all extremely embarrassed.
- 那个男孩讨厌 极了 ！
  Nàge nánhái tǎoyàn jíle!
  That boy is super annoying!

Similar to

- Expressing "excessively" with "tai" (A1)
- Expressing "really" with "zhen" (A2)
- Intensifying with "duo" (A2)
- Negative adjectives with "-si le" (A2)
- Special verbs with "hen" (A2)
- Superlative "zui" (A2)
- Adjectives with "name" and "zheme" (B1), page 83
- Degree complement (B1), page 206
- Expressing "quite" with "ting" (B1), page 85
- Adjectival complement "de budeliao" (B2)
- Adjectival complement "de hen" (B2)
- Advanced degree complements (B2)
- Complement "-huai le" (B2)

Expressing "not very" with "bu zenme" (B1)

When you use 不怎么 (bù zěnme) before an adjective, it means "not very." You might use it to say something like "not very good."

Structure

When used together with an adjective, 不怎么 becomes similar to 不太, which means that the degree of the adjective is not very high.

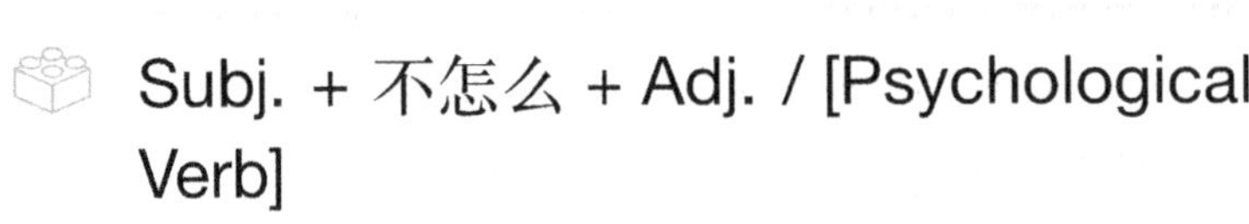

Subj. + 不怎么 + Adj. / [Psychological Verb]

Using this grammar structure is a way to indirectly or mildly state something. Instead of saying 他不聪明 (tā bù cōngming) you can say 他不怎么聪明 (tā bù zěnme cōngming), turning a very direct statement to a milder, more inoffensive comment.

Examples

- 最近 不怎么 忙。
  Zuìjìn bù zěnme máng.
  It hasn't been very busy lately.
- 这里的冬天 不怎么 冷。
  Zhèlǐ de dōngtiān bù zěnme lěng.
  It's not very cold here in winter.
- 他们好像 不怎么 高兴。
  Tāmen hǎoxiàng bù zěnme gāoxìng.
  They don't seem to be very happy.
- 这个学生 不怎么 努力。
  Zhège xuéshēng bù zěnme nǔlì.
  This student isn't very hard-working.
- 那家餐厅 不怎么 干净。
  Nà jiā cāntīng bù zěnme gānjìng.
  That restaurant isn't very clean.
- 这个老师 不怎么 专业。
  Zhège lǎoshī bù zěnme zhuānyè.
  This teacher isn't very professional.

- 你是不是昨天睡得 不怎么 好?
  Nǐ shì bu shì zuótiān shuì de bù zěnme hǎo?
  Did you not sleep very well last night?
- 我 不怎么 喜欢咖啡。
  Wǒ bù zěnme xǐhuan kāfēi.
  I'm not very into coffee.
- 他跟他父母长得 不怎么 像。
  Tā gēn tā fùmǔ zhǎng de bù zěnme xiàng.
  He and his parents don't look very much alike.
- 他去美国一年多了，不过 不怎么 想家。
  Tā qù Měiguó yì nián duō le, búguò bù zěnme xiǎngjiā.
  He's been in the USA for more than one year, but he's not very homesick.

Remember that to make 不怎么 mean "not very" you need to use it with an *adjective*. Using it with a verb will give it the meaning of "not often."

Similar to

- Asking why with "zenme" (A2)
- Expressing "not often" with "bu zenme" (B1), page 185

Indicating the whole with "quan" (B1)

One of the uses of 全 (quán) is to indicate the entirety of something. It could be used for something like a *whole* household, an *entire* country, the *whole* world, etc.

Used before Noun

Structure

Simply put 全 in front of the noun you want to emphasize "the whole" of. You cannot use it with 的. Pay attention to the types of nouns you can use with 全, since it is usually paired up with 身 (body), 家 (family), 国 (country), 世界 (world), 天 (day) and the like.

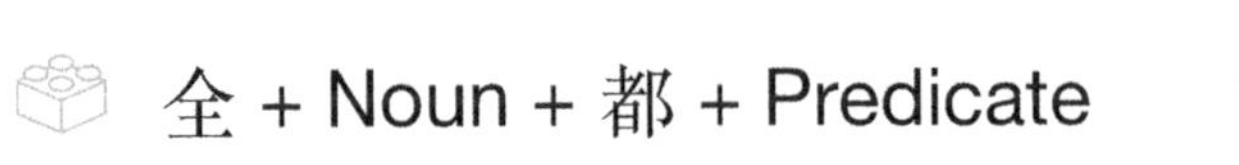

全 + Noun + 都 + Predicate

The predicate part of the pattern can be a verb or an adjective.

Examples

- 我们 全 家 都 去过北京。
  Wǒmen quán jiā dōu qù guo Běijīng.
  Our entire family has been to Beijing.
- 全 公司的人 都 不喜欢新老板。
  Quán gōngsī de rén dōu bù xǐhuan xīn lǎobǎn.
  The whole company doesn't like the new boss.
- 运动完以后我 全 身 都 是汗。
  Yùndòng wán yǐhòu wǒ quán shēn dōu shì hàn.
  My whole body was sweaty after I finished exercising.
- 全 校 都 放假了。
  Quán xiào dōu fàngjià le.
  The whole school is on break.
- 这个地方 全 年 都 很热。
  Zhège dìfang quán nián dōu hěn rè.
  This place is hot all year round.

Used before Predicate

Affirmative Form

Before a verb 全 can be omitted, but if it is used, the purpose is to emphasize the idea of "all" or "entire."

Structure

Subj. + 全都 + Predicate

Examples

- 大家 全 都 到了。

  Dàjiā quán dōu dào le.

  Everybody has arrived.

- 奶奶的头发 全 都 白了。

  Nǎinai de tóufà quán dōu bái le.

  All of grandma's hair has turned white.

- 我妈妈做的菜 全 都 好吃。

  Wǒ māma zuò de cài quán dōu hǎochī.

  All of the food that my mother makes is tasty.

- 作业 全 都 做完了吗?

  Zuòyè quán dōu zuò wán le ma?

  Have you finished all your homework?

- 你 全 都 拿走吧。

  Nǐ quán dōu názǒu ba.

  Take them all.

Negative Form: Total Negation

Structure

When you negate 全都 with 不 or 没 *after* it, you're not just saying "not entirely," you're saying "*none of it*" or "*not at all*."

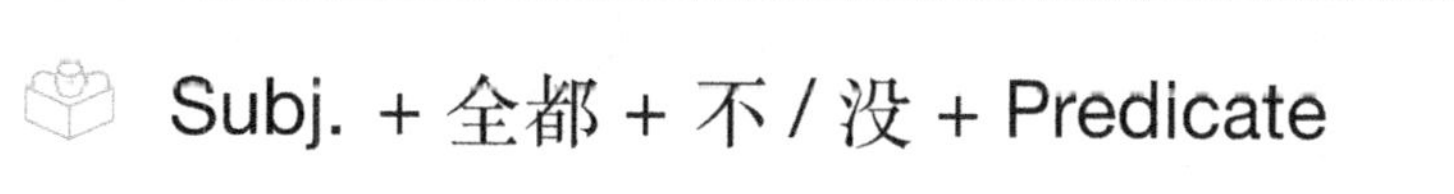
Subj. + 全都 + 不 / 没 + Predicate

Examples

- 他们 全 都 没去。

  Tāmen quán dōu méi qù.

  None of them went.

- 这个周末我们 全 都 不在家。
  Zhège zhōumò wǒmen quán dōu bú zài jiā.
  None of us will be home this weekend.
- 你们 全 都 不怕吗?
  Nǐmen quán dōu bú pà ma?
  Are none of you afraid?
- 这些菜 全 都 没熟。
  Zhèxiē cài quán dōu méi shú.
  None of these dishes is fully cooked.
- 他的话我 全 都 不相信。
  Tā de huà wǒ quán dōu bù xiāngxìn.
  I don't believe anything he says.

Negative Pattern: Partial Negation

Structure

When you negate by putting 不 or 没 *before* 全都, you're only *partially* negating. In other words, you're communicating "*not all*."

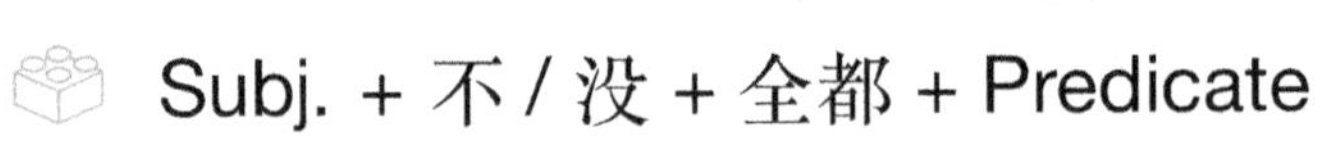
Subj. + 不 / 没 + 全都 + Predicate

Examples

- 他说得有道理，但我不 全 都 同意。
  Tā shuō de yǒu dàolǐ, dàn wǒ bù quán dōu tóngyì.
  He has a point, but I don't agree with all of it.
- 菜太多了，我们没 全 都 吃完。
  Cài tài duō le, wǒmen méi quán dōu chī wán.
  The food was too much. We didn't finish eating it all.
- 昨天作业太多了，我没 全 都 做完。
  Zuótiān zuòyè tài duō le, wǒ méi quán dōu zuò wán.
  I had too much homework yesterday. I didn't finish doing it all.
- 我的家人没 全 都 来参加我的婚礼。
  Wǒ de jiārén méi quán dōu lái cānjiā wǒ de hūnlǐ.
  Not all of my family came to my wedding.

- 你说得太快了，我没 全 都 记下来。
  Nǐ shuō de tài kuài le, wǒ méi quán dōu jì xiàlái.
  You spoke too fast. I didn't write down all of what you said.

Similar to

- Expressing “all” with “suoyou” (B1), page 232
- Expressing “double negation” (B1), page 268
- Expressing “less than” with “budao” (B1), page 143
- Expressing “no exception” with “yilu” (C1)

Reduplication of adjectives (B1)

One of the charming features of Chinese is reduplication (repeating, or doubling up) of certain words and characters, including adjectives. Reduplication can enhance the descriptive feeling of an adjective.

One-Syllable Adjectives (AA)

If an adjective is only one syllable (one character), then reduplicating it is a no-brainer. The only tricky part about this pattern is that not all adjectives can be reduplicated in natural speech. It's mostly for adjectives that describe the physical world: colors, sizes, shapes, and other physical descriptors.

Structure

Adj. + Adj. + 的 (+ Noun)

In most Chinese textbooks and grammar books, this is known as the "AA" pattern. We'll be using this form more extensively below:

A A + 的 (+ Noun)

Note that this pattern is also identical to single-syllable reduplication of verbs.

Examples

- 你的脸 红红的 。
  Nǐ de liǎn hóng hóng de.
  Your face is red.
- 宝宝的眼睛 大大的 。
  Bǎobao de yǎnjīng dà dà de.
  The baby's eyes are big.
- 今晚的月亮 圆圆的 。
  Jīnwǎn de yuèliàng yuán yuán de.
  The moon is round tonight.
- 她爸爸 高高胖胖的 。
  Tā bàba gāo gāo pàng pàng de.
  Her father is tall and fat.

- 我妹妹 瘦瘦小小的 。

  Wǒ mèimei shòu shòu xiǎo xiǎo de.

  My little sister is thin and small.

Two-Syllable Adjectives (AABB)

If the adjective has more than one character, then you should repeat each character individually (rather than the whole word). This is known as the "AABB" pattern.

Structure

In the structure below, the original two-character adjective (such as 高兴, 漂亮) is "AB," where the first character of the adjective is represented by "A," and the second by "B."

Examples

Not all two-syllable adjectives are used in AABB form, but here are some common examples of AB adjectives represented in AABB form.

- 高兴→ 高高兴兴

  gāoxìng → gāogāo-xìngxìng

  happy

- 热闹→ 热热闹闹

  rènao → rèrè-nāonāo

  noisy, boisterous

- 漂亮→ 漂漂亮亮

  piàoliang → piàopiào-liāngliāng

  pretty

- 舒服→ 舒舒服服

  shūfu → shūshū-fūfū

  comfortable

- 安静→ 安安静静

  ānjìng → ānān-jìngjìng

  quiet and still

Not all adjectives can take AABB form. Here are some examples of common adjectives that don't work in AABB form.

✘ 好吃→ 好好吃吃

hǎochī → hǎohǎo-chīchī

tasty

✘ 便宜→ 便便宜宜

piányi → piánpián-yíyí

cheap

✘ 麻烦→ 麻麻烦烦

máfan → mámá-fánfán

bothersome

Used as Adverbs (AABB)

When adjectives are used as adverbs to modify verbs, you can reduplicate the adjective using the AABB pattern.

Structure

AABB + 地 + Verb

Note: The "AABB" pattern for reduplication of two-syllable adjectives contrasts with the "ABAB" pattern for reduplication of two-syllable verbs.

Examples

- 我们 清清楚楚 地 看到他跟一个胖胖的男人上车了。

  Wǒmen qīngqīng-chǔchǔ de kàndào tā gēn yīgè pàng pàng de nánrén shàngchē le.

  We clearly saw him get in the car with a fat man.

- 我真想 舒舒服服 地 躺在沙发上看电视。

  Wǒ zhēn xiǎng shūshū-fūfū de tǎng zài shāfā shàng kàn diànshì.

  I'd really like to comfortably lie on the couch and watch TV.

- 你妈妈 辛辛苦苦 地 做了两个小时的饭，你怎么不吃?

  Nǐ māma xīnxīn-kǔkǔ de zuò le liǎng gè xiǎoshí de fàn, nǐ zěnme bù chī?

  Your mother labored over this meal for two hours, and you aren't going to eat it?

Used as Predicates (ABAB)

If you use an adjective as a predicate, then you're basically using the adjective like a verb, and you reduplicate it as you would a verb, which means ABAB form. Using an adjective in this way is roughly equivalent to using 一下 after the (non-reduplicated) adjective.

Structure

To use a reduplicated adjective as a predicate, follow this structure:

Subj. + ABAB

or

Subj. + AB + 一下

In the pattern above there's no verb because when an adjective serves as the predicate, it does the job of a verb. Notice also that there's no 的 after the ABAB, because 的 is used when modifying nouns.

Examples

- 妹妹快过生日了，我打算给她办一个生日派对，热闹热闹。
  Mèimei kuài guò shēngrì le, wǒ dǎsuàn gěi tā bàn yī gè shēngrì pàiduì, rènao rènao.
  My little sister's birthday is coming and I plan to throw her a birthday party and have a blast.
- 来，喝点酒，高兴高兴。
  Lái, hē diǎn jiǔ, gāoxìng gāoxìng.
  Come on, have a little wine and enjoy yourself.
- 到这里来凉快凉快。
  Dào zhèlǐ lái liángkuai liángkuai.
  Come over here and cool off.
- 我想去外面走走，安静一下。
  Wǒ xiǎng qù wàimiàn zǒuzou, ānjìng yīxià.
  I'd like to take a walk outside, get some quiet time.
- 想不想去做个按摩，放松一下。
  Xiǎng bu xiǎng qù zuò gè ànmó, fàngsōng yīxià.
  Would you like to go get a massage and unwind?

Similar to

- Simple "noun + adjective" sentences (A1)
- Reduplication of verbs (A2)

Turning adjectives into adverbs (B1)

You can easily convert most Chinese adjectives into adverbs with the particle 地 (de). This usage is very similar to the suffix *-ly* in English.

Structure

In Chinese, we place the structural particle 地 (de) after the adjective to make it function as an adverb.

Subj. + Adj. + 地 + Verb

Examples

- 你要 努力 地 学习。
  Nǐ yào nǔlì de xuéxí.
  You must study hard.
- 雨天地滑，慢慢 地 走。
  Yǔtiān dì huá, màn màn de zǒu.
  The floor is very slippery on rainy days. Walk slowly.
- 他 顺利 地 通过考试了。
  tā shùnlì de tōngguò kǎoshì le.
  He passed the exam successfully.
- 他 认真 地 对我说：“我喜欢你。”
  Tā rènzhēn de duì wǒ shuō: “wǒ xǐhuan nǐ.”
  In all seriousness, he said to me: "I like you."
- 他 热情 地 拥抱了我。
  Tā rèqíng de yōngbào le wǒ.
  He gave me a very warm embrace.
- 她 激动 地 对我说“谢谢”。
  Tā jīdòng de duì wǒ shuō “xièxie.”
  She said "thank you" to me excitedly.
- 老师 生气 地 看着我们。
  Lǎoshī shēngqì de kàn zhe wǒmen.
  The teacher is looking at us angrily.

- 孩子们 开心 地 唱了起来。
  Háizi men kāixīn de chàng le qǐlai.
  The children started to sing happily.
- 大家都在教室里 安安静静 地 看书。
  Dàjiā dōu zài jiàoshì lǐ ānān-jìngjìng de kàn shū.
  Everybody is reading quietly in the classroom.
- 我希望你 快快乐乐 地 长大。
  Wǒ xīwàng nǐ kuàikuài-lèlè de zhǎngdà.
  I hope that you grow up happily.

Similar to

- Modifying nouns with adjective + "de" (A2)

Coincidence with "zhenghao" (B1)

正好 (zhènghǎo) can be used as an adjective or adverb to help express a coincidence, and it could be related to time, size, volume, quantity, degree, etc. In English we might say something similar like, "oh, this shirt you gave me just happens to be in my favorite color."

Used as "happen to be"

You can also use 正好 to mean "happen to be."

Structure

 Subj. + 正好 + [Verb Phrase]

Examples

- 我 正好 要出去，垃圾我来扔吧。
  Wǒ zhènghǎo yào chūqù, lājī wǒ lái rēng ba.
  I'm just about to leave. I'll take out the trash.
- 你来了！我 正好 要找你。
  Nǐ lái le! Wǒ zhènghǎo yào zhǎo nǐ.
  You are here! I was just looking for you.
- 他 正好 问了我想问的问题。
  Tā zhènghǎo wèn le wǒ xiǎng wèn de wèntí.
  He happened to ask the question that I wanted to ask.
- 我 正好 也在这里实习。
  Wǒ zhènghǎo yě zài zhèlǐ shíxí.
  I happen to be interning here too.
- 正好 你们都是单身。
  Zhènghǎo nǐmen dōu shì dānshēn.
  You both happen to be single.
- 我明天见他，正好 可以问问他这件事。
  Wǒ míngtiān jiàn tā, zhènghǎo kěyǐ wènwen tā zhè jiàn shì.
  I'm going to meet with him tomorrow. I can just ask him about this matter.
- 我们 正好 也要去那儿，一起走吧。
  Wǒmen zhènghǎo yě yào qù nàr, yīqǐ zǒu ba.
  We just happen to be going there. Let's go together.

- 我敲门的时候，他 正好 出门。
  Wǒ qiāo mén de shíhou, tā zhènghǎo chūmén.
  He just happened to be leaving the house while I was knocking at the door.

Used as "just right"

You can also use 正好 by itself to mean "just right" or "just enough."

Examples of that usage:

- 这件衣服的大小 正好 。
  Zhè jiàn yīfu de dà xiǎo zhènghǎo.
  The size of these clothes is just right.
- 水温 正好 ，不冷也不热。
  Shuǐwēn zhènghǎo, bù lěng yě bù rè.
  The temperature of the water is perfect, not too cold, not too hot.

Continuation with "hai" (B1)

Although 还 (hái) has many meanings, the basic meaning of "still" to indicate a continuing action is essential to mastery of the word.

Affirmative Form

Usage of 还在

Often the auxiliary verb 在 (zài) will appear with 还 (hái), as it is natural to talk about *continuous* actions that are *still* happening.

Structure

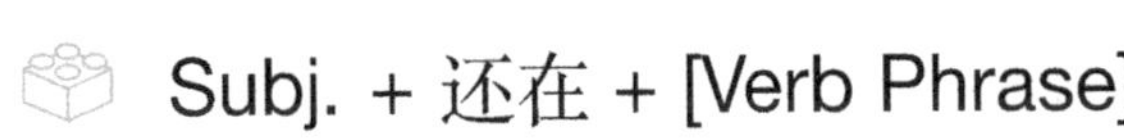

Examples

- 这件事情我 还在 考虑。
  Zhè jiàn shìqing wǒ hái zài kǎolǜ.
  I am still thinking over this matter.
- 已经中午了，他 还在 睡？
  Yǐjīng zhōngwǔ le, tā hái zài shuì?
  It's already noon and he's still sleeping?
- 她 还在 生气吗？
  Tā hái zài shēngqì ma?
  Is she still mad?
- 你怎么 还在 用那个旧手机？
  Nǐ zěnme hái zài yòng nàge jiù shǒujī?
  How come you're still using that old cell phone?
- 你 还在 玩游戏？明天不是有考试吗？
  Nǐ hái zài wán yóuxì? Míngtiān bù shì yǒu kǎoshì ma?
  You're still playing video games? Don't you have an exam tomorrow?

Usage of 还是

Here 还是 (háishì)–not literally "still is"–indicates what happened or will happen, *despite* the situation. The 是 (shì) here doesn't have a clear meaning here independent of 还 (hái).

Structure

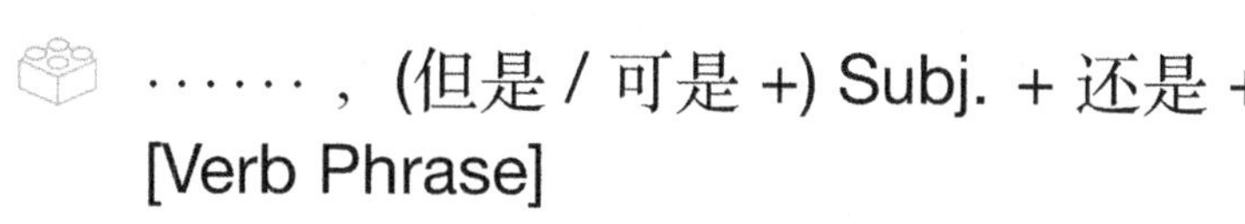
……，(但是 / 可是 +) Subj. + 还是 + [Verb Phrase]

Examples

- 我让他不要买，他 还是 买了。
  Wǒ ràng tā bùyào mǎi, tā háishì mǎi le.
  I told him not to buy it, but he still bought it.
- 他不想离婚，但是最后 还是 离婚了。
  Tā bù xiǎng líhūn, dànshì zuìhòu háishì líhūn le.
  He didn't want to get divorced, but in the end he still ended up getting divorced.
- 父母不同意他去，可是他 还是 去了。
  Fùmǔ bù tóngyì tā qù, kěshì tā háishì qù le.
  His parents didn't agree to it, but he still went.
- 医生不让她喝酒，她 还是 喝。
  Yīshēng bù ràng tā hējiǔ, tā háishì hē.
  The doctor told her to stop drinking, but she still drinks.
- 老师生病了，但是她 还是 来上课了。
  Lǎoshī shēngbìng le, dànshì tā háishì lái shàngkè le.
  The teacher is sick, but she still come to class.

Negative Form

Structure

When you put 不 or 没 after 还 (hái) in a question sentence, it can be used to emphasize the idea of what *should* be happening in a more idiomatic way.

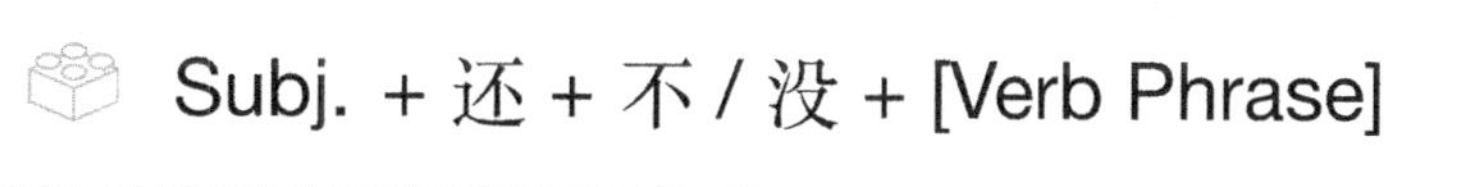
Subj. + 还 + 不 / 没 + [Verb Phrase]

Examples

- 我们等了半个小时了，老师 还没 到。
  Wǒmen děng le bàn gè xiǎoshí le. Lǎoshī hái méi dào.
  We've been waiting for half an hour, but the teacher still hasn't arrived.

- 电影已经开始了，你 还没 出门?
  Diànyǐng yǐjīng kāishǐ le, nǐ hái méi chūmén?
  The movie has started already, and you still haven't left the house?
- 你已经四十多了，还不 想结婚? *implying the listener should get married now*
  Nǐ yǐjīng sìshí duō le, hái bù xiǎng jiéhūn?
  You're in your forties, and you still don't want to get married?
- 我解释了这么多遍，你 还不 懂?
  Wǒ jiěshì le zhème duō biàn, nǐ hái bù dǒng?
  I've explained it so many times, and you still don't get it?
- 我对你这么好，你 还不 高兴? *implying the listener shouldn't be so upset*
  Wǒ duì nǐ zhème hǎo, nǐ hái bù gāoxìng?
  I treat you so well, but you're still not happy?

Similar to

- Expressing “and also” with “hai” (A2)
- Moderating positive adjectives with “hai” (A2)
- Advanced uses of “hai” (B2)

Emphasis with "jiushi" (B1)

As an adverb, 就 (jiù) can be placed before the predicate to add emphasis. It often has an intense or provocative feel to it, similar to "just." In English we might say, "it's *just* not right!" This emphasis very often appears as 就是 in Chinese.

Used as "Is Exactly"

Structure

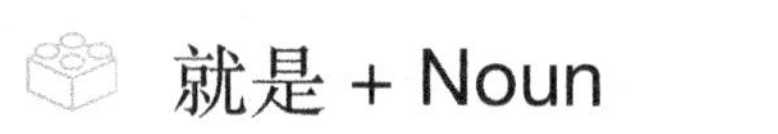

就是 + Noun

Examples

- 那个人 就是 她的新男朋友。
  Nàge rén jiùshì tā de xīn nánpéngyou.
  That guy is her new boyfriend.
- 他 就是 你要找的人。
  Tā jiùshì nǐ yào zhǎo de rén.
  He's just the person that you're looking for.
- 我们 就是 他的家人。
  Wǒmen jiùshì tā de jiārén.
  We're his family.
- 你 就是 个笨蛋！
  Nǐ jiùshì gè bèndàn!
  A moron is precisely what you are!
- 他 就是 那个骗子！
  Tā jiùshì nàge piànzi!
  That con man is him!

Used as "Only Because"

就是 can be used to intensify the predicate to mean "only (because of) that and nothing else." In this case, 是 can't be omitted. In many cases, you could also add in an 因为, but it's not required.

Examples

- 他不去旅游 就是 不想花钱。
  Tā bù qù lǚyóu jiùshì bù xiǎng huāqián.
  He didn't travel only because he doesn't want to spend the money.

- 你不参加比赛 就是 怕输吗?
  Nǐ bù cānjiā bǐsài jiùshì pà shū ma?
  You're not entering the competition just because you're afraid of losing?
- 他这样说 就是 不喜欢我。
  Tā zhèyàng shuō jiùshì bù xǐhuan wǒ.
  He said this only because he doesn't like me.
- 她问这么多, 就是 担心你。
  She asked so many questions only because she's worried about you.
- 她 就是 漂亮, 没别的优势。
  Tā jiùshì piàoliang, méi biéde yōushì.
  She's just pretty; she doesn't have any other strengths.

Other Usage

In the examples above, 就 pairs exclusively with the verb 是. But 就 can also come before other verbs, with similar emphatic effect. In these cases, it's also OK to use 就是 before the other verbs as well.

Structure

就 (是) + (不) + Verb

Examples

- 我 就 要去!
  Wǒ jiù yào qù!
  I just want to go!
- 我 就是 喜欢他。
  Wǒ jiù shì xǐhuan tā.
  I just like him.
- 我 就 不告诉你。
  Wǒ jiù bù gàosu nǐ.
  I'm just not going to tell you.
- 我父母 就是 不让我一个人去。
  Wǒ fùmǔ jiùshì bù ràng wǒ yīgèrén qù.
  My parents simply won't let me go alone.

- 这个学生 就是 不听老师的话。
  Zhège xuéshēng jiùshì bù tīng lǎoshī de huà.
  The student just wouldn't listen to his teacher.

As you may have noticed, many of these uses of 就 or 就是 carry a flippant, stubborn tone, referred to as 任性 (rènxìng) in Chinese.

Emphasizing negation with "you" (B1)

You already know that 不 (bù) and 没 (méi) can be used for negation. But you can also use the word 又 (yòu) to emphasize negation, giving your negative sentence a little kick!

Structure

In this structure, 又 is used to emphasize that something "*didn't* happen," "*is not*" the case, or "*will not* happen." It's most often used with 不 and 没. This grammar structure is often used in an accusatory context, and when used with other expressions like 干吗 (gànmá) can show annoyance.

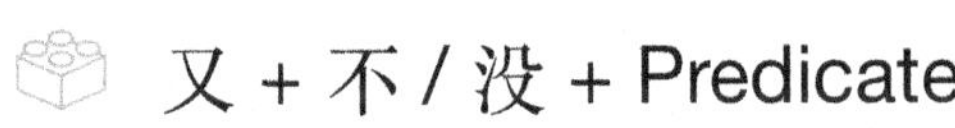

Examples

- 问我干吗？我 又 不 知道。
  Wèn wǒ gànmá? Wǒ yòu bù zhīdào.
  Why ask me? I definitely don't know.
- 这些菜 又 没 坏，为什么要扔？
  Zhèxiē cài yòu méi huài, wèishénme yào rēng?
  These dishes haven't gone bad. Why would you throw them away?
- 不要生气，我 又 不 是故意的。
  Bùyào shēngqì, wǒ yòu bù shì gùyì de.
  Don't be mad.It really wasn't on purpose.
- 今天 又 不 热，开空调干吗？
  Jīntiān yòu bù rè, kāi kōngtiáo gànmá?
  It's not hot today. Why turn on the air conditioner?
- 明天 又 不 上班，那么早起床干吗？
  Míngtiān yòu bù shàngbān, nàme zǎo qǐchuáng gànmá?
  You don't work tomorrow. Why get up so early?
- 你现在 又 不 忙，来帮我一下。
  Nǐ xiànzài yòu bù máng, lái bāng wǒ yīxià.
  You're not busy now. Come and help me.

- 我 又 没 吃过，怎么知道好不好吃？
  Wǒ yòu méi chī guo, zěnme zhīdào hǎo bu hǎochī?
  I haven't eaten it. How would I know if it is tasty or not?
- 孩子 又 没 做错，打他干吗？
  Háizi yòu méi zuò cuò, dǎ tā gànmá?
  The child didn't do anything wrong. Why are you spanking him?
- 又 没 下雨，带伞干吗？
  Yòu méi xiàyǔ, dài sǎn gànmá?
  It's not raining. Why are you bringing the umbrella?
- 又 不 关你的事，问那么多干吗？
  Yòu bù guān nǐ de shì, wèn nàme duō gànmá?
  It's none of your business. Why all the questions?

Similar to

- Expressing "again" in the past with "you" (B1), page 33
- Advanced use of "you" (B2)
- Emphasizing a negation with "bing" (B2)

Expressing "about to" with "jiuyao" (B1)

就要 (jiùyào) is similar to 快要 (kuàiyào), meaning "about to." They are interchangeable in some cases. But there is a major difference that you need to take a good look at.

Basic Pattern

Structure

(Subj. +) 就要 + Verb + 了 (，……)

Examples

- 就要下雨了。
  Jiù yào xiàyǔ le.
  It's about to rain.
- 他们就要结婚了。
  Tāmen jiù yào jiéhūn le.
  They are about to get married.
- 我就要出国了。
  Wǒ jiù yào chūguó le.
  I'm about to go abroad.
- 宝宝就要一岁了。
  Bǎobao jiù yào yī suì le.
  The baby is about to be one year old.
- 就要下课了，还有别的问题吗?
  Jiù yào xiàkè le, hái yǒu bié de wèntí ma?
  The class is almost over. Are there any other questions?

In this case, 就要 can be replaced by 快要 or 快.

Advanced Pattern

快要 (kuài yào) is generally "about to" [happen], but 就要 (jiù yào) could be used to mark a more specific time. 要 (yào) here can be omitted. For this one, you wouldn't normally use "about to" for this English translation, but the feeling is nevertheless that the impending event is coming up fast. This use of 就 (jiù) overlaps with its usage indicating earliness[1].

1. Expressing earliness with "jiu" (B1), page 69

Structure

> 还有 + Time (+ Subj.) + 就 (要) + Verb + 了

Examples

- 还有 十分钟我 就 下班 了 。
  Háiyǒu shí fēnzhōng wǒ jiù xiàbān le .
  I get off work in 10 minutes.
- 还有 两个星期我们 就要 考试 了 。
  Háiyǒu liǎng gè xīngqí wǒmen jiù yào kǎoshì le .
  We're just two weeks away from the exam date.
- 还有 一个月 就要 过年 了 。
  Háiyǒu yī gè yuè jiù yào guònián le .
  It will be Chinese New Year in another month.
- 还有 半个小时飞机 就 起飞 了 。
  Háiyǒu bàn gè xiǎoshí fēijī jiù qǐfēi le .
  The plane takes off in half an hour.
- 还有 五天 就要 放假 了 。
  Háiyǒu wǔ tiān jiù yào fàngjià le .
  I go on vacation in 5 days.

Similar to

- Expressing "be going to" with "yao" (A1)
- Expressing "about to happen" with "le" (A2)
- Expressing "nearly" with "jihu" (B2)

Expressing "again" in the future with "zai" (B1)

While 又 (yòu) is used for "again" in the past, 再 (zài) is used for "again" in the future. That is, 再 is used when something has happened once and it *will* happen again.

Used as "Again"

Remember this is the *future* "again."

Structure

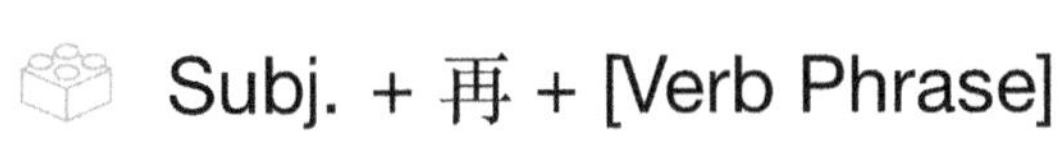
Subj. + 再 + [Verb Phrase]

Examples

- 我们明年 再 来。
  Wǒmen míngnián zài lái.
  We'll come again next year.
- 再 试一下。
  Zài shì yīxià.
  Try it again.
- 你可以 再 说一遍吗？
  Nǐ kěyǐ zài shuō yī biàn ma?
  Can you please say it again?
- 这本书我要 再 看一遍。
  Zhè běn shū wǒ yào zài kàn yī biàn.
  I want to read this book again.
- 你应该 再 复习一遍。
  Nǐ yīnggāi zài fùxí yī biàn.
  You should review it again.

In fact, this structure is present in one of the most common Chinese phrases: "再见!" In this case, it literally means "see you again."

Used as "Another" or "Some More"

The English word "another" is often avoided altogether by using 再.

Structure

Subj. + 再 + Verb + Obj.

In this case, the object includes a quantity phrase.

Examples

- 再吃一点。
  Zài chī yīdiǎn.
  Eat some more.
- 再点几个菜吧。
  Zài diǎn jǐ gè cài ba.
  Let's order some more dishes.
- 服务员，再来两瓶啤酒。
  Fúwùyuán, zài lái liǎng píng píjiǔ.
  Waiter, two more bottles of beer, please.
- 再给我三天时间。
  Zài gěi wǒ sān tiān shíjiān.
  Give me another three days.
- 我能不能再拿两个？
  Wǒ néng bu néng zài ná liǎng gè?
  Can I take two more?

Used for Continuous Action

Here 再 is similar to the English "for a while longer" or "keep [going/doing]."

Structure

Subj. + 再 + Verb + Verb

Examples

- 再找找。
  Zài zhǎozhao.
  Keep looking.

- 你 再 问问。
  Nǐ zài wènwen.
  Keep asking.
- 别急，再 想想。
  Bié jí, zài xiǎngxiang.
  Don't worry. Keep thinking.

You can also add 一会儿 after the verb to mean "keep doing something a little longer."

- 再 聊一会儿。
  Zài liáo yīhuǐr.
  Keep talking for a little bit.
- 再 等一会儿。
  Zài děng yīhuǐr.
  Wait a little longer.

You can use either the "Verb + Verb" pattern or the 一会儿 pattern with 再, but don't use them together.

Similar to

- Expressing "again" in the past with "you" (B1), page 33
- Expressing "the other" with "lingwai" (B1), page 237
- Sequencing with "xian" and "zai" (B1), page 74
- Comparing "zai" and "you" (B2)
- Expressing "never again" with "zai ye bu" (B2)
- Expressing "over and over again" with "zaisan" (B2)

Expressing "again" in the past with "you" (B1)

Whenever you want to express something that has happened again, as in, "oops, I did it *again*!" in Chinese, you generally want to use 又 (yòu). (You'll want to use 再 (zài) for "again" in the future[1].)

Affirmative Form

Structure

Normally, 又 is used to express an action that has already happened again for (at least) the second time. It doesn't have to be in quick succession; it happened before, and now it's happened again.

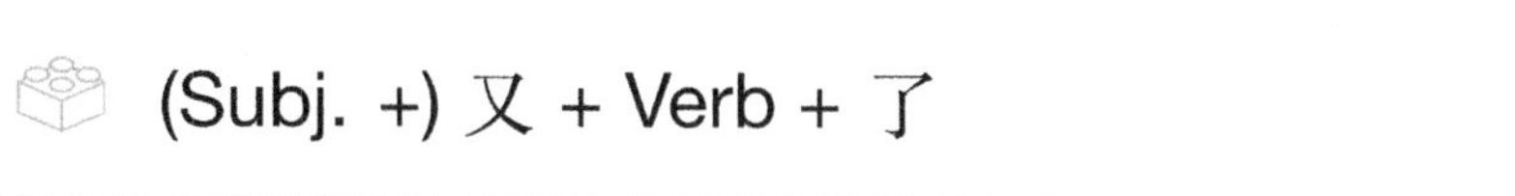

Examples

- 又下雨了！
  Yòu xiàyǔ le!
  It rained again!
- 你又迟到了。
  Nǐ yòu chídào le.
  You're late again.
- 宝宝又哭了。
  Bǎobao yòu kū le.
  The baby is crying again.
- 我又忘了。
  Wǒ yòu wàng le.
  I forgot again.

Negative Form

Structure

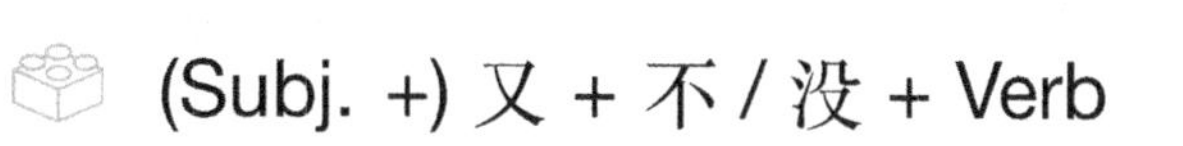

1. Expressing "again" in the future with "zai" (B1), page 30

Examples

- 他 又 没 来上课。
  Tā yòu méi lái shàngkè.
  He didn't come to class again.
- 你们 又 不 付钱?
  Nǐmen yòu bù fùqián?
  You're not paying again?
- 你 又 不 参加?
  Nǐ yòu bù cānjiā?
  You are not going to participate again?
- 对不起，我 又 没 带书。
  Duìbuqǐ, wǒ yòu méi dài shū.
  Sorry, I forgot to bring the book again.

Colloquial Saying 又来了

又来了 fits the above pattern, but is also a little tricky because it expresses something that is still ongoing, and has already started as the speaker is speaking. Literally it means "here it comes again," but it's more accurate to translate it as "there it is again," or "there [he] goes again." It indicates that the speaker is a bit annoyed that it happened *again*.

Other Usage

When it becomes clear that something is about to happen again, you can also use 又. It's almost as if it has already happened in your mind. In these cases, it's quite common for 又 to be immediately followed by 是 (shì), 要 (yào), 可以 (kěyǐ), or 能 (néng), and you'll notice that there's often a 了, indicating that something is about to happen.

Some examples:

- 今天 又 要 加班 了 !
  Jīntiān yòu yào jiābān le !
  We've got to work overtime again today!
- 老板请客，又 可以 吃大餐 了 !
  Lǎobǎn qǐngkè, yòu kěyǐ chī dàcān le !
  The boss is going to treat us. We can have a big meal again!
- 快过年了，我们 又 能 拿红包 了 !
  Kuài guònián le, wǒmen yòu néng ná hóngbāo le !
  It's almost Chinese New Year. We can get our red packets [of money] again!

Similar to

- Emphasizing negation with “you” (B1), page 26
- Expressing “again” in the future with “zai” (B1), page 30
- Advanced use of “you” (B2)

Expressing "all along" with "yuanlai" (B1)

原来 (yuánlái) means "originally" (similar to 本来) as an adverb, or "original" or "former" as an adjective. As an adverb it can also mean "all along" and can be used to indicate a sudden realization of something previously unknown — a bit like, "so it's been like that all along... how could I have not realized?"

Used as "Original" or "Originally"

Structure

When used as an adjective:

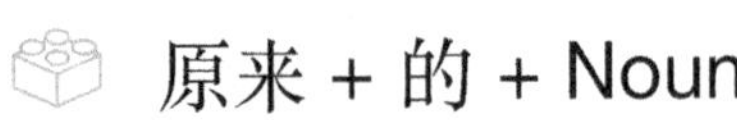

When used as an adverb:

Examples

- 你 原来 的发型也很可爱。
  Nǐ yuánlái de fàxíng yě hěn kě'ài.
  Your original hairstyle was also very cute.
- 这件衣服 原来 的价格是 999 块。
  Zhè jiàn yīfu yuánlái de jiàgé shì jiǔbǎi jiǔshí-jiǔ kuài.
  The original price of this piece of clothing was 999 RMB.
- 她们 原来 只是邻居，现在是很好的朋友。
  Tāmen yuánlái zhǐ shì línjū, xiànzài shì hěn hǎo de péngyou.
  Originally they were just neighbors. Now they're very good friends.
- 我们 原来 住在浦东，几个月以前搬到了这里。
  Wǒmen yuánlái zhù zài Pǔdōng, jǐ gè yuè yǐqián bān dào le zhèlǐ.
  Originally we lived in Pudong. We moved here a few months ago.
- 原来 她是他的中文老师，现在是他老婆。
  Yuánlái tā shì tā de Zhōngwén lǎoshī, xiànzài shì tā lǎopo.
  She was originally his Chinese teacher. She is now his wife.

Used as "All along"

Structure

 原来 + [New Information]

Examples

- 原来 是你！
  Yuánlái shì nǐ!
  So it was you all along!
- 原来 你们认识！
  Yuánlái nǐmen rènshi!
  So you both knew each other this whole time!
- 原来 是这样！
  Yuánlái shì zhèyàng!
  Oh, so it's like that!
- 原来 你这么有钱！
  Yuánlái nǐ zhème yǒuqián!
  It turns out you are so rich!
- 原来 你在骗我！我怎么那么傻?
  Yuánlái nǐ zài piàn wǒ! Wǒ zěnme nàme shǎ?
  You have been tricking me all along. How could I be so stupid?

The more formal expression 原来如此 (yuánlái rúcǐ) can be used like 原来是这样 in example 3.

Similar to

- Expressing "no wonder" (B1), page 319
- Comparing "benlai" and "yuanlai" (B2)
- Expressing "originally" with "benlai" (B2)

Expressing "all at once" with "yixiazi" (B1)

一下子 (yīxiàzi) can be used as an adverb, meaning "all at once." Because it inherently encompasses a sense of "completion," it's typically going to be followed by a 了 (le) later in the sentence.

Used as "All at Once"

一下子 (yīxiàzi) is a very informal expression to describe how fast things happened. It usually touches upon sudden or severe changes in a very short amount of time. Although 一下子 (yīxiàzi) is already quite informal, in colloquial Chinese 一下 (yīxià) can also be used to express the same thing.

Structure

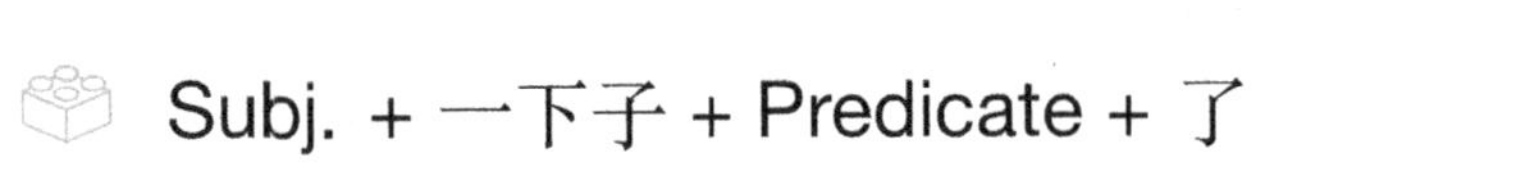

Examples

- 天气 一下子 变冷 了 。
  Tiānqì yīxiàzi biàn lěng le .
  The weather suddenly got cold.
- 他 一下子 吃 了 三碗米饭。
  Tā yīxiàzi chī le sān wǎn mǐfàn.
  He ate three bowls of rice all at once.
- 她下楼的时候 一下子 摔倒 了 。
  Tā xiàlóu de shíhou yīxiàzi shuāidǎo le .
  As she went down the stairs, she suddenly fell.
- 我们说话的时候，她 一下子 哭 了 。
  Wǒmen shuōhuà de shíhou, tā yīxiàzi kū le .
  She burst into tears when we were talking.
- 她上个月 一下子 瘦 了 很多。
  Tā shàng gè yuè yīxiàzi shòu le hěn duō.
  Last month, she lost a lot of weight all at once.

Used as "Quickly" and "Naturally"

一下子 (yīxiàzi), followed with 就 (jiù), usually implies that things happened very quickly, naturally, and easily. Again, 一下 (yīxià) can also be used instead of 一下子 (yīxiàzi).

Structure

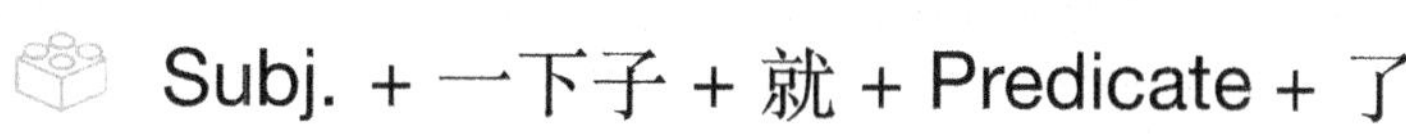
Subj. + 一下子 + 就 + Predicate + 了

Examples

- 老师进来以后，大家 一下子 就 安静 了 。
  Lǎoshī jìnlái yǐhòu, dàjiā yīxiàzi jiù ānjìng le .
  Everyone became silent after the teacher came in.
- 听他说完，我 一下子 就 明白 了 。
  Tīng tā shuō wán, wǒ yīxiàzi jiù míngbai le .
  After hearing him out, I understood everything all at once.
- 他是最高的，我 一下子 就 看到他 了 。
  Tā shì zuì gāo de, wǒ yīxiàzi jiù kàndào tā le .
  He is the tallest. I spotted him right away.
- 拍完那部电影，他 一下子 就 出名 了 。
  Pāi wán nà bù diànyǐng, tā yīxiàzi jiù chūmíng le .
  He became very famous soon after that movie came out.
- 看到那张照片，我 一下子 就 想起来 了 。
  Kàndào nà zhāng zhàopiàn, wǒ yīxiàzi jiù xiǎng qǐlái le .
  It all came back to me when I saw that picture.

Expressing "almost" using "chadian" (B1)

To say that something bad *almost* happened (but didn't), you can add the word 差点 (chàdiǎn) before the verb. You will also hear 差点儿 (chàdiǎnr) in northern China. There is no difference in meaning between 差点 and 差点儿.

Literal Meaning

It might help to understand the literal meaning of the structure. The word 差 has a lot of meanings. In this case, it means "to lack," or "to be short." So in Chinese, the way to say "almost" is to say, "lacking that little bit." If that "little bit" hadn't been lacking, it *would have* happened. But it *was* lacking, so it didn't happen; it *almost* happened. Just remember: the fact of what really happened is always *NOT* the verb phrase after 差点 (儿).

Structure

Note that the "Predicate" part of the structure is usually something bad or something you don't wish for, and that it **didn't happen**.

You can put 了 at the end of the sentence for emphasis. In this case, 就 is often used and it's optional.

Subj. + 差点 (+ 就) + Predicate + 了

The predicate part of the pattern can be a verb or an adjective.

Examples

- 车 差点 撞到我。
  Chē chàdiǎn zhuàngdào wǒ.
  The car almost hit me.
  The car didn't hit me.
- 我们 差点 相信他。
  Wǒmen chàdiǎn xiāngxìn tā.
  We almost believed him.
  We didn't believe him.
- 他们 差点 打起来。
  Tāmen chàdiǎn dǎ qǐlái.
  They almost started a fight.
  They didn't start fighting.

- 我 差点 忘 了 。
  Wǒ chàdiǎn wàng le .
  I almost forgot.
  I didn't forget.
- 我今天 差点 迟到 了 。
  Wǒ jīntiān chàdiǎn chídào le .
  I was almost late today.
  I wasn't late.
- 她 差点 疯 了 。
  Tā chàdiǎn fēng le .
  She almost went crazy.
  She didn't go crazy.
- 他 差点 就 死 了 。
  Tā chàdiǎn jiù sǐ le .
  He almost died.
  He didn't die.
- 菜 差点 糊 了 。
  Cài chàdiǎn hú le .
  The food was almost burned.
  It wasn't burned.
- 我们队 差点 输 了 。
  Wǒmen duì chàdiǎn shū le .
  Our team almost lost.
  The team didn't lose.
- 我 差点 就 打他 了 。
  Wǒ chàdiǎn jiù dǎ tā le .
  I almost hit him.
  I didn't actually do it.

Using 差点 with 没

This can get confusing, even though it's really the same pattern (and same logic) with a little added complexity. This pattern goes beyond the difficulty level of the needs of the B1 learner, so to learn more about this usage, see expressing "almost" using "chadian mei."

Similar to

- Expressing "almost" using "chadian mei" (B2)
- Expressing "nearly" with "jihu" (B2)

Expressing "already" with "dou" (B1)

都……了 (dōu... le) is a pattern used to express that something has already happened, similar to 已经 (yǐjīng)……了. However, 都……了 is used more emphatically, implying that the speaker holds some sort of attitude in relation to the event and is not merely objectively stating the facts, as with 已经……了. The two options can actually also be combined in the pattern 都已经……了. Here the meaning is the same as 都……了.

Used Before a Time

Structure

When 都……了 (dōu... le) is used at the beginning of a sentence, it will usually be followed with 还 (hái) or 还在 (hái zài). This implies that the other party should stop some kind of action.

 都 + Time + 了

Examples

- 都 九点 了，快点起床！
  Dōu jiǔ diǎn le, kuài diǎn qǐchuáng!
  It's already nine o'clock. Get out of bed!
- 都 十二点 了，你 还 不睡？
  Dōu shí'èr diǎn le, nǐ hái bù shuì?
  It's already 12 o'clock. Aren't you going to bed?
- 都 二十一世纪 了，你 还 这么想？
  Dōu èrshí-yī shìjì le, nǐ hái zhème xiǎng?
  It's already the 21st century and you still think this way?
- 都 一个小时 了，他 还 在厕所里。
  Dōu yī gè xiǎoshí le, tā hái zài cèsuǒ lǐ.
  It's already been an hour, and he's still in the bathroom.
- 都 一个星期 了，还在 下雨。
  Dōu yī gè xīngqī le, hái zài xiàyǔ.
  It's been a week and it's still raining.

Used Before the Predicate

Structure

Subj. + 都 + Predicate + 了

The predicate part of the pattern can be a verb or an adjective.

Examples

- 饭 都 凉 了 ，快吃吧。
  Fàn dōu liáng le , kuài chī ba.
  The food is cold already. Let's eat.
- 牛奶 都 坏 了 ，扔掉吧。
  Niúnǎi dōu huài le , rēngdiào ba.
  The milk's gone bad. Throw it out.
- 我 都 说了三遍 了 。别烦我！
  Wǒ dōu shuō le sān biàn le . Bié fán wǒ!
  I've said it three times already. Leave me alone!
- 这个电影你 都 看过 了 ，看别的吧。
  Zhège diànyǐng nǐ dōu kàn guo le , kàn biéde ba.
  You've seen this movie already. Let's watch something else.
- 他 都 道歉 了 ，你别生气了。
  Tā dōu dàoqiàn le , nǐ bié shēngqì le.
  He already apologized. Stop being so mad at him.

Similar to

- Expressing "already" with "yijing" (A2)
- Expressing "already" with just "le" (A2)
- Expressing duration of inaction (B1), page 67

Expressing "always" with "conglai" (B1)

Although perhaps more often used in the negative to mean "never," 从来 (cónglái) can be used with 都 (dōu) to mean "always" or "have always (done)."

Without the negative adverbs 不 and 没, 从来 takes on the meaning of "always." (Literally, 从来 means something like "from the beginning," although no one is really thinking that phrase when they use it.) When used in the positive, though, it is customary to put the adverb 都 after 从来.

Structure

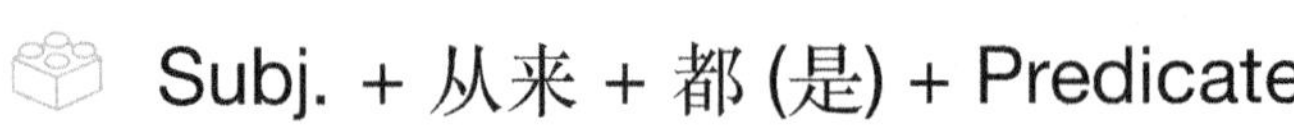

Subj. + 从来 + 都 (是) + Predicate

The predicate part of the pattern can be a verb or an adjective. It's also quite common to follow 从来都 with an additional 是 for emphasis.

Examples

- 他 从来都 这样。
  Tā cónglái dōu zhèyàng.
  He's always like this.
- 她 从来都 这么晚睡。
  Tā cónglái dōu zhème wǎn shuì.
  She's always gone to bed so late.
- 他说话 从来都 很大声。
  Tā shuōhuà cónglái dōu hěn dàshēng.
  He's always spoken very loudly.
- 我们学校的学生 从来都 只能穿校服。
  Wǒmen xuéxiào de xuéshēng cónglái dōu zhǐ néng chuān xiàofú.
  Students in our school can only wear school uniforms.
- 成功 从来都 要靠自己努力。
  Chénggōng cónglái dōu yào kào zìjǐ nǔlì.
  Success always depends on working hard by oneself.
- 我们下棋，从来都是 他赢。
  Wǒmen xiàqí, cónglái dōushì tā yíng.
  He always wins when we play chess.

- 她买衣服 从来都是 只买名牌。
  Tā mǎi yīfu cónglái dōushì zhǐ mǎi míngpái.
  She always buys brand-name clothes when she goes shopping.
- 我 从来都是 一个人住，已经习惯了。
  Wǒ cónglái dōushì yīgèrén zhù, yǐjīng xíguàn le.
  I've always lived alone; I'm used to it already.

Similar to

- Expressing "always" with "zongshi" (A2)
- Expressing "never" with "conglai" (A2)
- Using "always" as a complaint with "laoshi" (B1), page 77
- Expressing "always previously" with "xianglai" (C1)

Expressing "as a result" with "jieguo" (B1)

结果 (jiéguǒ) can be used as a conjunction or adverb, meaning "as a result" or "consequently." It normally starts the second half of a sentence and can also introduce an unexpected or undesirable result.

Indicating a Logical Result

Structure

Reason / Condition ，结果 + Result

Examples

- 她穿得很少，结果感冒了。
  Tā chuān de hěn shǎo, jiéguǒ gǎnmào le.
  She didn't dress warmly enough, and as a result, she caught a cold.
- 我太紧张了，结果说错了很多。
  Wǒ tài jǐnzhāng le, jiéguǒ shuō cuò le hěn duō.
  I was too nervous. As a result, I misspoke a lot.
- 他开得太快了，结果撞到了一个人。
  Tā kāi de tài kuài le, jiéguǒ zhuàngdào le yī gè rén.
  He drove too fast. As a result, he hit someone.
- 他没好好复习，结果考试没考好。
  Tā méi hǎohǎo fùxí, jiéguǒ kǎoshì méi kǎo hǎo.
  He didn't review well. As a result, he didn't do well in the exam.
- 他总是迟到，结果老板炒了他的鱿鱼。
  Tā zǒngshì chídào, jiéguǒ lǎobǎn chǎo le tā de yóuyú.
  He's always late for work. As a result, his boss fired him.

Indicating an Unexpected Result

Sometimes there is no cause-effect relationship between what comes before and after 结果 (no logical connection). In these sentences, the second half of the sentence usually emphasizes that what actually happened was unexpected or undesired.

Structure

Situation ，结果 + [Unexpected Result]

Examples

- 我去机场接他，结果没接到他。
  Wǒ qù jīchǎng jiē tā, jiéguǒ méi jiēdào tā.
  I went to the airport to pick him up. But in the end, I didn't find him there.
- 我跟朋友打赌，结果我输了。
  Wǒ gēn péngyou dǎdǔ, jiéguǒ wǒ shū le.
  I made a bet with a friend. I lost in the end.
- 我昨天跟朋友去喝酒，结果喝醉了。
  Wǒ zuótiān gēn péngyou qù hējiǔ, jiéguǒ hēzuì le.
  I went to have a drink with my friends yesterday. I ended up getting drunk.
- 他吃了很多药，结果都没有用。
  Tā chī le hěn duō yào, jiéguǒ dōu méiyǒu yòng.
  He took a lot of pills. None of them worked in the end.
- 我点的是牛肉汉堡，结果服务员给了我一个鸡肉的。
  Wǒ diǎn de shì niúròu hànbǎo, jiéguǒ fúwùyuán gěi le wǒ yī gè jīròu de.
  I ordered a burger. The waiter gave me a chicken sandwich instead.

Similar to

- Cause and effect with "yinwei" and "suoyi" (A2)
- Expressing "therefore" with "yinci" (B2)
- Stating the effect before the cause (B2)
- Using "because" with "er" to indicate effect (B2)

Expressing "each other" with "huxiang" (B1)

When some action is mutual, you can use the word 互相 (hùxiāng). The word "mutual" feels formal in English, but in Chinese, even everyday phrases such as "learn from each other" use the word 互相, which expresses this "each other" aspect.

Structure

Usually 互相 (hùxiāng) is used with two-syllable words, and for one-syllable words, some other information will be added after the verb to make it sound more natural (see below for examples of this.)

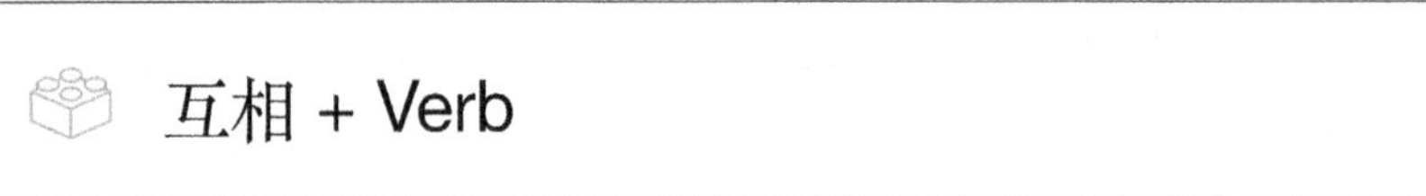

Examples

- 互相 帮助
  hùxiāng bāngzhù
  Help each other
- 互相 了解
  hùxiāng liǎojiě
  Know each other
- 互相 伤害
  hùxiāng shānghài
  Hurt each other
- 互相 尊重
  hùxiāng zūnzhòng
  Respect each other
- 互相 支持
  hùxiāng zhīchí
  Support each other
- 互相 鼓励
  hùxiāng gǔlì
  Encourage each other
- 互相 影响
  hùxiāng yǐngxiǎng
  Influence each other

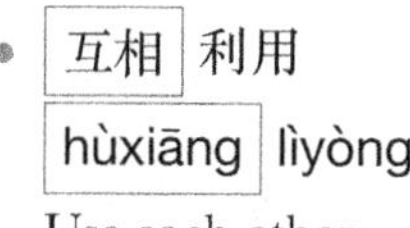

- 互相 利用
  hùxiāng lìyòng
  Use each other

Don't use 互相 (hùxiāng) with single-syllable verbs. If you really have to use 互相, you can make the verb longer by adding extra information after it.

✗ 互相 看
hùxiāng kàn
look at each other

✓ 互相 看了一眼
hùxiāng kàn le yī yǎn
glanced at each other

Note that for some verbs which are inherently "mutual," the use of 互相 (hùxiāng) is redundant and unnecessary. So the following phrases are not *wrong*, but a little strange.

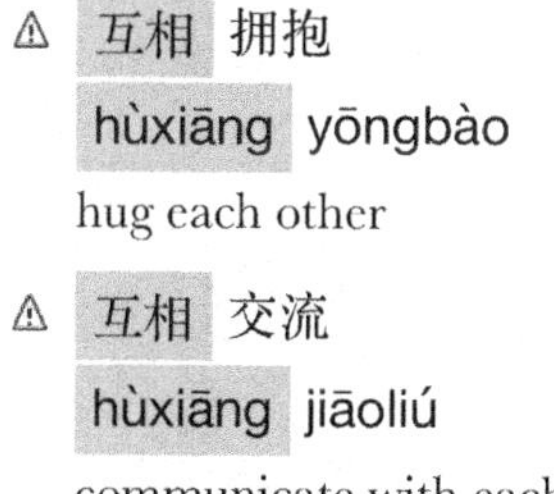

⚠ 互相 拥抱
hùxiāng yōngbào
hug each other

⚠ 互相 交流
hùxiāng jiāoliú
communicate with each other

Similar to

- Comparing "bici" and "duifang" (B2)
- Expressing "each other" with "bici" (B2)

Expressing "enough" with "gou" (B1)

In Chinese the word for "enough" is 够 (gòu). It also combines with other words and most often comes before verbs and adjectives, but there are a limited number of verbs that it can follow as well.

Affirmative Form

Structure

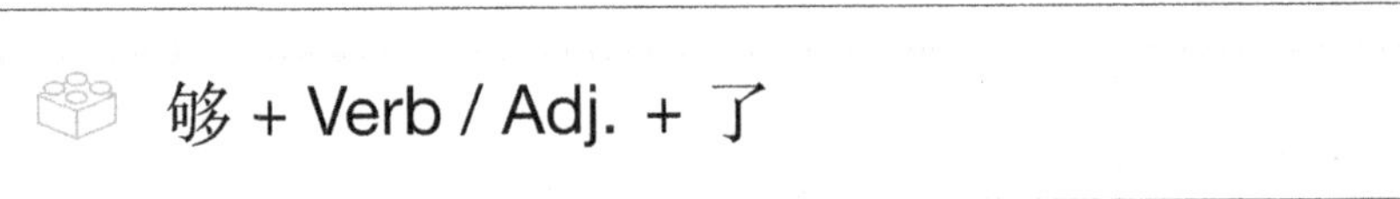

够 + Verb / Adj. + 了

The 了 is not strictly required, but it adds a sense of emphasis.

Examples

In these examples, 够 (gòu) comes before verbs. You'll notice that *who* is doing the verb to *what* is normally just understood in context.

- 我们买了很多菜，够吃了。
  Wǒmen mǎi le hěn duō cài, gòu chī le.
  We bought a lot of food. It's enough for us to eat.
- 这些纸够用吗？
  Zhèxiē zhǐ gòu yòng ma?
  Is this paper enough for us to use?
- 放心吧，我带的钱够花。
  Fàngxīn ba, wǒ dài de qián gòu huā.
  Don't worry. I've brought enough money to spend.

When it comes before an adjective, 了 is needed at the end of the sentence.

- 我对你够好了。
  Wǒ duì nǐ gòu hǎo le.
  I've been good enough to you.
- 别抱怨了，你够幸运了。
  Bié bàoyuàn le, nǐ gòu xìngyùn le.
  Stop complaining. You've been lucky enough.

Negative Form

In the negative form, you're not going to need a 了 (le).

Structure

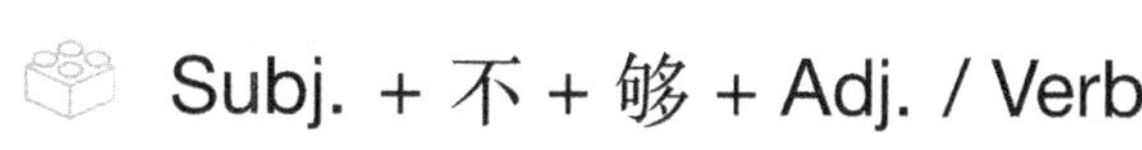

Subj. + 不 + 够 + Adj. / Verb

Note that 了 can't be used when it's negated.

Examples

- 他觉得他女朋友 不够 漂亮。
  Tā juéde tā nǚpéngyou bù gòu piàoliang.
  He thinks his girlfriend is not pretty enough.
- 你说得 不够 清楚。
  Nǐ shuō de bù gòu qīngchǔ.
  You didn't speak clearly enough.
- 这些菜 不够 吃，再点几个菜。
  Zhèxiē cài bù gòu chī, zài diǎn jǐ gè cài.
  This food is not enough for us to eat. Let's order a few more dishes.
- 这里太小了， 不够 坐。
  Zhèlǐ tài xiǎo le, bù gòu zuò.
  It's too cramped here. There's not enough room to sit.
- 你的包太小了，这些东西肯定 不够 放。
  Nǐ de bāo tài xiǎo le, zhèxiē dōngxi kěndìng bù gòu fàng.
  Your bag is too small. There's definitely not enough room to hold this stuff.

Translations feel looser here, as the Chinese frequently omits the details about what's not enough for what. The verb and the context makes it clear enough.

Colloquial Saying

Literally, 够了 means "it's enough." When the speaker is getting sick of doing something or feeling fed up, 够了 can be applied after a limited number of verbs.

A few common examples:

- 我 受 够了 ！
  Wǒ shòu gòu le!
  I've had enough!
- 天天吃外卖，我们都 吃 够了 。
  Tiāntiān chī wàimài, wǒmen dōu chī gòu le.
  We eat take-out every day. We're sick of eating it.

- 你 玩 够了 没有?
  Nǐ wán gòu le méiyǒu?
  Are you done playing?

Expressing "finally" with "zhongyu" (B1)

终于 (zhōngyú) expresses that something has *finally* happened after a long wait. Usually the speaker is looking forward to what is happening at long last, and thus, 终于 (zhōngyú) typically carries a sense of joy or relief.

Structure

Unlike the English word "finally," 终于 (zhōngyú) can never be used alone. It also can't be put in front of the subject or at the end of the sentence. 终于 (zhōngyú) needs to be used with 了 to express that the action is completed.

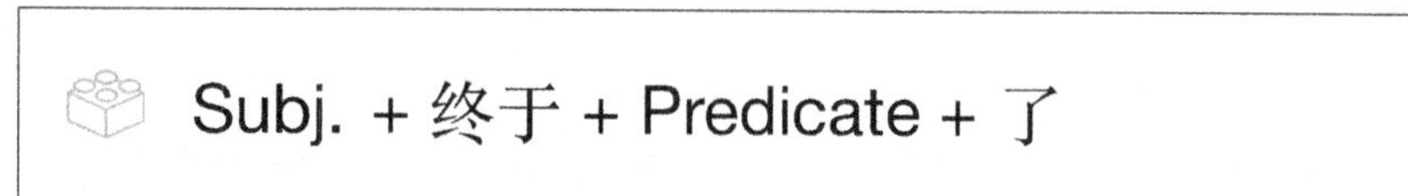

The predicate part of the pattern can be a verb or an adjective.

Examples

- 你 终于 到 了 !
  Nǐ zhōngyú dào le !
  You've finally arrived!
- 我们 终于 见面 了 !
  Wǒmen zhōngyú jiànmiàn le !
  We're finally meeting each other!
- 你们 终于 明白 了 。
  Nǐmen zhōngyú míngbai le .
  You've finally understood.
- 作业 终于 做完 了 !
  Zuòyè zhōngyú zuò wán le !
  I've finally finished my homework!
- 飞机 终于 起飞 了 !
  Fēijī zhōngyú qǐfēi le !
  The plane is finally taking off!
- 你们 终于 决定 了 。
  Nǐmen zhōngyú juédìng le .
  You've finally decided.

- 饭 终于 做好 了 。我快饿死了。
  Fàn zhōngyú zuò hǎo le . Wǒ kuài è sǐ le.
  Dinner is finally ready. I'm starving.
- 这个愿望 终于 实现 了 ！
  Zhège yuànwàng zhōngyú shíxiàn le !
  This dream has finally come true!
- 我们找了两个多小时， 终于 找到 了 那家店。
  Wǒmen zhǎo le liǎng gè duō xiǎoshí, zhōngyú zhǎodào le nà jiā diàn.
  We'd been looking for more than two hours, and we finally found that shop.
- 这些问题 终于 解决 了 。我们应该庆祝一下。
  Zhèxiē wèntí zhōngyú jiějué le . Wǒmen yīnggāi qìngzhù yīxià.
  The problems are finally solved. We should celebrate!

Similar to

- Comparing "zongsuan" and "zhongyu" (B2)

Expressing "had better" with "haishi" (B1)

One of the ways to use 还是 (háishì) is to have it mean "you had better," after having compared two options. Usually there's even a bit of deliberation before the speaker announces what "it would be better" to do, using 还是.

Structure

还是 as an adverb can express "had better" or "it would be better to." The idea is that the speaker has given the matter some thought, and after considering it, has finally come to a decision. The announcement of this decision will frequently include 还是, and it usually comes before a verb or a subject.

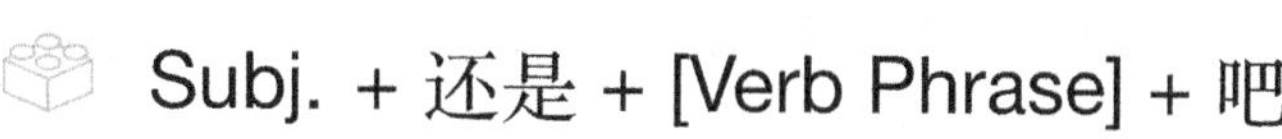

吧 is often placed after this structure, as it's a suggestion.

Examples

- 还是 明天去吧。
  Háishì míngtiān qù ba.
  We'd better go tomorrow.
- 还是 让她进来吧。
  Háishì ràng tā jìnlái ba.
  We'd better let her come in.
- 你 还是 快点走吧。
  Nǐ háishì kuài diǎn zǒu ba.
  You'd better leave now.
- 我们 还是 帮帮他吧。
  Wǒmen háishì bāngbang tā ba.
  We'd better help him.
- 太晚了，还是 先回家吧。
  Tài wǎn le, háishì xiān huíjiā ba.
  It's too late. We'd better go home now.
- 这里太脏了，我们 还是 走吧。
  Zhèlǐ tài zāng le, wǒmen háishì zǒu ba.
  It's too dirty here; we'd better leave.

- 快迟到了，我们 还是 打车吧。

  Kuài chídào le, wǒmen háishì dǎchē ba.

  We're running late. Let's take a taxi.

When the part after 还是 is a negative verb phrase, it's OK to drop the 吧 at the end.

- 太贵了，还是 别买了。

  Tài guì le, háishì bié mǎi le.

  It's too expensive. You'd better not buy it.

- 她不想说，还是 不要再问了。

  Tā bù xiǎng shuō, háishì bùyào zài wèn le.

  She doesn't want to say. We'd better not ask again.

- 他一定不同意，还是 别跟他说了。

  Tā yīdìng bù tóngyì, háishì bié gēn tā shuō le.

  He will definitely not agree to it. We'd better not say anything to him.

Similar to

- Offering choices with "haishi" (A1)
- Expressing "should" with "yinggai" (A2)
- Expressing "had better" with "zuihao" (B1), page 57
- Expressing "how about" with "yaobu" (B1), page 97

Expressing "had better" with "zuihao" (B1)

Sure, 最好 (zuìhǎo) means "best." But it can also be used to mean "it would be best to" or "had better." It is often used when giving advice to someone or even politely making demands.

Positive Form

Structure

Subj. + 最好 + Predicate

The predicate part of the pattern can be a verb or an adjective.

Examples

- 你 最好 先休息一下。
  Nǐ zuìhǎo xiān xiūxi yīxià.
  You'd better get some rest first.
- 你们 最好 给他打个电话问一下。
  Nǐmen zuìhǎo gěi tā dǎ gè diànhuà wèn yīxià.
  It would be best for you to give him a call and ask.
- 那个地方不好找，我们 最好 查一下百度地图。
  Nàge dìfang bù hǎo zhǎo, wǒmen zuìhǎo chá yīxià Bǎidù dìtú.
  It's not easy to find that place. We'd better search for it on Baidu Maps.
- 外面挺冷的，最好 多穿点。
  Wàimiàn tǐng lěng de, zuìhǎo duō chuān diǎn.
  It's pretty cold outside. Best to wear some more layers.
- 这个活动很重要，我们 最好 穿得正式一点。
  Zhège huódòng hěn zhòngyào, wǒmen zuìhǎo chuān de zhèngshì yīdiǎn.
  This is an important event. We'd better wear something more formal.

Negative Form

Structure

Subj. + 最好 + 别 / 不要 + Predicate

Examples

- 最好 别去。
  Zuìhǎo bié qù.
  You'd better not go.
- 最好 不要这样说。
  Zuìhǎo bùyào zhèyàng shuō.
  It's best not to say something like this.
- 晚饭 最好 不要吃那么多。
  Wǎnfàn zuìhǎo bùyào chī nàme duō.
  It's best not to eat so much for dinner.
- 雨这么大， 最好 别出门。
  Yǔ zhème dà, zuìhǎo bié chūmén.
  It's raining so heavily. It's best not to leave the house.
- 这个问题是隐私的， 最好 不要问。
  Zhège wèntí shì yǐnsī de, zuìhǎo bùyào wèn.
  This question is private. You'd better not ask.

Similar to

- Expressing "should" with "yinggai" (A2)
- Expressing "had better" with "haishi" (B1), page 55
- Expressing "must" with "dei" (B1), page 179

Expressing "in this way" with "zheyang" (B1)

这样 (zhèyàng) is used at the beginning of a phrase to express "this way" or "in this way."

Used as an Adverb

Structure

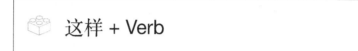

Examples

- 这样 做不对。
  Zhèyàng zuò bù duì.
  Doing it this way is not right.
- 这样 说不礼貌。
  Zhèyàng shuō bù lǐmào.
  It's not polite to say this.
- 这样 走过去更近。
  Zhèyàng zǒu guòqù gèng jìn.
  If you walk over this way, it's closer.
- 你们真的是 这样 想的吗?
  Nǐmen zhēnde shì zhèyàng xiǎng de ma?
  Do you guys really think so?

Used as a Conjunction

This use of 这样 corresponds to "in this way," which is another way of expressing "so that" or "thus."

Structure

You will often see 会 or 才 following 这样 to indicate "only in this way can or will something happen."

Examples

- 你要多鼓励学生，这样他们会更有自信。

  Nǐ yào duō gǔlì xuéshēng, zhèyàng tāmen huì gèng yǒu zìxìn.

  You need to encourage your students more. This will help them become more confident.

- 父母应该多陪孩子，这样孩子会更快乐。

  Fùmǔ yīnggāi duō péi háizi, zhèyàng háizi huì gèng kuàilè.

  Parents should spend more time with their children. This will make the children happier.

- 你要多说，这样才能越来越流利。

  Nǐ yào duō shuō, zhèyàng cái néng yuèláiyuè liúlì.

  You need to speak more. Only in this way will you become more and more fluent.

- 让他自己来，这样他才能学会。

  Ràng tā zìjǐ lái, zhèyàng tā cái néng xuéhuì.

  Let him do it by himself. This is the only way he will learn.

Colloquial Saying 这样的话

This use of 这样 corresponds to "this way," as in "if we do it this way." Adding 的话 gives the pattern more of a hypothetical "if" flavor. To make the "if" even more explicit, you can even add 如果是 before 这样的话.

 (如果是 +) 这样的话，……

A few examples:

- 这样的话，你还想去吗?

  Zhèyàng de huà, nǐ hái xiǎng qù ma?

  If this is the case, do you still want to go?

- 如果是这样的话，麻烦就大了。

  Rúguǒ shì zhèyàng dehuà, máfan jiù dà le.

  If this is the case, we're in for a heap of trouble.

- 我会住在美国朋友的家里。这样的话，我家人就不那么担心我了。

  Wǒ huì zhù zài Měiguó péngyou de jiā lǐ. Zhèyàng dehuà, wǒ jiārén jiù bù nàme dānxīn wǒ le.

  I will stay at my American friend's house when I go to visit the US. This way my family won't worry about me so much.

Expressing "one by one" with "yi" (B1)

The expression "one by one" is also simple in Chinese. It unsurprisingly features the word 一 (yī), but you don't even need the word "by." However, the pattern gets complicated somewhat by the concept of measure words.

Used as "One by One"

The most obvious way to express "one by one" is 一个一个 (yī gè yī gè), and this expression is, in fact, quite common, especially when referring to people doing things "one by one." But other measure words can be used in the same pattern instead of 个.

Structure

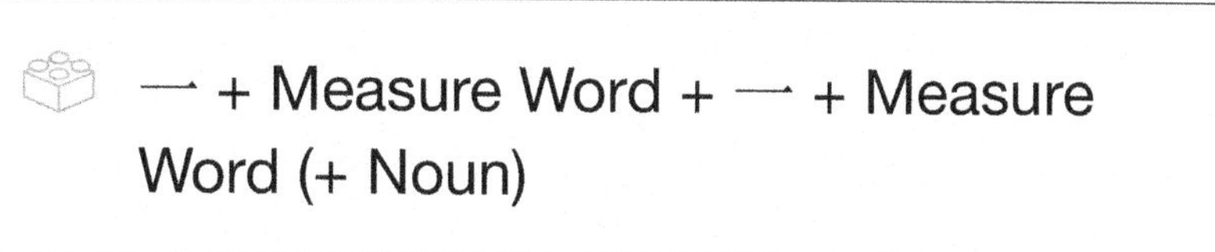
一 + Measure Word + 一 + Measure Word (+ Noun)

个 is the most likely candidate for the "Measure Word" slot here.

Examples

- 别吵，一个一个说。
  Bié chǎo, yī gè yī gè shuō.
  Don't argue. Speak one by one.
- 别着急，一点一点做。
  Bié zháojí, yī diǎn yī diǎn zuò.
  Don't worry, do it little by little.
- 请一个房间一个房间检查。
  Qǐng yī gè fángjiān yī gè fángjiān jiǎnchá.
  Please inspect room by room.
- 别拿那么多，一个一个拿。
  Bié ná nàme duō, yī gè yī gè ná.
  Don't carry so much. Carry them one at a time.

Used as "Little by Little"

Aside from just meaning "one by one," when 一 (yī) is used with a measure word that is a unit of time like "day" or "year," the meaning changes to "little by little" ("day by day," "year by year") or "gradually."

Structure

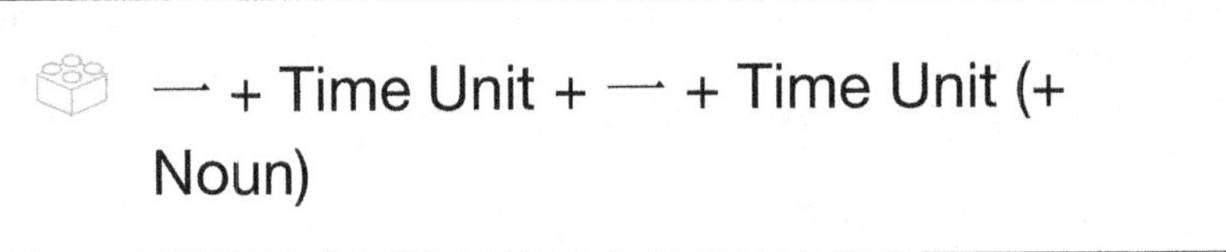
一 + Time Unit + 一 + Time Unit (+ Noun)

Examples

- 宝宝一天一天在长大。
  Bǎobao yī tiān yī tiān zài zhǎngdà.
  The baby is growing up day by day.
- 爸爸妈妈一年一年在变老。
  Bàba māma yī nián yī nián zài biàn lǎo.
  Year by year, mom and dad are growing old.

Used as "Over and Over Again"

When a measure word phrase like "one time" is repeated, the meaning also changes. When using a verb measure word like 次 (cì) or 遍 (biàn), using this pattern can indicate how the action is performed or indicate repetition of the the action.

Structure

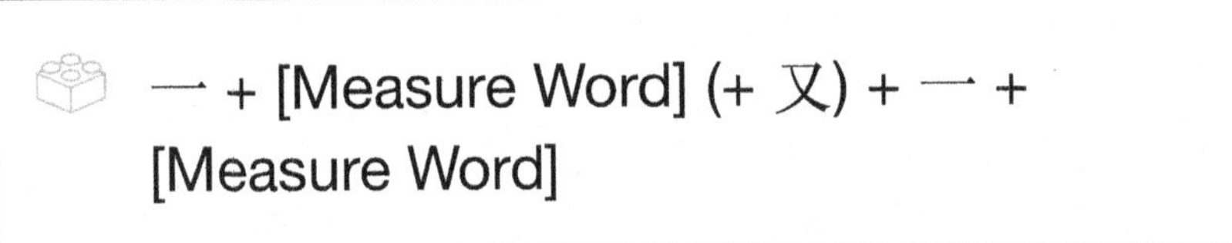
一 + [Measure Word] (+ 又) + 一 + [Measure Word]

If the speaker wants to emphasize that the action has been repeated many times, 又 (yòu) can add emphasis.

Examples

- 我一次一次问，他就是什么都不说。
  Wǒ yī cì yī cì wèn, tā jiùshì shénme dōu bù shuō.
  I asked him again and again, but he just wouldn't say anything.
- 我一遍一遍地跟他解释，他还是不听。
  Wǒ yī biàn yī biàn de gēn tā jiěshì, tā háishì bù tīng.
  I explained it to him again and again, but he still won't listen.

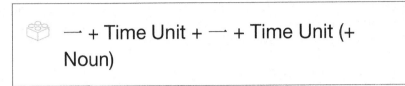

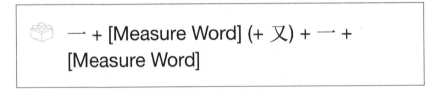

- 你为什么 一 遍 又 一 遍地听这首歌?
  Nǐ wèishénme yī biàn yòu yī biàn de tīng zhè shǒu gē?
  Why do you listen to this song over and over again?
- 他们 一 次 又 一 次犯这种小错误，让经理很头疼。
  Tāmen yī cì yòu yī cì fàn zhè zhǒng xiǎo cuòwù, ràng jīnglǐ hěn tóuténg.
  They keep making the same mistake over and over again, and it's giving their manager a headache.

Expressing "small quantity" with "jiu" (B1)

就 (jiù) is often translated simply as "just" or "only," but there are some nuances to how it is used.

Used as "Only"

就 can also be used to express one person or thing, similar to how we say in English "just one person" or "just one left." It is often paired with 一个 or similar in order to emphasize the small quantity.

Used Before the Subject

Structure

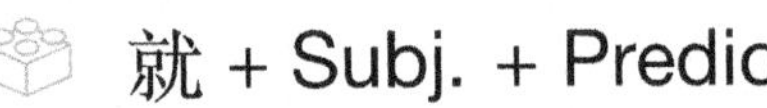

就 + Subj. + Predicate

The predicate part of the pattern can be a verb or an adjective.

Examples

- 这件事 就 我知道。
  Zhè jiàn shì jiù wǒ zhīdào.
  I'm the only person that knows about this.
- 我们都忘了，就 他还记得。
  Wǒmen dōu wàng le, jiù tā hái jìde.
  We all forgot. Only he still remembers it.
- 大家都下班了，就 老板还没走。
  Dàjiā dōu xiàbān le, jiù lǎobǎn hái méi zǒu.
  Everyone finished work and left. Only the boss hasn't left.
- 其他的菜都很好吃，就 这两个菜有点咸。
  Qítā de cài dōu hěn hǎochī, jiù zhè liǎng gè cài yǒudiǎn xián.
  The other dishes are great. Just these two dishes are a little salty.
- 你觉得别人都是傻子吗？就 你聪明？
  Nǐ juéde biérén dōu shì shǎzi ma? Jiù nǐ cōngming?
  Do you think everyone else is an idiot? That only you are smart?

In this case, the 就 comes before the verb, and what's being emphasized as "small quantity" comes after the verb, either as an object or some other kind of small quantity.

Used Before the Predicate

Structure

Subj. + 就 + [Verb Phrase]

In this structure, the verb phrase is going to include some kind of measure word.

Examples

- 我 就 去过一次。
  Wǒ jiù qù guo yī cì.
  I've only been there once.
- 我早饭 就 吃了一片面包。
  Wǒ zǎofàn jiù chī le yī piàn miànbāo.
  I only had a piece of bread for breakfast.
- 你 就 点了两个菜？
  Nǐ jiù diǎn le liǎng gè cài?
  You ordered only two dishes?
- 他的事，我们 就 知道一点点。
  Tā de shì, wǒmen jiù zhīdào yīdiǎndiǎn.
  We only know a little about his business.
- 她在我们公司 就 工作了两个月。
  Tā zài wǒmen gōngsī jiù gōngzuò le liǎng gè yuè.
  She has worked at our company for only two months.

Used as "Only Have"

In this case, 就 means "only have," similar in meaning to 只有. (In these cases, however, 就有 would not be correct. Just use 就.)

Structure

Subj. + 就 + Number + [Measure Word] + Noun

Examples

- 这里 就 一个厕所?
  Zhèlǐ jiù yī gè cèsuǒ?
  Does this place only have one bathroom?
- 你们家 就 一个孩子吗?
  Nǐmen jiā jiù yī gè háizi ma?
  Does your family only have one child?
- 我 就 一个哥哥。
  Wǒ jiù yī gè gēge.
  I only have one brother.
- 他在上海 就 一个朋友。
  Tā zài Shànghǎi jiù yī gè péngyou.
  He only has one friend in Shanghai.
- 我们公司 就 三个员工。
  Wǒmen gōngsī jiù sān gè yuángōng.
  There are only three employees in our company.

Similar to

- Comparing “cai” and “jiu” (B2)

Expressing duration of inaction (B1)

Saying how long you have *not* done something is not difficult, but the word order is different from the regular pattern for expressing duration. If there's a consistent keyword in this pattern, it's going to be 没 (méi), since it almost always plays a role.

Structure

Remember, this pattern differs from both simple pattern for expressing duration and the pattern for ongoing duration.

> Subj. + (已经 +) Duration + 没 + Verb + 了

So now the duration comes right after the subject and 了 is at the end of the sentence. The verb has to be negated with 没, as the action *hasn't* happened.

Note that 已经 can be omitted.

Examples

- 他们 已经 两天 没 吃东西 了 。
  Tāmen yǐjīng liǎng tiān méi chī dōngxi le .
  They haven't eating anything for two days already.
- 我们 已经 十年 没 见 了 。
  Wǒmen yǐjīng shí nián méi jiàn le .
  We haven't seen each other for ten years already.
- 他 已经 一个星期 没 洗澡 了 。
  Tā yǐjīng yī gè xīngqī méi xǐzǎo le .
  He has already gone a whole week without showering.
- 你多长时间 没 刮胡子 了 ?
  Nǐ duō cháng shíjiān méi guā húzi le ?
  How long has it been since you last shaved?
- 她半个月 没 出门 了 。
  Tā bàn gè yuè méi chūmén le .
  It's been half a month since she's left the house.
- 你们多久 没 回家 了 ?
  Nǐmen duōjiǔ méi huíjiā le ?
  How long has it been since you returned home?

- 你多久 没 休假 了 ?
  Nǐ duōjiǔ méi xiūjià le ?
  How long has it been since your last vacation?
- 买吧，你 已经 一年多 没 买新衣服 了 。
  Mǎi ba, nǐ yǐjīng yī nián duō méi mǎi xīn yīfu le .
  Just buy it. It's been more than one year since you last bought new clothes.
- 你好像很久 没 这么开心 了 。
  Nǐ hǎoxiàng hěnjiǔ méi zhème kāixīn le .
  It seems like it's been a long time since you were this happy.

In English, we may say something like, "I haven't eaten since 9:00 this morning" or "I haven't been to China since the year 2000." Note that the Chinese do not tend to say somebody hasn't done something since a *certain point in time*. Instead, you should either express it as a duration of time that one hasn't done something (as in the above examples), or you can say "the last time somebody did something was [a certain point in time]."

- 我已经十年 没 来中国 了 。
  Wǒ yǐjīng shí nián méi lái Zhōngguó le .
  It's been 10 years since I came to China last.
- 我 上次 来中国 是 2010 年。
  Wǒ shàngcì lái Zhōngguó shì èr-líng-yī-líng nián.
  The last time I came to China was 2010.

Similar to

- Expressing duration with "le" (A2)
- Expressing ongoing duration with double "le" (A2)
- Expressing "already" with "dou" (B1), page 42

Expressing earliness with "jiu" (B1)

Just as 才 (cái) can express lateness[1], 就 (jiù) can be used to indicate that something happened earlier or sooner than expected. It can also be used in the near future to indicate something will happen very soon.

Used as "Right Away" (in the Future)

When something happens "right away," you're talking about "very soon" in the *future*.

Structure

The pattern is as follows:

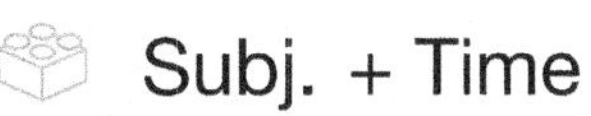

Subj. + Time + 就 + Verb

Examples

- 我马上 就 来。
  Wǒ mǎshàng jiù lái.
  I'll be there in a second.
- 米饭二十分钟 就 好。
  Mǐfàn èrshí fēnzhōng jiù hǎo.
  The rice will be ready in 20 minutes.
- 你们现在 就 出门吗？
  Nǐmen xiànzài jiù chūmén ma?
  Are you leaving the house right now?
- 他们一会儿 就 到。
  Tāmen yīhuìr jiù dào.
  They will be here in a few minutes.
- 老板明天 就 回来。
  Lǎobǎn míngtiān jiù huílái.
  The boss will be back tomorrow.

Note that it can sometimes be hard to translate the feeling of "soonness" into English, but in every one of these examples, the time given in the sentences *feels "soon"* to the speaker.

---

1. Expressing lateness with "cai" (B1), page 72

Used as "Early" (in the Past)

Structure

This use of 就 might be translated "as early as," but usually the earliness is not specifically marked in English.

Examples

- 我们九点上课，他八点 就 来 了 。
  Wǒmen jiǔ diǎn shàngkè, tā bā diǎn jiù lái le .
  We have class at nine, but he came in at eight.
- 飞机十点起飞，他六点 就 到机场 了 。
  Fēijī shí diǎn qǐfēi, tā liù diǎn jiù dào jīchǎng le .
  The plane takes off at ten o'clock, but he arrived at the airport at six.
- 我昨晚八点半 就 睡觉 了 。
  Wǒ zuówǎn bā diǎn bàn jiù shuìjiào le .
  I went to bed at eight thirty last night.
- 她十八岁 就 大学毕业 了 。
  Tā shíbā suì jiù dàxué bìyè le .
  She graduated from college when she was only 18 years old.

Not only can 就 emphasize a "point in time," but it can also emphasize a "time period," indicating that something happened very quickly.

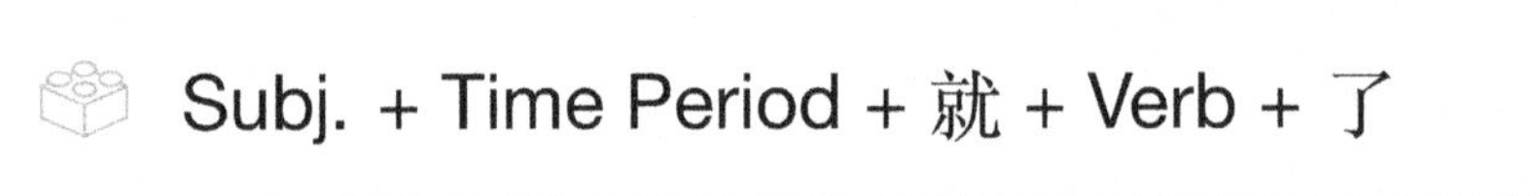

A few examples:

- 你 一个晚上 就 看完 了 ?
  Nǐ yī gè wǎnshang jiù kàn wán le ?
  It only took you just one night to finish reading it?
- 他 十分钟 就 做完 了 。
  Tā shí fēnzhōng jiù zuò wán le .
  It only took him ten minutes to finish doing it.

From the example sentences it is clear that 了 naturally occurs with a verb used after 就. This is because verbs following 就 generally have the feeling of being completed.

Colloquial Saying 早就

早就 means "long ago," and is usually used to express a kind of impatience or surprise on the part of the speaker. It comes before the verb.

- 我 早就 知道 了 ！
  Wǒ zǎo jiù zhīdào le !
  I knew that long ago!
- 她 早就 结婚 了 。
  Tā zǎo jiù jiéhūn le .
  She got married a long time ago.
- 他们 早就 分手 了 。
  Tāmen zǎo jiù fēnshǒu le .
  They broke up a long time ago.
- 我们 早就 毕业 了 。
  Wǒmen zǎo jiù bìyè le .
  We graduated a long time ago!
- 我 早就 跟你说 过 ，他不是好人。
  Wǒ zǎo jiù gēn nǐ shuō guo , tā bù shì hǎo rén.
  I told you a long time ago that he's not a good guy.

Similar to

- Events in quick succession with "yi… jiu…" (B1), page 307
- Expressing lateness with "cai" (B1), page 72
- Comparing "cai" and "jiu" (B2)

Expressing lateness with "cai" (B1)

To express that something happened later than expected, you can use 才 (cái). In English, this might be expressed with "as late as" or "not until." This form is often used with a time of some sort, like a specific time of day, age, etc. This pattern is essentially the opposite of using 就 (jiù) to express earliness[1].

Structure

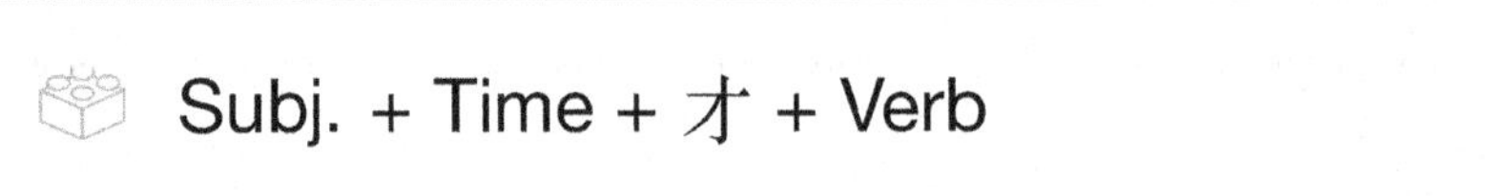

Examples

- 我昨天晚上十一点 才 到家。
  Wǒ zuótiān wǎnshang shíyī diǎn cái dào jiā.
  I didn't arrive at home until eleven o'clock last night.
- 他二十五岁 才 上大学。
  Tā èrshí-wǔ suì cái shàng dàxué.
  He didn't go to college until he was 25.
- 她四十岁 才 结婚。
  Tā sìshí suì cái jiéhūn.
  She didn't get married until she was forty.
- 我女儿昨天十二点 才 睡觉，作业太多了。
  Wǒ nǚ'ér zuótiān shí'èr diǎn cái shuìjiào, zuòyè tài duō le.
  My daughter didn't go to bed until 12 o'clock yesterday. Too much homework.
- 你九点上班，八点半 才 起床？
  Nǐ jiǔ diǎn shàngbān, bā diǎn bàn cái qǐchuáng?
  You start work at nine o'clock, but don't get up until 8:30?
- 飞机刚刚 才 起飞，晚点了两个小时。
  Fēijī gānggāng cái qǐfēi, wǎndiǎn le liǎng gè xiǎoshí.
  The airplane just took off. It was delayed for two hours.
- 电影七点半开始，可是因为堵车，我们八点 才 到。
  Diànyǐng qī diǎn bàn kāishǐ, kěshì yīnwèi dǔchē, wǒmen bā diǎn cái dào.
  The movie began at 7:30, but we didn't arrive until eight because of traffic.

---

1. Expressing earliness with "jiu" (B1), page 69

You can use 才 alone with the verb to indicate the lateness when the context is clear:

- 你怎么 才 吃晚饭？已经十点了。
  Nǐ zěnme cái chī wǎnfàn? Yǐjīng shí diǎn le.
  How come you are eating dinner now? It's 10 pm.
- 你怎么 才 来？我们等了半个多小时。
  Nǐ zěnme cái lái? Wǒmen děng le bàn gè duō xiǎoshí.
  How come you came here so late? We've waited for more than half an hour.

Note that verbs following 才 should not take 了.

- ✘ 我昨天晚上十一点 才 到家 了 。
  Wǒ zuótiān wǎnshang shíyī diǎn cái dào jiā le .
- ✘ 她四十岁 才 结婚 了 。
  Tā sìshí suì cái jiéhūn le .

Similar to

- Expressing "all the way until" with "zhidao" (B1), page 137
- Expressing "when" with "dengdao" (B1), page 325
- Expressing earliness with "jiu" (B1), page 69
- Comparing "cai" and "jiu" (B2)

Sequencing with "xian" and "zai" (B1)

The word 再 (zài) actually has a lot of uses, beyond just "again," and in this pattern it means something like "and then." 先……，再…… (xiān..., zài...) is a pattern used for sequencing events, much like "first..., then..." in English. This pattern can also include 然后 (ránhòu), meaning "and after that."

Basic Usage

In the pattern below, 先 means "first" and 再 has a meaning of "then" or "and then."

Structure

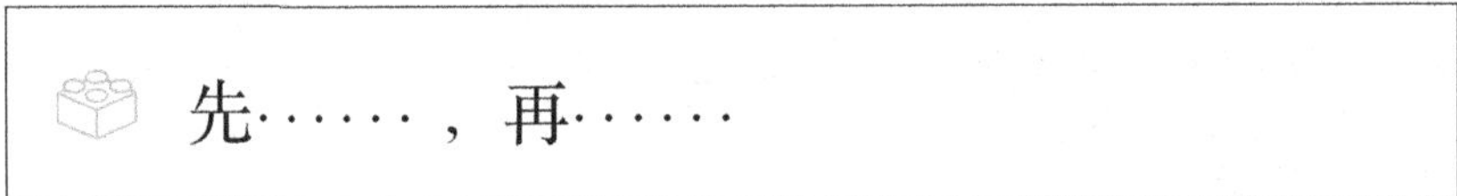

Examples

- 先 洗手 再 吃。
  Xiān xǐ shǒu zài chī.
  Wash your hands first, and then eat.
- 我喜欢 先 洗澡，再 睡觉。
  Wǒ xǐhuan xiān xǐzǎo, zài shuìjiào.
  I prefer to take a bath first and then go to bed.
- 请你 先 买票 再 进去。
  Qǐng nǐ xiān mǎi piào zài jìnqù.
  Please buy a ticket first and then enter.
- 你要 先 做作业，再 看电视。
  Nǐ yào xiān zuò zuòyè, zài kàn diànshì.
  You need to do your homework first, and then watch TV.
- 我想 先 找工作，再 搬家。
  Wǒ xiǎng xiān zhǎo gōngzuò, zài bānjiā.
  I want to find a job first, and then move.

Colloquial Usage with 再说

You may have learned that 再说 can mean "in addition." Well, the usage of 再 here is a more literal combination of 再说, fitting into the 先…… 再…… pattern.

So in this usage, 再说 doesn't really mean "in addition." Rather, it most literally means, "and then we'll talk." In other words, "let's just do this now," and then after we see the result, we can talk some more about next steps. There's a "let's see how this goes first" feeling to the expression.

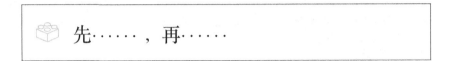

Structure

Note that in the pattern below, the sentence normally ends with 再说.

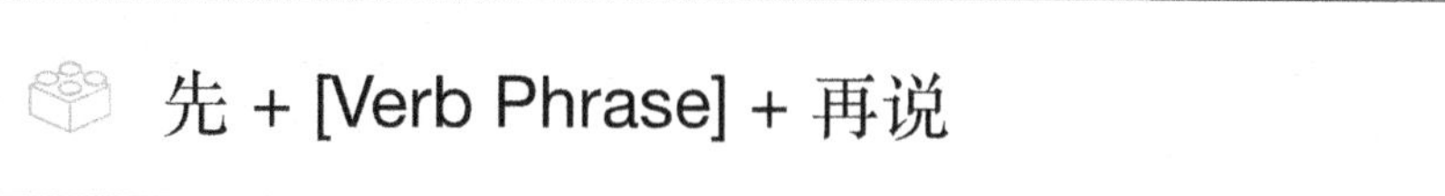

Examples

The 再说 part in the following sentences can be a little tricky to translate into English.

- 先 吃饭 再说 。
  Xiān chīfàn zài shuō.
  Let's eat first, then we'll talk.
- 先 休息一下 再说 。
  Xiān xiūxi yīxià zàishuō.
  Let's rest a little first, then we'll see.
- 你 先 看完 再说 。
  Nǐ xiān kàn wán zàishuō.
  Finish reading first, and then we'll see.
- 我 先 问一下老板 再说 。
  Wǒ xiān wèn yīxià lǎobǎn zàishuō.
  I'm going to ask the boss first before doing anything else.
- 你们 先 讨论一下 再说 。
  Nǐmen xiān tǎolùn yīxià zàishuō.
  You guys discuss a little first, then we'll figure out what to do next.

"and then..." with 接着

When describing a series of actions, steps, or consecutive events, your Chinese will sound more natural if you can diversify your conjunctions. 然后 (ránhòu) is most commonly used, a conjunction which means "and then." Alternatively, you can use 接着 (jiezhe), as a conjunction that means "next," or "afterwards."

A longer example to help you understand how they can all work together:

- 今天早上我起床以后 先 准备早饭， 再 叫孩子们起床， 接着 我们一起吃早饭， 然后 我送他们去学校。
  Jīntiān zǎoshang wǒ qǐchuáng yǐhòu xiān zhǔnbèi zǎofàn, zài jiào háizi men qǐchuáng, jiēzhe wǒmen yīqǐ chī zǎofàn, ránhòu wǒ sòng tāmen qù xuéxiào.
  After I got up this morning, I first prepared breakfast, and then I woke up the kids. Next, we ate breakfast together. After that, I took them to school.

Similar to

- Expressing "again" in the future with "zai" (B1), page 30
- Expressing "again" in the past with "you" (B1), page 33
- Comparing "zai" and "you" (B2)
- Expressing "never again" with "zai ye bu" (B2)

Using "always" as a complaint with "laoshi" (B1)

We have a few ways to say "always" in Chinese, and one of them is to use the word 老是 (lǎoshì). 老是 is usually used in the context of a complaint, like how your sister is "always" hogging the bathroom.

Structure

老是 is an adverb, usually translated into English as "always." It expresses that an action or a condition constantly repeats or continues and can be interchanged with the word 总是. However, 老是 also has an unsatisfied or frustrated tone.

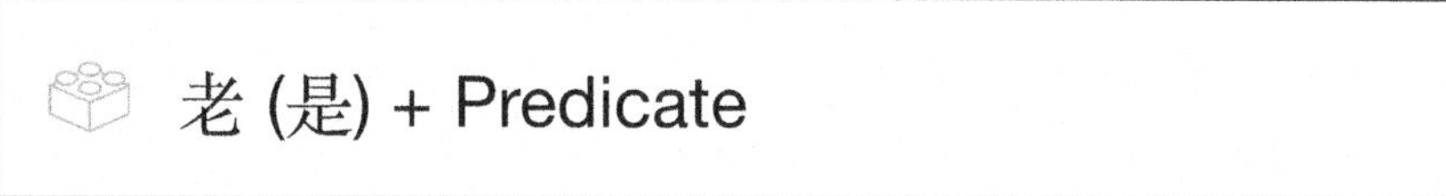

You can also use 老 instead of 老是. The predicate part of the pattern can be a verb or an adjective.

When 老是 is used together with an adjective, 老是 is usually followed by an adverb such as 不, 很, 非常, 这么, 那 etc.

Examples

- 你怎么 老是 加班?
  Nǐ zěnme lǎoshì jiābān?
  Why are you always working late?
- 那个孩子 老 说脏话。
  Nàge háizi lǎo shuō zānghuà.
  That kid always says bad words.
- 你怎么 老是 不高兴?
  Nǐ zěnme lǎoshì bù gāoxìng?
  How are you always unhappy?
- 你儿子上课的时候 老是 说话。
  Nǐ érzi shàngkè de shíhou lǎoshì shuōhuà.
  Your son talks all the time in class.
- 这个老师 老是 这么严肃。
  Zhège lǎoshī lǎoshì zhème yánsù.
  This teacher is always so serious.
- 别 老是 抱怨。
  Bié lǎoshì bàoyuàn.
  Stop complaining all the time.

- 这个机器 老是 出问题。
  Zhège jīqì lǎoshì chū wèntí.
  There is always something wrong with this machine.
- 他经常迟到，还 老是 找借口。
  Tā jīngcháng chídào, hái lǎoshì zhǎo jièkǒu.
  He's always late. And he always makes excuses.
- 奶奶 老是 忘带钥匙。
  Nǎinai lǎoshì wàng dài yàoshi.
  Grandma forgets to take her keys all the time.
- 你 老是 这么凶干吗?
  Nǐ lǎoshì zhème xiōng gànmá?
  Why are you always so mean?
- 他真讨厌，老是 跟朋友借钱。
  Tā zhēn tǎoyàn, lǎoshì gēn péngyou jièqián.
  He's such a nuisance. He's always borrowing money from his friends.

Similar to

- Expressing “always” with “zongshi” (A2)
- Expressing “always” with “conglai” (B1), page 44
- Comparing “buduan” and “buting” (B2)

Using "cai" for small numbers (B1)

The character 才 (cái) can be used to emphasize that a number is small, or less than expected.

Used as a Verb

Structure

In this case, 才 means "is only" or "only have."

才 + Number + [Measure Word] + Noun

In English, we often express this by using "only" or "just" to emphasize that the number is small.

Examples

- 你 才 二十岁?
  Nǐ cái èrshí suì?
  You're only twenty?
- 这个班 才 两个学生。
  Zhège bān cái liǎng gè xuéshēng.
  This class only has two students.
- 你的工资 才 两千? *Probably RMB, per month*
  Nǐ de gōngzī cái liǎng qiān?
  Your salary is only two thousand?
- 这顿饭 才 二十块，太便宜了！
  Zhè dùn fàn cái èrshí kuài. Tài piányi le!
  This meal only cost twenty kuai. It's too cheap!
- 你 才 一百斤，还要减肥? *One "jin" = 500g*
  Nǐ cái yī bǎi jīn, hái yào jiǎnféi?
  You're only 100 jin and you still want to lose some weight?

Used with a Verb

Structure

才 + Verb + Number + Measure Word + Noun

In this pattern, adding a 了 after the verb is optional.

Examples

- 她 才 来了两个月。
  Tā cái lái le liǎng gè yuè.
  She's been here for only two months.
- 这家店关门了？可是它 才 开业一个星期。
  Zhè jiā diàn guānmén le? Kěshì tā cái kāiyè yī gè xīngqī.
  This shop is out of business? But it's only been one week since it opened.
- 已经两天了，你 才 看完一页？
  Yǐjīng liǎng tiān le, nǐ cái kàn wán yī yè?
  It's been two days and you only finished reading one page?
- 我们 才 玩了一会儿，再玩一会儿吧？
  Wǒmen cái wán le yīhuìr, zài wán yīhuìr ba?
  We've only played for a short while. Can we play a little bit longer?
- 他们结婚了？他们 才 认识三个月！
  Tāmen jiéhūn le? Tāmen cái rènshi sān gè yuè!
  They got married? They've only known each other for three months!

Similar to

- Expressing "small quantity" with "jiu" (B1), page 64
- Expressing lateness with "cai" (B1), page 72

Using "ye" and "dou" together (B1)

If you are trying to call attention to similarities between multiple things, you will want to use 也 (yě) first followed by 都 (dōu) to express that these multiple things have something in common.

Positive Form

Structure

When using 也 (yě) and 都 (dōu) in the same sentence, remember to put 也 (yě) first:

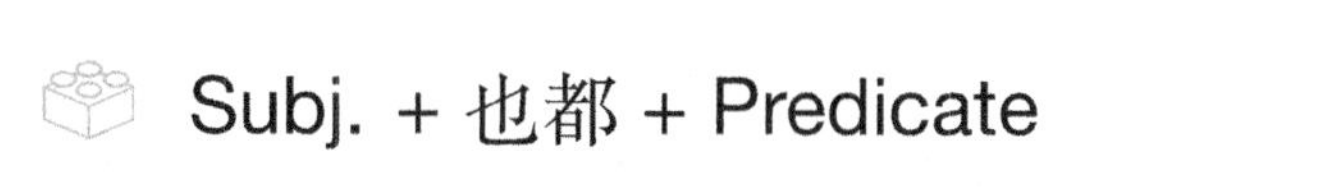

The predicate part of the pattern can be a verb or an adjective.

Examples

- 我很好，我的家人 也都 很好。
  Wǒ hěn hǎo, wǒ de jiārén yě dōu hěn hǎo.
  I'm good. So is everyone in my family.
- 大人很喜欢这个餐厅，孩子们 也都 很喜欢。
  Dàren hěn xǐhuan zhège cāntīng, háizi men yě dōu hěn xǐhuan.
  Adults all like this restaurant, and the children all like it too.
- 我老板是美国人，很多客户 也都 是美国人。
  Wǒ lǎobǎn shì Měiguó rén, hěn duō kèhù yě dōu shì Měiguó rén.
  My boss is American. Lots of our clients are also Americans.
- 他很高，他的两个弟弟 也都 比较高。
  Tā hěn gāo, tā de liǎng gè dìdi yě dōu bǐjiào gāo.
  He's tall. His two younger brothers are also pretty tall.
- 老板加班，你们 也都 要加班吗?
  Lǎobǎn jiābān, nǐmen yě dōu yào jiābān ma?
  The boss will be working late. Will you all need to work late too?

Negative Form

Structure

If you're using 不 (bù) or 没 (méi) with 也都 (yě dōu) in the same sentence, remember to put 不 (bù) or 没 (méi) after 也都 (yě dōu):

 Subj. + 也都 + 不 / 没 + Predicate

Examples

- 我们 也都没 吃饭，一起去吧。
  Wǒmen yě dōu méi chīfàn, yīqǐ qù ba.
  We all haven't eaten either. Let's go together.
- 这些不贵，那些 也都不 贵。
  Zhèxiē bù guì, nàxiē yě dōu bù guì.
  These are not expensive. Those aren't expensive, either.
- 我不喜欢蝙蝠侠，我的朋友 也都不 喜欢他。
  Wǒ bù xǐhuan Biānfú-xiá, wǒ de péngyou yě dōu bù xǐhuan tā.
  I don't like Batman. My friends don't like him, either.
- 你觉得你不容易？我们 也都不 容易。
  Nǐ juéde nǐ bù róngyì? Wǒmen yě dōu bù róngyì.
  You're saying it isn't easy for you? It isn't easy for us, either.
- 我没去过美国，我的家人 也都没 去过。
  Wǒ méi qù guo Měiguó, wǒ de jiārén yě dōu méi qù guo.
  I've never been to the USA. My family has never been there, either.

Similar to

- The "all" adverb "dou" (A1)
- The "also" adverb "ye" (A1)

Adjectives with "name" and "zheme" (B1)

In English, the words "that" and "so" are often used to emphasize the degree of an adjective (ex. "he is so tall" or "the food is so good"). In Chinese, 那么 (nàme) and 这么 (zhème) serve the same function.

Structure

All you have to do to use this grammar structure is put the 那么 or 这么 in front of the adjective.

 Subj. + 那么 / 这么 + Adj.

Examples

You could think of 这么 as "this" or "so," and 那么 as "that" or "so."

- 他说得 这么 快，你们听得懂吗？
  Tā shuō de zhème kuài, nǐmen tīng de dǒng ma?
  He speaks so fast. Can you guys understand?
- 我没想到这个考试 这么 难。
  Wǒ méi xiǎng dào zhège kǎoshì zhème nán.
  I didn't expect this exam would be this difficult.
- 雨 这么 大，明天再去吧。
  Yǔ zhème dà, míngtiān zài qù ba.
  The rain is so heavy. How about we go tomorrow?
- 你 那么 聪明，一定能猜到。
  Nǐ nàme cōngming, yīdìng néng cāi dào.
  You're so smart. You can definitely guess it.
- 老板 那么 忙，肯定没时间。
  Lǎobǎn nàme máng, kěndìng méi shíjiān.
  The boss is so busy. He definitely won't have time for this.
- 今天怎么 这么 冷？
  Jīntiān zěnme zhème lěng?
  Why is it so cold today?
- 你怎么 这么 没礼貌？
  Nǐ zěnme zhème méi lǐmào?
  How can you be this impolite?

- 这个外国人怎么会了解 那么 多中国历史?

  Zhège wàiguórén zěnme huì liǎojiě nàme duō Zhōngguó lìshǐ?

  How could this foreigner know that much about Chinese history?

- 中国人口 这么 多，当然会有很多社会问题。

  Zhōngguó rénkǒu zhème duō, dāngrán huì yǒu hěn duō shèhuì wèntí.

  China has such a big population. Of course there will be many social problems.

- 科技 那么 发达，什么都是有可能的。

  Kējì nàme fādá, shénme dōu shì yǒu kěnéng de.

  Science and technology is so developed. Anything is possible.

When to use which one

You might be thinking that since 这 ("this") and 那 ("that") have totally different meanings, how could they be used in an essentially interchangeable way? Well, there are some differences. 这么 is used when the subject is close by (either in space or in time), when you would say "this" or 这个. On the other hand, if the subject is far away (or in the past), you would likely use 那么.

Similar to

- Simple "noun + adjective" sentences (A1)
- Expressing "really" with "zhen" (A2)
- Intensifying with "duo" (A2)
- Superlative "zui" (A2)
- Adjectives with "-ji le" (B1), page 4

Expressing "quite" with "ting" (B1)

挺 (tǐng) can be used before an adjective to mean "quite," "rather," or "pretty," as in "pretty good." This pattern is quite common in spoken Chinese.

Used with Adjectives

Using 挺 with an adjective means "quite."

Structure

挺 + Adj. + 的

Examples

- 这个老师挺年轻的。
  Zhège lǎoshī tǐng niánqīng de.
  This teacher is quite young.
- 你男朋友挺帅的。
  Nǐ nánpéngyou tǐng shuài de.
  Your boyfriend is pretty handsome.
- 最近大家都挺忙的。
  Zuìjìn dàjiā dōu tǐng máng de.
  We've all been quite busy lately.
- 这件衣服大小挺合适的。
  Zhè jiàn yīfu dàxiǎo tǐng héshì de.
  The size of this piece of clothing is quite suitable.
- 他家不是挺有钱的吗?
  Tā jiā bù shì tǐng yǒuqián de ma?
  Isn't his family rather rich?

Used with Verbs

In English, we're limited on what words come after the word "quite." Though Chinese is open to taking on verbs after 挺, these verbs are mostly psychological verbs.

Structure

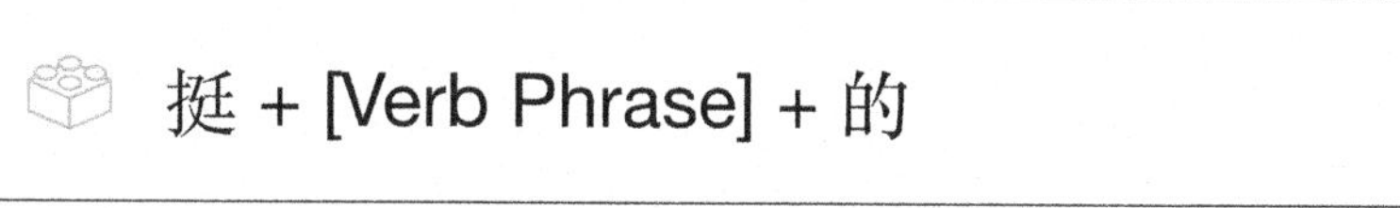

挺 + [Verb Phrase] + 的

Examples

- 我们都 挺 想你 的 。
  Wǒmen dōu tǐng xiǎng nǐ de .
  We all quite miss you.
- 我 挺 喜欢这份工作 的 。
  Wǒ tǐng xǐhuan zhè fèn gōngzuò de .
  I quite like this job.
- 我女儿 挺 怕他爸爸 的 。
  Wǒ nǚ'ér tǐng pà tā bàba de .
  My daughter is quite afraid of his father.
- 那件事我 挺 后悔 的 。
  Nà jiàn shì wǒ tǐng hòuhuǐ de .
  I rather regret that incident.
- 你不是 挺 爱他 的 吗？怎么分手了？
  Nǐ bù shì tǐng ài tā de ma? Zěnme fēnshǒu le?
  Weren't you quite in love with him? How come you broke up?

Similar to

- Expressing "excessively" with "tai" (A1)
- Expressing "really" with "zhen" (A2)
- Expressing "rather" with "bijiao" (B1), page 87

Expressing "rather" with "bijiao" (B1)

The word 比较 (bǐjiào) can be a verb which means "to compare." But it can also be an adverb meaning "comparatively" or "rather."

Used with Adjectives

Structure

The adverb 比较 can be used to express "quite," "rather," or "relatively."

 Subj. + 比较 + Adj.

Examples

- 这个问题 比较 简单。
  Zhège wèntí bǐjiào jiǎndān.
  This question is quite easy.
- 我觉得这个价格 比较 贵。
  Wǒ juéde zhège jiàgé bǐjiào guì.
  I think this price is rather expensive.
- 我家离市中心 比较 近。
  Wǒ jiā lí shìzhōngxīn bǐjiào jìn.
  My place is relatively close to downtown.
- 大城市的工作压力 比较 大。
  Dà chéngshì de gōngzuò yālì bǐjiào dà.
  Jobs in big cities have quite a lot of pressure.
- 你上班坐地铁 比较 方便吧?
  Nǐ shàngbān zuò dìtiě bǐjiào fāngbiàn ba?
  To get to work, it's quite convenient for you to take the subway, right?

Used with Verbs

比较 can also be used with psychological verbs.

Structure

 Subj. + 比较 + [Verb Phrase]

Examples

- 我 比较 讨厌男人说脏话。

  Wǒ bǐjiào tǎoyàn nánrén shuō zānghuà.

  I quite hate it when men use foul language.

- 你 比较 喜欢用 Gmail 还是 Hotmail？ *Note that for this phrase, the translation is a totally different verb.*

  Nǐ bǐjiào xǐhuan yòng Gmail háishì Hotmail?

  Do you prefer to use Gmail or Hotmail?

- 我父母 比较 反对我找外国男朋友。

  Wǒ fùmǔ bǐjiào fǎnduì wǒ zhǎo wàiguó nánpéngyou.

  My parents rather object to me seeking a foreign boyfriend.

- 民众 比较 支持新的就业政策。

  Mínzhòng bǐjiào zhīchí xīn de jiùyè zhèngcè.

  The public rather supports the new employment policy.

- 老板通常 比较 关注结果，不是过程。

  Lǎobǎn tōngcháng bǐjiào guānzhù jiéguǒ, bù shì guòchéng.

  The boss usually pays more attention to results and not process.

Similar to

- Expressing “a little too” with “you dian” (A2)
- Moderating positive adjectives with “hai” (A2)
- Special verbs with “hen” (A2)
- Superlative “zui” (A2)
- Expressing “quite” with “ting” (B1), page 85
- Making judgments with “suan” (B1), page 172
- Expressing “a bit too” (B2)

Ending a non-exhaustive list with "shenme de" (B1)

什么的 (shénme de) is an informal way to express "and so on," and is used to end a list of items when it is obvious to the listener what class of things the speaker is talking about. 什么的 can also be used after a single item if it is obvious enough what might follow.

Structure

Noun 1, Noun 2 (+ Noun 3) + 什么的

Examples

- 我奶奶不吃肉，只吃蔬菜、豆腐 什么的 。
  Wǒ nǎinai bù chī ròu, zhǐ chī shūcài, dòufu shénme de.
  My grandma doesn't eat meat. She only eats vegetables, tofu, and so on.
- 养狗很麻烦，你要喂它，给它洗澡，跟它玩 什么的 。
  Yǎng gǒu hěn máfan, nǐ yào wèi tā, gěi tā xǐzǎo, gēn tā wán shénme de.
  Having a dog is too much trouble. You need to feed it, give it a bath, play with it, and so on.
- 数学、物理、化学 什么的 ，我都不感兴趣。
  Shùxué, wùlǐ, huàxué shénme de, wǒ dōu bù gǎnxìngqù.
  Math, physics, chemistry, and so on. I'm not interested in any of them.
- 我喜欢实用的礼物，手表、衣服、书 什么的 。
  Wǒ xǐhuan shíyòng de lǐwù, shǒubiǎo, yīfu, shū shénme de.
  I like practical presents: watches, clothes, books, and so on.
- 我们见面一般就是吃饭、聊天 什么的 。
  Wǒmen jiànmiàn yībān jiùshì chīfàn, liáotiān shénme de.
  When we meet, we just eat a meal, chat, and so on.
- 明天去野餐，我们要不要买一些水果、零食 什么的 ？
  Míngtiān qù yěcān, wǒmen yào bu yào mǎi yīxiē shuǐguǒ, língshí shénme de?
  We are going on picnic tomorrow. Shall we buy some fruits, snacks, and so on?
- 跑步、游泳、篮球 什么的 ，这些运动他都喜欢。
  Pǎobù, yóuyǒng, lánqiú shénme de, zhèxiē yùndòng tā dōu xǐhuan.
  Running, swimming, basketball, and so on. He likes all these sports.

- 长城、故宫 什么的 ，都是北京很有名的景点。

  Chángchéng, Gùgōng shénme de, dōu shì Běijīng hěn yǒumíng de jǐngdiǎn.

  The Great Wall, the Forbidden City, and so on. They're all very famous tourist attractions in Beijing.

- 一个人住，洗衣服、做饭 什么的 都要自己做。

  Yīgèrén zhù, xǐ yīfu, zuòfàn shénme de dōu yào zìjǐ zuò.

  When you live alone, laundry, cooking, and so on all need to be done yourself.

- 电视、洗衣机 什么的 ，我爸爸都会修。

  Diànshì, xǐyījī shénme de, wǒ bàba dōu huì xiū.

  Televisions, washing machines, and so on. My father can fix all those.

It can be a little impolite to use 什么的 after a list of peoples names, in which case 等[1] can be used in place of 什么的. When referring to a list of friends in informal contexts there is no problem using 什么的.

Similar to

- Expressing "stuff like that" with "zhileide" (B1), page 91
- Non-exhaustive lists with "dengdeng" (B1), page 93
- Listing things with "a" (B2)

1. Non-exhaustive lists with "dengdeng" (B1), page 93

Expressing "stuff like that" with "zhileide" (B1)

之类的 (zhī lèi de) can be translated as "and so on" or "and stuff like that." As in English, this grammar point is used to continue a list without explicitly mentioning further items within it.

Structure

像……之类的 + [Category]

The 像 can also be left out:

……之类的 + [Category]

Examples

- 我家附近有很多 像 KFC 之类的 快餐店。
  Wǒ jiā fùjìn yǒu hěn duō xiàng KFC zhī lèi de kuàicān diàn.
  There are many fast-food restaurants in my neighborhood, like KFC and others like it.
- 你喜欢《星球大战》之类的 电影吗?
  Nǐ xǐhuan "Xīngqiú Dà Zhàn" zhī lèi de diànyǐng ma?
  Do you like movies like Star Wars?
- 我没看过 像 吸血鬼 之类的 故事。
  Wǒ méi kàn guo xiàng xīxuèguǐ zhī lèi de gùshi.
  I haven't read stories about vampires and stuff like that.
- 你们公司谁负责管理 之类的 工作?
  Nǐmen gōngsī shéi fùzé guǎnlǐ zhī lèi de gōngzuò?
  In your company, who is in charge of management and stuff like that?
- 她很适合做 像 市场推广 之类的 工作。
  Tā hěn shìhé zuò xiàng shìchǎng tuīguǎng zhī lèi de gōngzuò.
  She's very suitable for jobs like marketing and similar.
- 她穿的衣服都是 Gucci、Chanel 之类的 名牌。
  Tā chuān de yīfu dōu shì Gucci, Chanel zhī lèi de míngpái.
  The clothes she wears are all famous brands like Gucci, Chanel, and the like.

- 年轻人很喜欢用 像 支付宝 之类的 电子支付方式。

  Niánqīng rén hěn xǐhuan yòng xiàng Zhīfùbǎo zhī lèi de diànzǐ zhīfù fāngshì.

  Young people love using electronic methods of payment like Alipay and similar.

- 很多中国老人喜欢广场舞、太极 之类的 运动。

  Hěn duō Zhōngguó lǎorén xǐhuan guǎngchǎng wǔ, Tàijí zhī lèi de yùndòng.

  Many old Chinese people are fond of exercises like plaza dancing, tai chi, and stuff like that.

- 我们学校很少办才艺比赛 之类的 活动。

  Wǒmen xuéxiào hěnshǎo bàn cáiyì bǐsài zhī lèi de huódòng.

  Our school rarely holds activities like talent shows or similar.

- 中国女孩会怎么回应 像 "你真漂亮" 之类的 话?

  Zhōngguó nǚhái huì zěnme huíyìng xiàng "nǐ zhēn piàoliang" zhī lèi de huà?

  How would Chinese girls respond to lines like, "you are really pretty" and the like?

Similar to

- Ending a non-exhaustive list with "shenme de" (B1), page 89
- Non-exhaustive lists with "dengdeng" (B1), page 93
- Listing things with "a" (B2)

Non-exhaustive lists with "dengdeng" (B1)

等等 (děng děng) or simply 等 (děng), is just like saying "and so on" or "etc." in English, but it's just a bit more formal. Both are placed after listing a series of items (generally with a list that exceeds two items).

Structure

The basic structure is easy. Just make a list of things and add 等 (děng) or 等等 (děng děng) to the end of the list. It's the same as in English when we use "etc." at the end of a list, except in Chinese you don't put a final comma before the 等 or 等等.

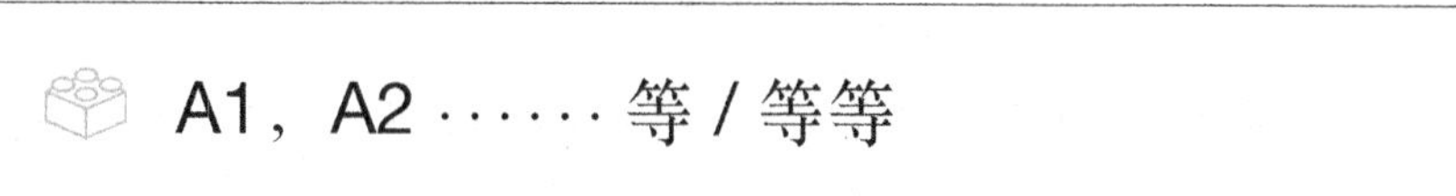

Examples

- 西瓜、菠萝、葡萄 等等 ，我都喜欢吃。
  Xīguā, bōluó, pútao, děngděng, wǒ dōu xǐhuan chī.
  Watermelons, pineapples, apples, grapes, and so on… I like them all.
- 我爸爸很喜欢运动，比如跑步、游泳、打羽毛球 等等 。
  Wǒ bàba hěn xǐhuan yùndòng, bǐrú pǎobù, yóuyǒng, dǎ yǔmáoqiú, děngděng.
  My father likes different sports, for example, running, swimming, playing badminton, etc.
- Bruce Li、Jackie Chan、Jet Li 等 都是功夫明星。
  Bruce Li, Jackie Chan, Jet Li děng dōu shì gōngfu míngxīng.
  Bruce Li, Jackie Chan, Jet Li, etc. are all kung fu stars.
- 我们公司有市场部、设计部、技术部 等等 。
  Wǒmen gōngsī yǒu shìchǎng bù, shèjì bù, jìshù bù děngděng.
  Our company has a marketing department, design department, technology department, etc.
- 联合国的工作语言有英语、法语、西班牙语 等 。
  Liánhéguó de gōngzuò yǔyán yǒu Yīngyǔ, Fǎyǔ, Xībānyáyǔ děng.
  The working languages of the UN are English, French, Spanish, etc.

等 (děng) can also be added to the end of a list and is followed by a noun that represents the list. In this case, you can only use 等:

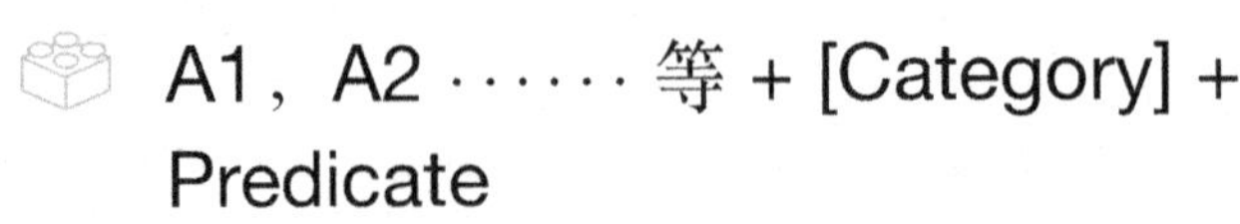

The predicate part of the pattern can be a verb or an adjective.

- 长城、故宫 等 景点都是北京有名的景点。
  Chángchéng, Gùgōng děng jǐngdiǎn dōu shì Běijīng yǒumíng de jǐngdiǎn.
  The Great Wall, the Forbidden City, etc. are all famous tourist attractions in Beijing.
- 北京、上海、广州 等 城市的经济都很发达。
  Běijīng, Shànghǎi, Guǎngzhōu děng chéngshì de jīngjì dōu hěn fādá.
  Beijing, Shanghai, Guangzhou and so on are economically developed cities.
- 牛津、剑桥 等 大学是英国最有名的大学。
  Niújīn, Jiànqiáo děng dàxué shì Yīngguó zuì yǒumíng de dàxué.
  Oxford, Cambridge and so on are the most famous British universities.
- 中国、印度、巴西 等 国家都是发展中国家。
  Zhōngguó, Yìndù, Bāxī děng guójiā dōu shì fāzhǎn zhōng guójiā.
  China, India, Brazil and so on are all developing countries.
- 食品安全、空气污染、人工智能 等 话题都是热点话题。
  Shípǐn ānquán, kōngqì wūrǎn, réngōng zhìnéng děng huàtí dōu shì rèdiǎn huàtí.
  Food safety, air pollution, artificial intelligence, and so on are all hot topics.

Similar to

- Expressing "stuff like that" with "zhileide" (B1), page 91
- Listing things with "a" (B2)

A softer "but" with "buguo" (B1)

Instead of just using 可是 or 但是, you can also use the softer and more informal 不过 (búguò), which also means "but."

Structure

Just like its counterparts, 不过 is a conjunction that comes between two distinct clauses.

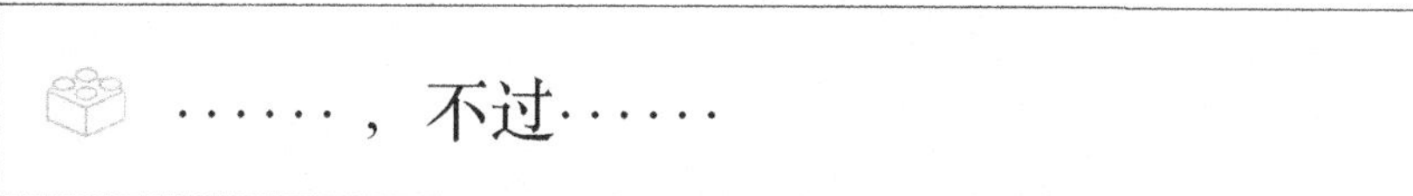

Examples

- 这件衣服我很喜欢，不过有点贵。
  Zhè jiàn yīfu wǒ hěn xǐhuan, bùguò yǒudiǎn guì.
  I like this piece of clothing, but it's a little bit expensive.
- 这家餐厅我没去过，不过我听说还不错。
  Zhè jiā cāntīng wǒ méi qù guo, bùguò wǒ tīngshuō hái bùcuò.
  I've never been to this restaurant, but I heard it's pretty good.
- 这个学生很聪明，不过有点懒。
  Zhège xuéshēng hěn cōngming, bùguò yǒudiǎn lǎn.
  This student is very smart, but he's a little lazy.
- 那儿的天气不太好，不过我们玩得很开心。
  Nàr de tiānqì bù tài hǎo, bùguò wǒmen wán de hěn kāixīn.
  The weather there was not very good, but we had a lot of fun.
- 他是东北人，不过他没有口音。
  Tā shì dōngběi rén, bùguò tā méiyǒu kǒuyīn.
  He's from the northeast, but he doesn't have the accent.
- 他说得不错，不过不认识汉字。
  Tā shuō de bùcuò, bùguò bù rènshi Hànzì.
  He can speak well, but he doesn't know any Chinese characters.
- 我的钱包丢了，不过没丢什么重要的东西。
  Wǒ de qiánbāo diū le, bùguò méi diū shénme zhòngyào de dōngxi.
  I lost my wallet, but I didn't lose anything important.

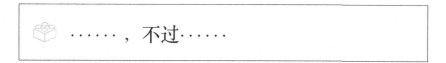

- 刚来的时候很想家，不过现在习惯了。
  Gāng lái de shíhou hěn xiǎng jiā, bùguò xiànzài xíguàn le.
  I was homesick when I first got here, but I'm used to it now.
- 你可以参加，不过有个条件。
  Nǐ kěyǐ cānjiā, bùguò yǒu gè tiáojiàn.
  You can participate, but there is a condition.
- 他还在考虑，不过我已经决定了。
  Tā hái zài kǎolǜ, bùguò wǒ yǐjīng juédìng le.
  He's still considering it, but I've already decided.

Similar to

- Expressing "although" with "suiran" and "danshi" (B1), page 309
- Expressing "however" with "ran'er"

Expressing "how about" with "yaobu" (B1)

Colloquially, 要不 (yàobù) can be used for making suggestions, like how we use "how about" in English.

Structure

要不 can be used as an indirect way of giving a suggestion, as the speaker is using 要不 to seek consent of the listener. When using 要不 in this way, it can come either at the beginning of the sentence or in the middle, after explaining the situation.

Reason / Situation，要不 + Suggestion

or

要不 + Suggestion，Reason / Situation

Examples

- 大家都有点累了，要不休息一会儿吧。
  Dàjiā dōu yǒudiǎn lèi le, yàobù xiūxi yīhuìr ba.
  Everyone is a little tired. Let's rest for a while.
- 要不我们一起去吧，一个人去没意思。
  Yàobù wǒmen yīqǐ qù ba, yīgèrén qù méi yìsi.
  How about we go together? It's no fun to go by myself.
- 这个星期我比较忙，要不下个星期见？
  Zhège xīngqī wǒ bǐjiào máng, yàobù xià gè xīngqī jiàn?
  I'm pretty busy this week. How about we meet up next week?
- 要不我们换个地方吧，这里太吵了。
  Yàobù wǒmen huàn gè dìfang ba, zhèlǐ tài chǎo le.
  How about we go to somewhere else? It's too loud here.
- 要不你先走吧，我还没做完。
  Yàobù nǐ xiān zǒu ba, wǒ hái méi zuò wán.
  How about you leave first? I haven't finished yet.

- 下雨了，要不明天去吧。
  Xiàyǔ le, yàobù míngtiān qù ba.
  It's raining. How about we go tomorrow?
- 这么远，要不我开车送你去？
  Zhème yuǎn, yàobù wǒ kāichē sòng nǐ qù?
  It's so far. How about I drive you there?

Multiple Meanings

When 要不 (yàobù) is used to mean "otherwise," it's a shortened form of 要不然 (yàobùrán), which literally means "if that's not the case."

Note 要不 (yàobù) can also be used to offer "either/or" choices to others, similar to 要么[1] (yàome).

Here are a few examples of 要不 used as "otherwise":

- 你先吃吧，要不然饭就凉了。
  Nǐ xiān chī ba, yàobùrán fàn jiù liáng le.
  You should eat; otherwise, the food will get cold.
- 打车吧，要不会迟到的。
  Dǎchē ba, yàobù huì chídào de.
  Take a taxi. Otherwise, you'll be late.
- 快回家吧，要不你爸妈会担心的。
  Kuài huíjiā ba, yàobù nǐ bà mā huì dānxīn de.
  Hurry home, or your parents will worry about you.

Similar to

- Suggestions with "ba" (A1)
- Expressing "or" in statements (A2)
- Expressing "either… or…" with "yaome" (B1), page 311
- Expressing "had better" with "haishi" (B1), page 55
- Expressing good luck with "haihao" (B1), page 327
- Expressing "unless" with "chufei" (B2)
- Providing two options with double "huozhe" (B2)

---

1. Expressing "either… or…" with "yaome" (B1), page 311

Expressing "in addition" with "haiyou" (B1)

还有 (háiyǒu) is used to express "in addition..." or "and also..." in a conversation. It is for introducing new information as an afterthought.

Structure

It's as simple as using 还有 before the new clause or sentence. 还有 can also be used with a comma, similar to how we can say "in addition..." in English.

Examples

- 你需要吃药。还有，要多休息。
  Nǐ xūyào chī yào. Háiyǒu, yào duō xiūxi.
  You need to take medicine. Also, you should get more rest.
- 我要大杯，不要冰，还有，少放糖。
  Wǒ yào dà bēi,bùyào bīng. Háiyǒu, shǎo fàng táng.
  I want a large drink, no ice. Also, just a little sugar, please.
- 不要一边吃饭一边说话。还有，别吃那么快。
  Bùyào yībiān chīfàn yībiān shuōhuà. Háiyǒu, bié chī nàme kuài.
  Don't talk while you eat. Also, don't eat so fast.
- 考试的时候不要说话。还有，不要用手机。
  Kǎoshì de shíhou bùyào shuōhuà. Háiyǒu, bùyào yòng shǒujī.
  No talking while taking a test. Also, no using your cell phones.
- 他们不想要孩子。还有，他们也没时间照顾孩子。
  Tāmen bù xiǎng yào háizi. Háiyǒu, tāmen yě méi shíjiān zhàogù háizi.
  They don't want to have kids. Plus, they wouldn't have time to look after a kid.
- 酒店谁来订？还有，机票买了吗？
  Jiǔdiàn shéi lái dìng? Háiyǒu, jīpiào mǎi hǎo le ma?
  Who's going to book the hotel room? Also, did you buy the plane tickets?
- 下班以后早点回来。还有，回来的路上买点水果。
  Xiàbān yǐhòu zǎo diǎn huílái. Háiyǒu, huílái de lùshàng mǎi diǎn shuǐguǒ.
  Come back early after work. Also, buy some fruit on your way back.

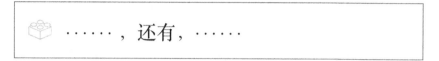

- 今天要做完这个报告。还有，明天开会前打印三份。

  Jīntiān yào zuò wán zhège bàogào. Háiyǒu, míngtiān kāihuì qián dǎyìn sān fèn.

  You need to finish this report today. In addition, print three copies before the meeting tomorrow.

- 入住前要付押金。还有，不能带宠物。

  Rùzhù qián yào fù yājīn. Háiyǒu, bù néng dài chǒngwù.

  You need to pay the deposit before using the room. Also, you're not allowed to have pets here.

- 先生，这里不能抽烟。还有，请你们声音小一点。

  Xiānsheng, zhèlǐ bù néng chōuyān. Háiyǒu, qǐng nǐmen shēngyīn xiǎo yīdiǎn.

  Sir, you can't smoke in here. Also, lower your voices, please.

Similar to

- Expressing "and" with "he" (A1)
- Expressing "and also" with "hai" (A2)
- Expressing "except" and "in addition" with "chule··· yiwai" (B1), page 313
- Expressing "in addition" with "lingwai" (B2), page 101
- Expressing "in addition" with "zaishuo" (B1), page 103
- Expressing "not only... but also" (B1), page 322
- Using "budan... geng" to express "not only... but also"
- Expressing "and" with "he" (advanced) (B2)
- Expressing "as well as" with "yiji" (C1)

Expressing "in addition" with "lingwai" (B1)

另外 (lìngwài) can be used to express "in addition" or "besides," and is often followed by 还 (hái) or 也 (yě).

Using as a Conjunction

As a conjunction, 另外 can link two sentences.

Structure

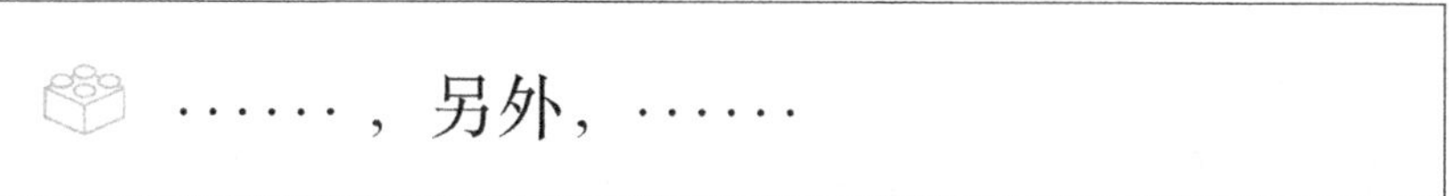

Note that 还 or 也 is often used after 另外.

Examples

- 这个课文太难了，我不想学。另外，我也没准备。
  Zhège kèwén tài nán le, wǒ bù xiǎng xué. Lìngwài, wǒ yě méi zhǔnbèi.
  This lesson is too difficult and I don't want to read it. Besides, I didn't prepare for it.
- 希望你不要再迟到了。另外，你应该穿得正式一点。
  Xīwàng nǐ bùyào zài chídào le. Lìngwài, nǐ yīnggāi chuān de zhèngshì yīdiǎn.
  I hope you won't be late again. In addition, you should also dress a bit more formally.
- 这个航班经常晚点。另外，他们的飞机餐也很难吃。
  Zhège hángbān jīngcháng wǎndiǎn. Lìngwài, tāmen de fēijī cān yě hěn nánchī.
  This flight is frequently delayed. In addition, their in-flight food is terrible.
- 我没时间参加这个活动。另外，我也不太感兴趣。
  Wǒ méi shíjiān cānjiā zhège huódòng. Lìngwài, wǒ yě bù tài gǎn xìngqù.
  I don't have time to attend this activity. Besides, I'm not really interested.
- 幼儿园提供午餐。另外，每天下午还有点心和水果。
  Yòuéryuán tígōng wǔcān. Lìngwài, měi tiān xiàwǔ hái yǒu diǎnxin hé shuǐguǒ.
  The kindergarten provides lunch. In addition, there are also snacks and fruit every afternoon.

Used as an Adverb

As an adverb, 另外 adds the meaning of "additionally" (although that's probably not going to be the most natural English translation for most sentences).

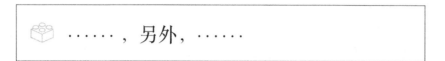

Structure

 另外 + [Verb Phrase]

Examples

- 今天我没空，能不能 另外 安排时间？

  Jīntiān wǒ méi kòng, néng bu néng lìngwài ānpái shíjiān?

  I don't have time today. Can you schedule it another time?

- 在我家开会不方便，我们 另外 找地方吧。

  Zài wǒ jiā kāi huì bù fāngbiàn, wǒmen lìngwài zhǎo dìfang ba.

  It's not very convenient to have a meeting at my place. Let's find some other place.

- 这个项目他们做得不好，我建议你们 另外 找人来做。

  Zhège xiàngmù tāmen zuò de bu hǎo, wǒ jiànyì nǐmen lìngwài zhǎo rén lái zuò.

  They aren't doing a good job on this project. I suggest you find some other people to do it.

- 这里是 VIP 室，要 另外 付费才能用。

  Zhèlǐ shì VIP shì, yào lìngwài fùfèi cái néng yòng.

  This is the VIP room. You will have to pay extra in order to use it.

- 如果学生觉得不难，老师可以 另外 加一些学习内容。

  Rúguǒ xuéshēng juéde bù nán, lǎoshī kěyǐ lìngwài jiā yīxiē xuéxí nèiróng.

  If the students don't find it difficult, the teacher can add more study material.

Similar to

- Expressing "and" with "he" (A1)
- Expressing "except" and "in addition" with "chule⋯yiwai" (B1), page 313
- Expressing "in addition" with "haiyou" (B1), page 99
- Expressing "in addition" with "zaishuo" (B1), page 103
- Expressing "not only… but also" (B1), page 322
- Expressing "the other" with "lingwai" (B1), page 237
- Using "budan… geng" to express "not only… but also"
- Expressing "and" with "he" (advanced) (B2)

Expressing "in addition" with "zaishuo" (B1)

再说 (zàishuō) is used in a similar way as "in addition" or "moreover" in that it adds supporting information or reasons to the topic at hand.

Structure

Just add 再说 to the beginning of the second clause of your sentence. Remember that the parts of the sentence before and after 再说 should be logically related to each other.

Note that 也 is often used in the second clause.

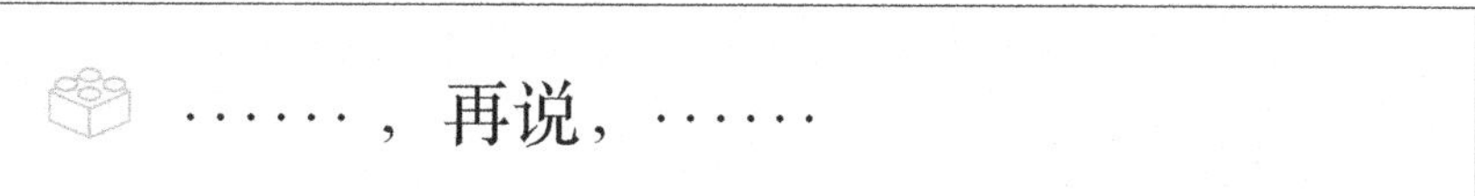

Examples

- 这么晚，别走了。再说，外面正在下雪。
  Zhème wǎn, bié zǒu le. Zàishuō, wàimiàn zhèngzài xiàxuě.
  It's so late. Stay. Besides, it's snowing outside.
- 他喜欢，就让他去吧。再说，他在家也没事干。
  Tā xǐhuan, jiù ràng tā qù ba. Zàishuō, tā zài jiā yě méi shì gàn.
  He likes it. Just let him go. Besides, he's got nothing to do at home.
- 那件衣服太贵了，我没买。再说，我也不是很喜欢。
  Nà jiàn yīfu tài guì le, wǒ méi mǎi. Zàishuō, wǒ yě bù shì hěn xǐhuan.
  That piece of clothing is too expensive. I didn't buy it. Besides, I didn't like it so much.
- 对不起，我没时间。再说，我也没兴趣。
  Duìbuqǐ, wǒ méi shíjiān. Zàishuō, wǒ yě méi xìngqù.
  Sorry, I don't have time for this. Besides, I'm not interested.
- 别吃了，你已经吃了五个了。再说，我们还没吃呢。
  Bié chī le, nǐ yǐjīng chī le wǔ gè le. Zàishuō, wǒmen hái méi chī ne.
  Stop eating. You've already eaten five. Besides, the rest of us haven't eaten yet.
- 住我家吧，可以省点钱。再说，孩子们也可以一起玩。
  Zhù wǒ jiā ba, kěyǐ shěng diǎn qián. Zàishuō, háizi men yě kěyǐ yīqǐ wán.
  Stay with me. You can save some money. Besides, the kids can play together.

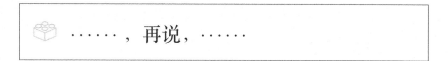

- 我不想干了。天天加班，再说，我在这儿也没有未来。

  Wǒ bù xiǎng gàn le. Tiāntiān jiābān, zàishuō, wǒ zài zhèr yě méiyǒu wèilái.

  I want to do this anymore. I work overtime every day. Besides, I don't even have a future here.

- 明天去买吧，今天太累了。再说，超市也快关门了。

  Míngtiān qù mǎi ba, jīntiān tài lèi le. Zàishuō, chāoshì yě kuài guānmén le.

  Let's go and buy it tomorrow. I'm too tired today. Besides, the supermarket is about to close.

- 别怪他。不是他的错。再说，这也不是什么大事。

  Bié guài tā. Bù shì tā de cuò. Zàishuō, zhè yě bù shì shénme dà shì.

  Don't blame him. It's not his fault. Besides, it's not even a big deal.

- 这个项目的风险太大了。再说，现在很难找到投资。

  Zhège xiàngmù de fēngxiǎn tài dà le. Zàishuō, xiànzài hěn nán zhǎodào tóuzī.

  This project is too risky. Besides, it's very hard to find investment now.

Similar to

- Expressing "except" and "in addition" with "chule⋯yiwai" (B1), page 313
- Expressing "in addition" with "haiyou" (B1), page 99
- Expressing "in addition" with "lingwai" (B2), page 101
- Expressing "not only... but also" (B1), page 322

Expressing "then..." with "name" (B1)

English speakers often like to connect sentences together with "so..." and also try to do this in Chinese with the word 所以 (suǒyǐ). In reality, they should mostly be using 那么 (nàme).

Structure

When expressing "so...," you can use 那么 or 那 in order to begin a judgment or result from previous context. An example of this in English would be: "so, what should we do?"

Situation ，那么 + Suggestion / Decision

Examples

- 他不听，那 我应该怎么办？
  Tā bù tīng, nà wǒ yīnggāi zěnme bàn?
  He won't listen. So what should I do?
- 你说这个办法不行，那 你有别的办法吗？
  Nǐ shuō zhège bànfǎ bù xíng, nà nǐ yǒu bié de bànfǎ ma?
  You said this idea is not going to work. So do you have any other ideas?
- 大家都到了，那么 我们开始吧。
  Dàjiā dōu dào le, nàme wǒmen kāishǐ ba.
  Everybody is here, so let's begin.
- 雨停了，那 我们走吧。
  Yǔ tíng le, nà wǒmen zǒu ba.
  The rain has stopped, so let's leave.
- 你说得有道理，那么 就这么办吧。
  Nǐ shuō de yǒu dàolǐ, nàme jiù zhème bàn ba.
  What you said makes sense, so let's just do that.
- 他学过十年中文？那 他的中文说得很好吧？
  Tā xué guo shí nián Zhōngwén? Nà tā de Zhōngwén shuō de hěn hǎo ba?
  He's studied Chinese for ten years? So he must speak Chinese really well, then?

- 他表现不错，那么让他通过吧。
  Tā biǎoxiàn bùcuò, nàme ràng tā tōngguò ba.
  He performed well, so let's let him pass.
- 会议时间已经确定了，那你快点去安排吧。
  Huìyì shíjiān yǐjīng quèdìng le, nà nǐ kuài diǎn qù ānpái ba.
  The meeting time has been set, so please arrange it soon.
- 他们没有提前通知我们，那么这是他们的责任。
  Tāmen méiyǒu tíqián tōngzhī wǒmen, nàme zhè shì tāmen de zérèn.
  They didn't notify us in advance, so this is their responsibility.
- 实现这个目标应该不难，那么我们一起努力吧。
  Shíxiàn zhège mùbiāo yīnggāi bù nán, nàme wǒmen yīqǐ nǔlì ba.
  It shouldn't be difficult to reach this goal, so let's all really make an effort.

Similar to

- Cause and effect with “yinwei” and “suoyi” (A2)

Using "lai" to connect two verb phrases (B1)

The word 来 (lái) can be used to connect two verb phrases, relating the actions to each other. It can be translated as "in order to" or "so that," and it can help in explaining reasoning.

Structure

Connecting two verb phrases is very straightforward. All you need to do is place 来 in between them. This has the meaning of doing the first verb to achieve the second verb and is often used with words expressing a way or a method, e.g. 通过 (tōngguò) or 用 (yòng).

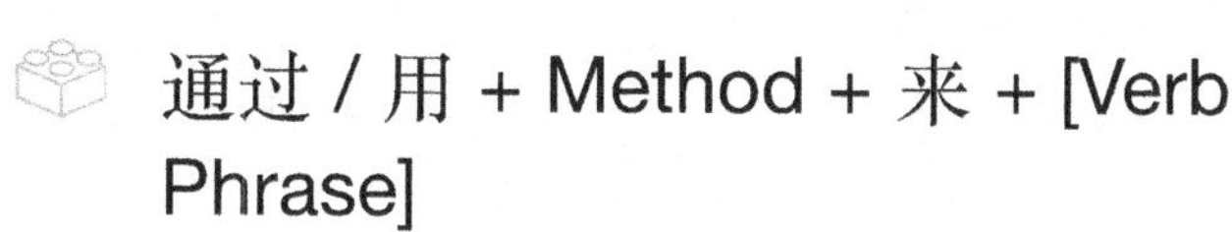
通过 / 用 + Method + 来 + [Verb Phrase]

Examples

- 用 这种方法 来 赚钱，真丢人。
  Yòng zhè zhǒng fāngfǎ lái zhuànqián, zhēn diūrén.
  It's shameful to earn money in this way.
- 很多年轻人 用 手机 APP 来 点外卖。
  Hěn duō niánqīng rén yòng shǒujī APP lái diǎn wàimài.
  A lot of young people use apps on their cell phones to order food.
- 父母不应该经常 用 钱 来 奖励孩子。
  Fùmǔ bù yīnggāi jīngcháng yòng qián lái jiǎnglì háizi.
  Parents shouldn't often use money to reward their children.
- 用 这个 APP 来 学汉字更容易。
  Yòng zhège APP lái xué Hànzì gèng róngyì.
  It's easier to use this app to study Chinese characters.
- 你可以 通过 微信 来 关注我们。
  Nǐ kěyǐ tōngguò Wēixìn lái guānzhù wǒmen.
  You can follow us on WeChat.
- 很多人都是 通过 这个网站 来 找工作的。
  Hěn duō rén dōu shì tōngguò zhège wǎngzhàn lái zhǎo gōngzuò de.
  A lot of people look for a job through this website.

- 商店经常 通过 打折 来 吸引顾客。
  Shāngdiàn jīngcháng tōngguò dǎzhé lái xīyǐn gùkè.
  Shops often use discounts to attract customers.
- 你们是 通过 什么平台 来 推广新产品的?
  Nǐmen shì tōngguò shénme píngtái lái tuīguǎng xīn chǎnpǐn de?
  What platform did you use to promote the new product?
- 我们需要 通过 培训 来 提高服务质量。
  Wǒmen xūyào tōngguò péixùn lái tígāo fúwù zhìliàng.
  We need to improve our service quality through training.
- 双方都希望 通过 谈判 来 解决问题。
  Shuāngfāng dōu xīwàng tōngguò tánpàn lái jiějué wèntí.
  Both sides hope to work out the issues through negotiation.

Similar to

- Expressing purpose with “weile” (B1), page 291
- Expressing purpose with “hao” (B2)
- Facilitating an outcome with “yibian” (B2)

Expressing "before" and "after" with "zhiqian" and "zhihou" (B1)

The words "before" and "after" can be expressed using 之前 (zhīqián) and 之后 (zhīhòu). They are very similar to 以前 (yǐqián) and 以后 (yǐhòu), but are slightly more formal.

Used at the End of a Phrase

In this pattern, 之前 and 之后 come at the start of a sentence, right after mention of some kind of event or thing that happened.

Structure

Examples

- 来中国 之前 ，我的汉语很一般。
  Lái Zhōngguó zhīqián, wǒ de Hànyǔ hěn yībān.
  Before I came to China, my Chinese was really mediocre.
- 下班 之后 给我打个电话。
  Xiàbān zhīhòu gěi wǒ dǎ gè diànhuà.
  Give me a call after you get off work.
- 吃完饭 之后 去看电影吧？
  Chī wán fàn zhīhòu qù kàn diànyǐng ba?
  What about going to the movies after eating dinner?
- 出国 之前 ，他和女朋友分手了。
  Chūguó zhīqián, tā hé nǚpéngyou fēnshǒu le.
  Before he went abroad, he broke up with his girlfriend.
- 她每天放学 之后 都要去上钢琴课。
  Tā měi tiān fàngxué zhīhòu dōu yào qù shàng gāngqín kè.
  She needs to go to piano lessons every day after school.

Used as a Time Word

In this pattern, 之前 and 之后 usually come at the start of a phrase, in the middle of a sentence.

Structure

……，之前 / 之后……

Examples

- 他在英国读完了大学，之后 回上海了。

  Tā zài Yīngguó dú wán le dàxué, zhīhòu huí Shànghǎi le.

  He finished university in England. Afterwards, he returned to Shanghai.

- 她当汉语老师四年多了，之前 是教英语的。

  Tā dāng Hànyǔ lǎoshī sì nián duō le, zhīqián shì jiāo Yīngyǔ de.

  She's been a Chinese teacher for more than four years. She used to be an English teacher.

- 老板刚刚回来，之前 在休假。

  Lǎobǎn gānggāng huílái, zhīqián zài xiūjià.

  The boss just came back. He was on vacation before.

- 我们都不知道，他 之前 什么也没说。

  Wǒmen dōu bù zhīdào, tā zhīqián shénme yě méi shuō.

  None of us knew. He didn't say anything before.

- 我现在去吃饭，之后 去见客户。

  Wǒ xiànzài qù chīfàn, zhīhòu qù jiàn kèhù.

  I'm going to eat now. After that I will go meet a client.

Slight Differences between 之前/之后 and 以前/以后

One difference between the two pairs is that 之前/之后 feel more formal simply because they contain 之, which is a word common in classical Chinese. Both words are still used in everyday spoken Chinese, however.

In addition, while all four words can mean "before and "after" (referring to time), 之前/之后 also sometimes mean "in front of" or "behind," referring to physical location. (之前/之后 aren't used in this way, but the single characters 前/后 are.) We haven't included examples of the "physical location" usage here, because it's less common and more formal.

Similar to

- In the future in general with "yihou" (A2)
- Comparing "yihou" and "zhihou" (B2)
- Expressing "ever since" with "zicong" (B2)

Expressing "ever since" with "yilai" (B1)

You can express "ever since" in Chinese using 以来 (yǐlái) after a time in the past. Just the word 来 (lái) can also play a similar role.

Pattern with 以来

To express "ever since," all one needs to do is put 以来 after a specific event or time. It expresses what has happened since the stated event until the time that the speaker talks (in other words, referring to a certain continuous time period leading up to the present).

Structure

This grammar pattern is usually used to start a statement.

Although we won't go into detail here, note that when using 以来 in a more formal or written context, you can add 自, 从, or 自从 (or other similar words) before the time or event to make it into a "sandwich pattern."

Examples

- 今年八月 以来 ，这里一直没下过雨。
  Jīnnián Bāyuè yǐlái, zhèlǐ yīzhí méi xià guo yǔ.
  It hasn't rained since August of this year.
- 结婚 以来 ，我们没吵过架。
  Jiéhūn yǐlái, wǒmen méi chǎo guo jià.
  Since we got married we haven't had a fight.
- 上大学 以来 ，他变了很多。
  Shàng dàxué yǐlái, tā biàn le hěn duō.
  Since starting college, he's changed a lot.
- 从 他爸爸去世 以来 ，他就没有回过家。
  Cóng tā bàba qùshì yǐlái, tā jiù méiyǒu huí guo jiā.
  He hasn't returned home since his father passed away.
- 从 我学汉语 以来 ，我认识了很多中国朋友。
  Cóng wǒ xué Hànyǔ yǐlái, wǒ rènshi le hěn duō Zhōngguó péngyou.
  Since I started studying Chinese, I've made a lot of Chinese friends.

Pattern with 来

Using 来 to mean "ever since" is basically the same as 以来. However, there is one key difference: you can only use 来 after a length of time, rather than a specific date. In other words, it needs to be used with a certain number of years, months, days, hours, etc. In English, this would be like saying "Ever since three days ago, I've had a constant headache." It doesn't have to be a specific number either; it could be "a few" (几).

Structure

Time Period + 来，……

This form cannot be used with 自, 从, or 自从 (or other similar words).

Examples

- 十年 来 ，房价一直在涨。
  Shí nián lái, fángjià yīzhí zài zhǎng.
  For the past decade, housing prices have been continuously going up.
- 几年 来 ，我们公司的收入一直在增加。
  Jǐ nián lái, wǒmen gōngsī de shōurù yīzhí zài zēngjiā.
  Our company's income has been steadily increasing over the past few years.
- 实习几个月 来 ，我学到了很多。
  Shíxí jǐ gè yuè lái, wǒ xuédào le hěn duō.
  I've learned a lot from my internship during the last few months.
- 出国几个月 来 ，她一点也不想家。
  Chūguó jǐ gè yuè lái, tā yīdiǎn yě bù xiǎng jiā.
  She hasn't missed home at all since she went abroad a few month ago.
- 离婚这几年 来 ，他从没去看过孩子。
  Líhūn zhè jǐ nián lái, tā cóng méi qù kàn guo háizi.
  Since getting divorced these past few years, he's never visited his child.
- 这三个月 来 ，我每天都在想她。
  Zhè sān ge yuè lái, wǒ měitiān dōu zài xiǎng tā.
  I've been missing her every day these past three months.

Similar to

- Comparing "li" and "cong" (B1), page 355
- Expressing "as early as" using "zaozai……"

- Expressing "before" and "after" with "zhiqian" and "zhihou" (B1), page 109
- Sequencing past events with "houlai" (B1), page 116
- Expressing "ever since" with "zicong" (B2)

Expressing "when" with "shi" (B1)

By now you should now how to express "when" using 的时候 (de shíhou). But there's also a slightly shorter, more formal way to do it: simply use 时 (shí) all by itself. (No 的!)

Structure

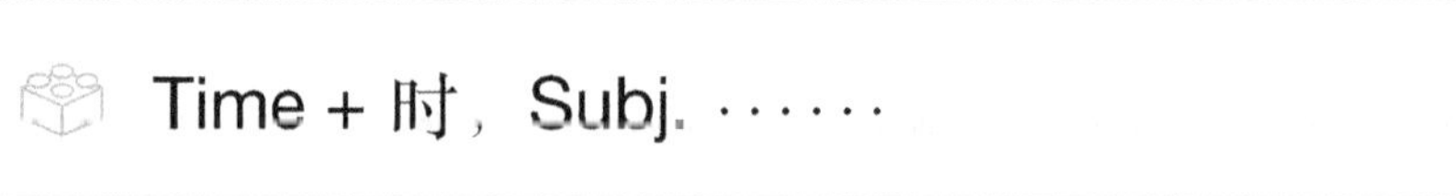

Time + 时，Subj. ……

As time words can appear before or after the subject, you can also place the "Time + 时" phrase after the subject.

Examples

- 考试 时 不要说话。
  Kǎoshì shí bùyào shuōhuà.
  Don't talk when you're taking a test.
- 我面试 时 经常会问这个问题。
  Wǒ miànshì shí jīngcháng huì wèn zhège wèntí.
  I often ask this question during job interviews.
- 会议结束 时 老板才来。
  Huìyì jiéshù shí lǎobǎn cái lái.
  The boss didn't show up until the meeting was over.
- 我生气 时 不想说话。
  Wǒ shēngqì shí bù xiǎng shuōhuà.
  I don't want to talk when I'm angry.
- 他们大学毕业 时 就分手了。
  Tāmen dàxué bìyè shí jiù fēnshǒu le.
  They broke up when they graduated from college.
- 飞机起飞 时 ，他关了手机和电脑。
  Fēijī qǐfēi shí, tā guān le shǒujī hé diànnǎo.
  When the plane took off, he turned off his cell phone and computer.
- 他太太提出离婚 时 ，他很惊讶。
  Tā tàitai tíchū líhūn shí, tā hěn jīngyà.
  He was very surprised when his wife asked for a divorce.

- 他去世 时 ，他的孩子都不在身边。
  Tā qùshì shí, tā de háizi dōu bù zài shēnbiān.
  His children weren't with him when he passed away.
- 我们公司成立 时 只有三个人。
  Wǒmen gōngsī chénglì shí zhǐyǒu sān gè rén.
  There were only three people when this company was founded.
- 跟别人说话 时 不要玩手机。
  Gēn biérén shuōhuà shí bùyào wán shǒujī.
  Don't play with your cell phone when you're talking with other people.

There are also two great examples of this pattern in the poem below:

你

一会儿看我

一会儿看云

你看我时很远

你看云时很近

Similar to

- Expressing "when" with "de shihou" (A2)

Sequencing past events with "houlai" (B1)

The word 后来 (hòulái) is used to sequence past events in the same way that "afterward" is in English. Something very important to note is that 后来 can only be used with two events **that have already occurred**.

Structure

 [Past Event 1]，后来，[Past Event 2]

Examples

Here are some examples of this pattern in action:

- 他说他会来，后来又说不来了。
  Tā shuō tā huì lái, hòulái yòu shuō bù lái le.
  He said he would come, but later he said that he's not coming.
- 他们上周吵架了，后来和好了。
  Tāmen shàng zhōu chǎojià le, hòulái hé hǎo le.
  They had a fight last week, and they made up afterwards.
- 他以前是厨师，后来当了老板。
  Tā yǐqián shì chúshī, hòulái dāng le lǎobǎn.
  He used to be a chef. Afterwards, he became the owner.
- 我昨晚走得早，不知道后来发生了什么。
  Wǒ zuówǎn zǒu de zǎo, bù zhīdào hòulái fāshēng le shénme.
  I left early yesterday evening, so I don't know what happened afterwards.
- 开始我父母不同意，后来他们同意了。
  Kāishǐ wǒ fùmǔ bù tóngyì, hòulái tāmen tóngyì le.
  My parents disapproved in the beginning, but they approved later.
- 空调我上个月修好了，后来又坏了。
  Kōngtiáo wǒ shàng gè yuè xiū hǎo le, hòulái yòu huài le.
  I fixed the air conditioner last month, but it broke again afterwards.
- 他们在一起差不多三年，后来分手了。
  Tāmen zài yīqǐ chàbuduō sān nián, hòulái fēnshǒu le.
  They had been together for about three years. But they broke up afterwards.

- 她以前是兼职老师，后来 做了全职。
  Tā yǐqián shì jiānzhí lǎoshī, hòulái zuò le quánzhí.
  She used to be a part-time teacher. Afterwards, she became full-time.
- 我的大学老师辞职了，后来 去上海做生意了。
  Wǒ de dàxué lǎoshī cízhí le, hòulái qù Shànghǎi zuò shēngyi le.
  My college professor quit his job. Afterwards, he went to Shanghai to do business.
- 北京以前叫北平，后来 改成了北京。
  Běijīng yǐqián jiào Běipíng, hòulái gǎi chéng le Běijīng.
  Beijing used to be called Beiping. Later, the name was changed to Beijing.

Similar to

- In the future in general with "yihou" (A2)
- Expressing "before" and "after" with "zhiqian" and "zhihou" (B1), page 109
- Expressing "ever since" with "yilai" (B1), page 111
- Comparing "yihou" "ranhou" "houlai" (B2)

Expressing fractions with "fenzhi" (B1)

分之 (fēn zhī) is used to express fractions in Chinese. When expressing a fraction, the denominator is always said before the numerator. This pattern is also the way percentages are expressed in Chinese.

So "$\frac{1}{2}$" is read 二分之一 (èr fēn zhī yī), literally "1 of 2 portions." Note the order: it's *NOT* 一分之二 (yī fēn zhī èr). So "$\frac{3}{4}$" is 四分之三 (sì fēn zhī sān), and "$\frac{5}{6}$" is 六分之五 (liù fēn zhī wǔ). To say a percentage, for example, 50 percent, you would say 百分之五十 (bǎi fēn zhī wǔshí), which is literally the same as how you would pronounce the equivalent fraction "50 hundredths."

Basic Pattern

Structure

 Denominator + 分之 + Numerator

Remember that the *denominator* is the *bottom* number in a fraction, but it comes *first* in spoken Chinese. Knowing that this order actually totally fits the overall "big to small" Chinese cultural pattern might help you to remember.

Examples

- 我的手机电量只有百 分之 五了。
  Wǒ de shǒujī diànliàng zhǐ yǒu bǎi fēn zhī wǔ le.
  My phone only has 5% power left.
- 这个文件已经下载了三 分之 二。
  Zhège wénjiàn yǐjīng xiàzǎi le sān fēn zhī èr.
  This document is two-thirds downloaded.
- 这篇文章有五 分之 三是抄别人的。
  Zhè piān wénzhāng yǒu wǔ fēn zhī sān shì chāo biérén de.
  Three fifths of this article has been copied from others.
- 差不多三 分之 一的美国人有护照。
  Chàbuduō sān fēn zhī yī de Měiguó rén yǒu hùzhào.
  About one third of Americans have passports.
- 我们学校四 分之 三的老师都是男老师。
  Wǒmen xuéxiào sì fēn zhī sān de lǎoshī dōu shì nán lǎoshī.
  Three fourths of the teachers at our school are male teachers.

Advanced Pattern

Structure

This structure is what you'll often see in news stories that use statistics. The word 占 (zhàn) is a bit more formal, and means something like "comprises" or "makes up" or "accounts for."

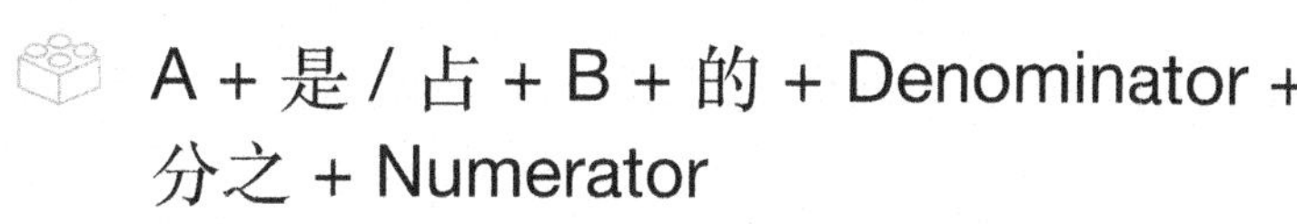
A + 是 / 占 + B + 的 + Denominator + 分之 + Numerator

Examples

- 我们公司的外国员工 占 三 分之 一。
  Wǒmen gōngsī de wàiguó yuángōng zhàn sān fēn zhī yī.
  One third of our company's employees are foreigners.
- 美国人口 是 中国的五 分之 一。
  Měiguó rénkǒu shì Zhōngguó de wǔ fēn zhī yī.
  The USA's population is one fifth of China's.
- 押金 是 房租的百 分之 二十。
  Yājīn shì fángzū de bǎifēn zhī èrshí.
  The deposit is 20% of the rent.
- 期末考试成绩 占 总成绩的百 分之 三十。
  Qīmò kǎoshì chéngjì zhàn zǒng chéngjì de bǎi fēn zhī sānshí.
  The final exam grade accounts for 30% of the final grade.
- 在美国，全职妈妈差不多 占 五 分之 二。
  Zài Měiguó, quánzhí māma chàbuduō zhàn wǔ fēn zhī èr.
  In the US, full-time mothers are about two fifths of all mothers.

Similar to

- Expressing "multiples" with "bei" (B1), page 283

Indicating a number in excess (B1)

A number in excess of a certain amount is expressed by adding "多" (duō) to the end of a number. This is usually translated as "more than..." in English.

Structure

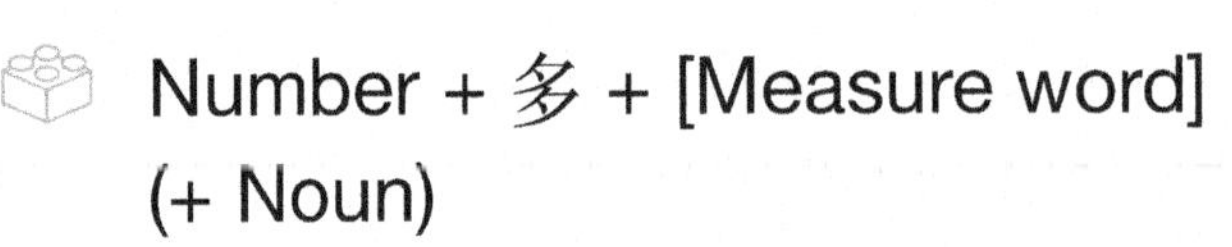

Number + 多 + [Measure word] (+ Noun)

Examples

- 我妈妈已经五十 多 岁了。
  Wǒ māma yǐjīng wǔshí duō suì le.
  My mother is over fifty.
- 我们走了两个 多 小时。
  Wǒmen zǒu le liǎng gè duō xiǎoshí.
  We walked for more than two hours.
- 这个班有两百 多 个学生。
  Zhège bān yǒu liǎng bǎi duō gè xuéshēng.
  There are more than two hundred students in this class.
- 这个包三万 多 块钱。
  Zhège bāo sān wàn duō kuài qián.
  This bag costs more than thirty thousand kuai.
- 这本书有一千 多 页。
  Zhè běn shū yǒu yī qiān duō yè.
  This book has more than a thousand pages.
- 他在国外住了二十 多 年了。
  Tā zài guówài zhù le èrshí duō nián le.
  He has been living abroad for more than twenty years.
- 他在那儿住了二十 多 天了。
  Tā zài nàr zhù le èrshí duō tiān le.
  He's been staying there for over 20 days.

- 我昨天收到了三十 多 条垃圾短信。

  Wǒ zuótiān shōudào le sānshí duō tiáo lājī duǎnxìn.

  I received more than thirty spam text messages yesterday.

- 这个城市有两千 多 年的历史。

  Zhège chéngshì yǒu liǎng qiān duō nián de lìshǐ.

  This city has a history of more than two thousand years.

In the above examples, 岁, 年 and 天 do not take a measure word.

When the number is smaller than eleven, the 多 can be put after the measure word. However, if the number is bigger than eleven, the 多 has to be put before the measure word:

✔ 五岁 多

wǔ suì duō

✘ 五十岁 多

wǔshí suì duō

✔ 五十 多 岁

wǔshí duō suì

✘ 九十块钱 多

jiǔshí kuàiqián duō

✔ 九十 多 块钱

jiǔshí duō kuàiqián

Similar to

- Approximating with sequential numbers (A2)
- Asking about degree with “duo” (A2)
- Big numbers in Chinese (A2)
- Counting money (A2)
- Intensifying with “duo” (A2)
- Using “ji” to mean “several” (A2)
- Doing something more with “duo” (B1), page 183
- Expressing “less than” with “budao” (B1), page 143

Advanced yes-no questions with "ma" (B1)

The question particle 吗 (ma) is a very simple way to convert simple statements into "yes/no" questions, and beginners will learn *not to use 吗 with other question words*, because it's redundant. More advanced students, however, will note that 吗 has some more complicated structures that *do* involve combining 吗 with question words in order to ask very specific types of confirming questions.

Structure

You'll remember that this is the simple pattern for yes/no questions:

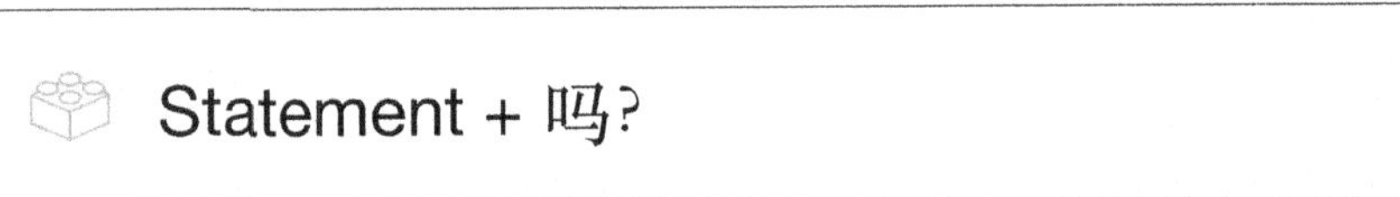

If you embed a *question that uses a question word* instead of a statement, you can create a more complex kind of "confirming" 吗 (ma) question:

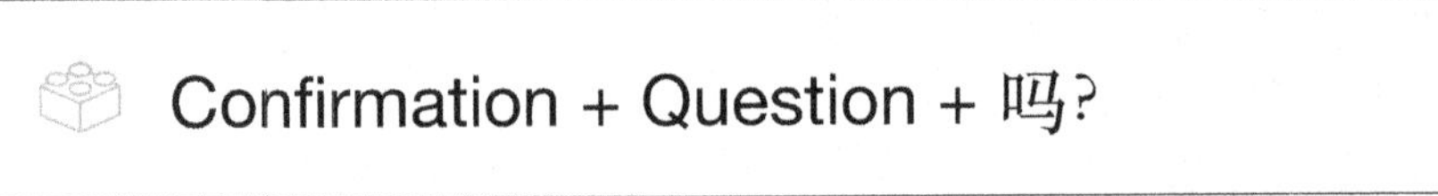

The "Confirmation" part include typically contains some kind of "verb of understanding" such as 知道 (zhīdào), 了解 (liǎojiě), 明白 (míngbai), 认识 (rènshi), etc. Examples of common question words to use in the "Question" part include 什么 (shénme), 谁 (shéi), and 哪里 (nǎlǐ). Then "吗" (ma) can still be added at the end of the question, turning the whole structure into a kind of confirmation yes/no question.

Examples

- 这是什么?

  Zhè shì shénme?

  What is this?

- 你 知道 这是什么 吗 ?

  Nǐ zhīdào zhè shì shénme ma ?

  Do you know what this is?

- 他是谁?

  Tā shì shéi?

  Who is he?

- 你 知道 他是谁 吗 ?

  Nǐ zhīdào tā shì shéi ma ?

  Do you know who he is?

- 他叫什么名字?
  Tā jiào shénme míngzi?
  What is his name?
- 你 知道 他叫什么名字 吗 ?
  Nǐ zhīdào tā jiào shénme míngzi ma ?
  Do you know what his name is?
- 她住在哪儿?
  Tā zhù zài nǎr?
  Where does she live?
- 她 说过 她住在哪儿 吗 ?
  Tā shuō guo tā zhù zài nǎr ma ?
  Did she say where she lives?
- 这个标志是什么意思?
  Zhège biāozhì shì shénme yìsi?
  What does this symbol mean?
- 你们 明白 这个标志是什么意思 吗 ?
  Nǐmen míngbai zhège biāozhì shì shénme yìsi ma ?
  Do you all understand what this symbol means?
- 我们想要什么?
  Wǒmen xiǎng yào shénme?
  What do we want?
- 他 问过 我们想要什么 吗 ?
  Tā wèn guo wǒmen xiǎng yào shénme ma ?
  Did he ask what we want?
- 你的问题是什么?
  Nǐ de wèntí shì shénme?
  What is your question?
- 你能 再说一遍 你的问题是什么 吗 ?
  Nǐ néng zài shuō yī biàn nǐ de wèntí shì shénme ma ?
  Can you repeat what your question is?
- 他是什么时候开始学中文的?
  Tā shì shénme shíhou kāishǐ xué Zhōngwén de?
  When did he start to learn Chinese?

- 你 知道 他是什么时候开始学中文的 吗 ?
  Nǐ zhīdào tā shì shénme shíhou kāishǐ xué Zhōngwén de ma ?
  Do you know when he started to learn Chinese?
- 这是在哪儿买的?
  Zhè shì zài nǎr mǎi de?
  Where did you buy this?
- 你能 告诉 我这是在哪儿买的 吗 ?
  Nǐ néng gàosu wǒ zhè shì zài nǎr mǎi de ma ?
  Can I tell me where you bought this?
- 老板的孩子多大了?
  Lǎobǎn de háizi duō dà le?
  How old is the boss's child now?
- 你 知道 老板的孩子多大了 吗 ?
  Nǐ zhīdào lǎobǎn de háizi duō dà le ma ?
  Do you know how old the boss's child is now?

Similar to

- Expressing "some" with question words (B1), page 287

Aspect particle "zhe" (B1)

The particle 着 (zhe) is one way of indicating the *continuous aspect* in Mandarin Chinese (another common way is using the adverb 在 in front of verbs). You may have heard that the Chinese particle 着 added onto the end of verbs is similar to the use of *-ing* in English. This isn't particularly helpful, however, because the use of 着 in Chinese is not nearly so commonly used, and can also be quite idiomatic.

Basic Usage

The main idea here is that the action won't just happen and stop immediately; it will continue for a while.

Structure

Examples

This basic pattern is often used with commands involving certain verbs where the action persists for a while.

- 我读，你听 着 。
  Wǒ dú, nǐ tīng zhe.
  I'll read, and you listen.
- 我们做，你们看 着 。
  Wǒmen zuò, nǐmen kàn zhe.
  We will do it, and you all watch.
- 你们坐 着 ，我马上回来。
  Nǐmen zuò zhe, wǒ mǎshàng huílái.
  Sit for a while. I'll be right back.
- 我出去一下，你帮我看 着 行李。
  Wǒ chūqù yīxià, nǐ bāng wǒ kān zhe xíngli.
  I'll go out for a second, and you watch the luggage for me.

Used for Manner or State in which an Action is Performed

This pattern is used when you want to use one verb to describe how *another* action is performed.

Structure

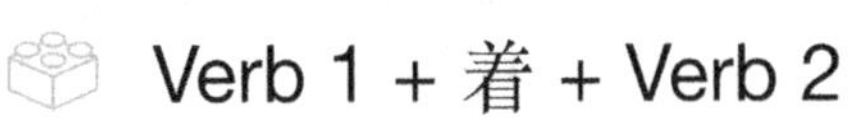

Note that the **first verb** (followed by 着) describes the **state**; the second verb is the action verb. In this case, the "-ing" translation can be useful for the state.

Examples

- 她喜欢站 着 吃饭。
  Tā xǐhuan zhàn zhe chīfàn.
  He likes to eat standing up.
  "standing + eat = eating while standing"
- 他笑 着 说"对不起"。
  Tā xiào zhe shuō "duìbuqǐ".
  Smiling, he said, "I'm sorry."
  "smiling + say = saying "I'm sorry" while smiling
- 孩子抱 着 爸爸哭了起来。
  Háizi bào zhe bàba kū le qǐlái.
  Hugging his daddy, the child started to cry.
  "hugging + cry = crying while hugging

Note: If you want to make a sentence where both verbs are action verbs (neither is truly a state), then you don't want this pattern; you want 一边⋯⋯, 一边⋯⋯ (yībiān..., yībiān...).

Used for Continuous State

While it's true that the "full progressive pattern[1]" can make use of 着, this is not a pattern you're going to want to use all the time.

Usage Examples

The verbs most commonly used with 着 are the ones below:

- 开 (kāi) alone can mean "to open" or "to turn on." Adding 着 allows one to express that something "is open" or "is on."
- 关 (guān) alone can mean "to close" or "to turn off." Adding 着 allows one to express that something "is closed" or "is off."
- 穿 (chuān) alone means "to wear." Adding 着 allows one to express that one "is wearing" something (on one's person).
- 戴 (dài) alone means "to wear" (an accessory). Adding 着 allows one to express that one "is wearing" a hat, jewelry, or accessory (on one's person).

1. Expressing actions in progress (full form) (B1), page 189

- 躺 (tǎng) alone means "to lie on one's back." Adding 着 allows one to express that someone "is lying down."

Sentence Examples

✔ 公司的门开 着 ，可是没人在。
Gōngsī de mén kāi zhe, kěshì méi rén zài.
The office door is open but no one is in there.
"Being open" is a state, so using 着 is natural.)

✘ 公司的门 在 开，可是没人在。
Gōngsī de mén zài kāi, kěshì méi rén zài.
"Being open" is not an action, so don't use 在.)

✔ 她穿 着 一条小黑裙。
Tā chuān zhe yī tiáo xiǎo hēi qún.
She's wearing a little black dress.
"Be wearing" is a state, so using 着 is natural.)

✘ 她 在 穿一条小黑裙。
Tā zài chuān yī tiáo xiǎo hēi qún.
"Be wearing" is not an action, so don't use 在.)

✔ 躺 着 最舒服。
Tǎng zhe zuì shūfu.
It's most comfortable just lying down.
"Lying down" is a state, so using 着 is natural.)

✘ 在 躺最舒服。
Zài tǎng zuì shūfu.
"Lying here" is not strictly an action, so don't use 在.)

Colloquial Sayings

Certain verbs tend to take 着 more frequently than others, and what the 着 exactly is *doing* might not be apparent at all. It's best to think of these usages as set phrases.

Examples

- 听 着 ！
  Tīng zhe!
  "to listen and keep listening"
- 别客气，拿 着 吧。
  Bié kèqi, ná zhe ba.
  "to take and keep it"
- 你们等 着 ！
  Nǐmen děng zhe!
  "to wait and keeping waiting"

Verb + 着 + 玩 "For Fun"

There's also one colloquial usage of 着 that's often chosen for special treatment by Chinese textbooks, so we'll cover it here as well:

Subj. + 是 + Verb + 着 + 玩 + 的

This pattern may look like that "doing an action in a particular state" pattern already covered above, but in practice it doesn't really work that way. It just means "[Verb] for fun" or "[Verb] as a joke."

Examples of Verb + 着 + 玩

- 你不要生气，我是说 着 玩的。
  Nǐ bùyào shēngqì, wǒ shì shuō zhe wán de!
  Don't be mad. I was just joking.
- 我听不懂英文歌，只是听 着 玩的。
  Wǒ tīng bu dǒng Yīngwén gē, zhǐshì tīng zhe wán de.
  I don't understand English songs. I just listen to them for fun.

Similar to

- Expressing actions in progress with "zai" (A2)
- Simultaneous tasks with "yibian" (A2)
- Alternative existential sentences (B1), page 264
- Expressing actions in progress (full form) (B1), page 189
- Using "zhe" when "verbing away" (B2)

Expressing the self-evident with "ma" (B1)

The particle 嘛 (ma) is a sentence-final particle identical in pronunciation to the simple "yes/no question" particle 吗 (ma) you learned back in the day, but with a rather different function. It can be used when the speaker feels what he is saying is obvious (from his point of view).

Structure

Examples

- 你妹妹很漂亮 嘛 。
  Nǐ mèimei hěn piàoliang ma .
  Your sister is pretty.
  She's clearly pretty.
- 他挺有钱的 嘛 。
  Tā tǐng yǒuqián de ma .
  He is pretty rich.
  He has shown that's he's rich.
- 不想去就不要去 嘛 。
  Bù xiǎng qù jiù bùyào qù ma .
  If you don't wanna go, don't go.
  Clearly you don't have to.
- 你别太谦虚 嘛 。
  Nǐ bié tài qiānxū ma .
  Don't be too modest.
  Obviously you're being super modest.
- 大家有话就说 嘛 。
  Dàjiā yǒu huà jiù shuō ma .
  Guys, just say whatever you have to say.
  Clearly you can just say it.
- 你跟他很熟 嘛 。
  Nǐ gēn tā hěn shú ma .
  You two know each other well.
  You two are obviously well acquainted.
- 开慢点，安全第一 嘛 。
  Kāi màn diǎn, ānquán dìyī ma .
  Drive slowly. Safety first.
  We all know: safety first!

- 不用塑料袋更环保 嘛 。 *You know you should be eco-friendly!*
  Bùyòng sùliàodài gèng huánbǎo ma .
  It's more environmentally friendly not to use plastic bags.
- 这个外国人很了解中国文化 嘛 。 *He has amazed us all.*
  Zhège wàiguórén hěn liǎojiě Zhōngguó wénhuà ma .
  This foreigner knows a lot about Chinese culture.
- 别担心，一边工作一边学 嘛 。 *Clearly this takes time to learn.*
  Bié dānxīn, yībiān gōngzuò yībiān xué ma .
  Don't worry. You can learn as you work.

Similar to

- Advanced yes-no questions with “ma” (B1), page 122
- Marking a topic with “ma” (B2)

Reviewing options with "ba" (B1)

When 吧 (ba) is used twice in a sentence, it is used to list two options that the speaker is debating. It gives the sentence an indecisive feel, as though the speaker doesn't know which one to choose. This construction often has a negative connotation, since the options usually are not ideal.

Structure

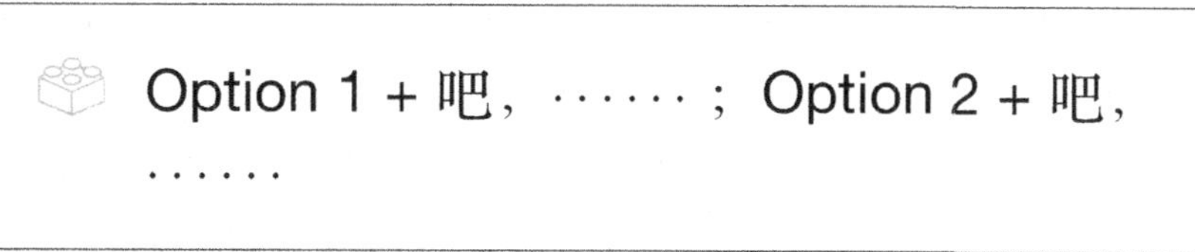

If this structure doesn't seem clear to you, the examples will help.

Examples

- 冬天去 吧 ，太冷；夏天去 吧 ，太热。
  Dōngtiān qù ba , tài lěng; xiàtiān qù ba , tài rè.
  If we go in the winter, it's too cold. If we go in the summer, it's too hot.
- 早点去 吧 ，要等；晚点去 吧 ，会堵车。
  Zǎo diǎn qù ba , yào děng; wǎn diǎn qù ba , huì dǔchē.
  If we go early, we'll have to wait. If we go later, there will be bad traffic.
- 穿得多一点 吧 ，会热；穿得少一点 吧 ，会冷。
  Chuān de duō yīdiǎn ba , huì rè; chuān de shǎo yīdiǎn ba , huì lěng.
  If I wear a little more, it will be hot. If I wear a little less, it will be cold.
- 去 吧 ，要给红包；不去 吧 ，他没面子。
  Qù ba , yào gěi hóngbāo; bù qù ba , tā méi miànzi.
  I need to give a red envelope if I go early. If I don't go, he will lose face.
- 不说 吧 ，他还会做错；说 吧 ，他肯定不高兴。
  Bù shuō ba , tā hái huì zuò cuò; shuō ba , tā kěndìng bù gāoxìng.
  If I don't tell him, he will still do it wrong next time. If I do tell him, he will get upset.
- 回去 吧 ，机票太贵；不回去 吧 ，家人肯定会想我。
  Huíqù ba , jīpiào tài guì; bù huíqù ba , jiārén kěndìng huì xiǎng wǒ.
  If I go back, the plane ticket is too expensive. If I don't go back, my family will definitely miss me.

- 带你去 吧，你总是不听话；不带你去 吧，你一个人肯定无聊。

  Dài nǐ qù ba, nǐ zǒngshì bù tīnghuà; bù dài nǐ qù ba, nǐ yīgèrén kěndìng wúliáo.

  If I take you with me, you will be naughty like always. If I don't take you with me, you will definitely be bored.

- 见面 吧，常常吵架；不见面 吧，还是会想他。

  Jiànmiàn ba, chángcháng chǎojià; bù jiànmiàn ba, háishì huì xiǎng tā.

  If we see each other, we fight a lot. If we don't see each other, I miss him anyway.

- 不说真话 吧，老婆不高兴；说真话 吧，老婆也不高兴。

  Bù shuō zhēn huà ba, lǎopo bù gāoxìng; shuō zhēn huà ba, lǎopo yě bù gāoxìng.

  If I don't speak the truth, my wife will be upset. If I tell her the truth, my wife will also be upset.

- 这个老房子，卖 吧，怕父母不同意；不卖 吧，就没钱买新车。

  Zhège lǎo fángzi, mài ba, pà fùmǔ bù tóngyì; bù mài ba, jiù méi qián mǎi xīn chē.

  If I sell this old house, I'm afraid my parents will disagree. If I don't sell it, I don't have money to buy a new car.

Using "de" (modal particle) (B1)

The particle 的 (de) is most often a structural particle, but it can also be a sentence-final particle which indicates that the speaker is certain about what he is saying. When it serves this purpose, it's expressing a type of "mood" and thus is called a "modal particle."

Structure

Frequently, the statement will include 会 (huì) or 一定会 (yīdìng huì) to emphasize the speaker's certainty.

Examples

- 他会好 的 。
  Tā huì hǎo de.
  He will get better.
- 你可以 的 。
  Nǐ kěyǐ de.
  You can do this.
- 她一定会来 的 。
  Tā yīdìng huì lái de.
  She's definitely coming.
- 我们能搞定 的 。
  Wǒmen néng gǎodìng de.
  We can handle it.
- 他不会道歉 的 。
  Tā bù huì dàoqiàn de.
  He's not going to apologize.
- 这个地方我们来过 的 。
  Zhège dìfang wǒmen lái guo de.
  We've been here before.
- 我跟你说过 的 ，你不记得了？
  Wǒ gēn nǐ shuō guo de, nǐ bù jìde le?
  I've told you this before. Do you not remember?

- 我不会骗你 的 。
  Wǒ bù huì piàn nǐ de .
  I won't lie to you.
- 你们会成功 的 。
  Nǐmen huì chénggōng de .
  You will succeed.
- 你的建议我们会考虑 的 。
  Nǐ de jiànyì wǒmen huì kǎolǜ de .
  We will consider your suggestion.

Similar to

- The "shi... de" construction for emphasizing details (B1), page 239
- The "shi... de" construction for indicating purpose (B1), page 245
- The "shi... de" patterns: an overview (B1), page 247

Expressing "about" with "guanyu" (B1)

关于 (guānyú) means "about." It can be used in a few ways, often marking a topic of a statement or modifying a noun.

Used for Topic-Marking

Structure

As an adverb/adverbial clause, it can only be placed at the beginning of the sentence.

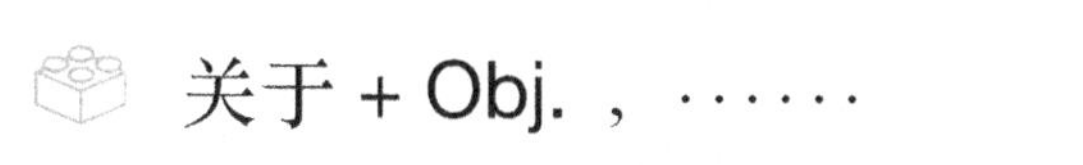

关于 + Obj. ，……

Examples

- 关于 中国历史，我知道的不多。
  Guānyú Zhōngguó lìshǐ, wǒ zhīdào de bù duō.
  As for Chinese history, I don't know a lot.
- 关于 这次考试，我还有几个问题要问。
  Guānyú zhè cì kǎoshì, wǒ hái yǒu jǐ gè wèntí yào wèn.
  As for this exam, I still have a few questions that I need to ask.
- 关于 这个问题，你们还是问他吧。
  Guānyú zhège wèntí, nǐmen háishì wèn tā ba.
  As for this question, you'd better ask him.
- 关于 你的建议，老板还在考虑。
  Guānyú nǐ de jiànyì, lǎobǎn hái zài kǎolǜ.
  As for your suggestion, the boss is still thinking it over.
- 关于 调查结果，我们也不太清楚。
  Guānyú diàochá jiéguǒ, wǒmen yě bù tài qīngchu.
  As for the result of that investigation, we don't know much either.

Used as Part of a Modifier

As an attributive modifier, 关于 (guānyú) is placed before the noun phrase (rather than after, as in English), and you should always add a 的.

Structure

关于……的 + Noun

Examples

- 网上有很多 关于 这件事情的评论。
  Wǎngshang yǒu hěn duō guānyú zhè jiàn shìqing de pínglùn.
  There are lots of comments about this matter online.
- 他写过很多 关于 男女平等的文章。
  Tā xiě guo hěn duō guānyú nánnǚ píngděng de wénzhāng.
  He wrote many articles about gender equality.
- 汉语有很多 关于 饮食的成语。
  Hànyǔ yǒu hěn duō guānyú yǐnshí de chéngyǔ.
  There are lots of idioms about food in Chinese.
- 我昨天看了一部 关于 动物保护的纪录片。
  Wǒ zuótiān kàn le yī bù guānyú dòngwù bǎohù de jìlùpiàn.
  I saw a documentary about animal protection yesterday.
- 这是一份 关于 中国奢侈品市场的报告。
  Zhè shì yī fèn guānyú Zhōngguó shēchǐpǐn shìchǎng de bàogào.
  This is a report about the Chinese luxury market.

The Unspoken "About"

The word "about" often follows verbs in English, such as "talk about" or "ask about." In Chinese, however, this "about" meaning is built into the verb and no additional "about" word is needed, much like we don't say "discuss about" in English.

A few examples:

- 我们聊聊你的新工作吧。
  Wǒmen liáoliao nǐ de xīn gōngzuò ba.
  Let's talk about your new job.
- 今天开会要说说公司下个月的培训。
  Jīntiān kāihuì yào shuōshuo gōngsī xià gè yuè de péixùn.
  Today, we need to hold a meeting about the company training next month.

Similar to

- Expressing "related to…" with "you guan de" (B2)

Expressing "all the way until" with "zhidao" (B1)

直到 (zhídào) is for describing a time frame that began in the past and continued until a point closer to the present. It is like the English phrase, "all the way until." It can be used in an affirmative or negative form, expressing that something has taken a while or is late. The word 才 (cái) often teams up with 直到, and serves to emphasize the lateness aspect[1].

Affirmative Form

In the positive form, which uses 才, it may be more natural in English to express the idea as "not until... did" something happen.

Structure

直到 + Time / Event ， Subj. + 才……

This subject can also be placed before 直到.

Examples

- 直到 十二点半，我 才 做完作业。
  Zhídào shí'èr diǎn bàn, wǒ cái zuò wán zuòyè.
  It wasn't until twelve thirty in the morning that I finished my homework.
- 直到 半个月以后，我的感冒 才 好。
  Zhídào bàn gè yuè yǐhòu, wǒ de gǎnmào cái hǎo.
  It took me half a month to recover from the cold.
- 她 直到 十八岁 才 见到亲生父母。
  Tā zhídào shíbā suì cái jiàndào qīnshēng fùmǔ.
  It wasn't until she was eighteen that she met her biological parents.
- 我 直到 大学毕业 才 开始独立生活。
  Wǒ zhídào dàxué bìyè cái kāishǐ dúlì shēnghuó.
  It wasn't until I graduated from college that I started living independently.
- 直到 去了北京，他 才 知道一个人在大城市多辛苦。
  Zhídào qù le Běijīng, tā cái zhīdào yīgèrén zài dà chéngshì duō xīnkǔ.
  It wasn't until he went to Beijing that he understood how hard it is to be alone in a big city.

---

1. Expressing lateness with "cai" (B1), page 72

Negative Form

Structure

直到 + Time / Event ， Subj. + 都 + 不 / 没……

Examples

- 直到 他搬到上海，我们 都没 见过。
  Zhídào tā bān dào Shànghǎi, wǒmen dōu méi jiàn guo.
  We didn't meet until he moved to Shanghai.
- 他们是同学，但是 直到 毕业， 都没 说过话。
  Tāmen shì tóngxué, dànshì zhídào bìyè, dōu méi shuō guo huà.
  They were classmates, but they had never spoken until they graduated.
- 直到 电影结束，他 都没 来。
  Zhídào diànyǐng jiéshù, tā dōu méi lái.
  He didn't show up until the movie was over.
- 直到 我弟弟上大学，他 都不 会洗衣服。
  Zhídào wǒ dìdi shàng dàxué, tā dōu bù huì xǐ yīfu.
  My younger brother didn't know how to wash clothes until he went to college.
- 我认识他一年多了，直到 现在，我 都不 知道他的全名。
  Wǒ rènshi tā yī nián duō le, zhídào xiànzài, wǒ dōu bù zhīdào tā de quánmíng.
  I've known him for over a year, but even now I still don't know his full name.

Similar to

- Expressing “until” with “dao” (B1), page 187
- Expressing “when” with “dengdao” (B1), page 325
- Expressing lateness with “cai” (B1), page 72

Expressing "for" with "gei" (B1)

The preposition 给 (gěi) can mean "for," as in, "everything I do, I do it *for* you." You can also think of it as meaning "give," like to give a service or to give something to someone. In this case, the default position of the character is before the verb, although it sometimes comes after, depending on the verb.

Structure

The meaning of 给 is very similar to 为 (wèi) in Chinese, but 给 is more informal than 为, and there are many cases where it's simply based on convention and general practice to decide to use one or the other.

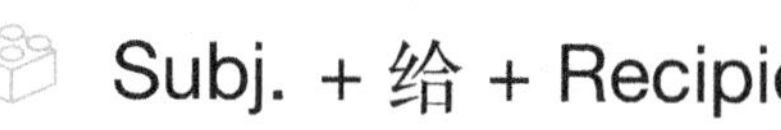

Subj. + 给 + Recipient + [Verb Phrase]

Note that the "recipient" in the pattern above is usually a person but isn't necessarily a person. It could be an animal, company, or any number of other types of recipients.

Examples

- 给 客人 倒茶 。
  Gěi kèrén dàochá .
  Pour tea for the guests.
- 妈妈在 给 孩子们 做饭 。
  Māma zài gěi háizi men zuòfàn .
  Mom cooks for the kids.
- 我儿子喜欢 给 小狗 洗澡 。
  Wǒ érzi xǐhuan gěi xiǎogǒu xǐzǎo .
  My son likes giving our dog a bath.
- 请 给 我 拿 一双筷子。
  Qǐng gěi wǒ ná yī shuāng kuàizi.
  Please get a pair of chopsticks for me.
- 可以 给 我 买 一杯咖啡吗?
  Kěyǐ gěi wǒ mǎi yī bēi kāfēi ma?
  Could you buy me a cup of coffee?
- 可以 给 我 拿一下 行李吗?
  Kěyǐ gěi wǒ ná yīxià xíngli ma?
  Can you take my luggage for me?

- 这个周末我们 给 儿子 开生日派对 。
  Zhège zhōumò wǒmen gěi érzi kāi shēngrì pàiduì .
  We're going to hold a birthday party for our son this weekend.
- 我没带钥匙，你能 给 我 开一下门 吗?
  Wǒ méi dài yàoshi, nǐ néng gěi wǒ kāi yīxià mén ma?
  I didn't bring the key. Could you open the door for me?
- 你想 给 我 打扫 房间吗?
  Nǐ xiǎng gěi wǒ dǎsǎo fángjiān ma?
  Would you like to clean the room for me?
- 如果你来中国玩，我 给 你 当导游 。
  Rúguǒ nǐ lái Zhōngguó wán, wǒ gěi nǐ dāng dǎoyóu .
  If you come visit China, I'll be your tour guide.

Similar to

- Expressing “for” with “wei” (B1), page 141
- Using “dui” with verbs (B1), page 153
- Verbs followed by “gei” (B1), page 201

Expressing "for" with "wei" (B1)

When you work *for* a company or do other sorts of physical (and even mental) activities for another party, you're likely to use the Chinese preposition 为 (wèi). This character is often translated into English as "for," but is sometimes unnatural or unnecessary, depending on the particular phrase. For example, the super common Mao-era phrase, 为人民服务 (wèi rénmín fúwù), "serve the people," doesn't need the word "for" in English.

Don't confuse this preposition with 为了[1], which is a bit different.

Structure

为 + Party + Verb / Adj.

Examples

- 我们都为你高兴。
  Wǒmen dōu wèi nǐ gāoxìng.
  We are all happy for you.
- 谁为我考虑过?
  Shéi wèi wǒ kǎolǜ guo?
  Who has ever considered me?
- 你们可以来为我们加油。
  Nǐmen kěyǐ lái wèi wǒmen jiāyóu.
  You guys can come to cheer us on.
- 她是为美国政府工作的。
  Tā shì wèi Měiguó zhèngfǔ gōngzuò de.
  She works for the United States government.
- 这个生日蛋糕是为你准备的。
  Zhège shēngrì dàngāo shì wèi nǐ zhǔnbèi de.
  This birthday cake has been prepared for you.
- 父母为家庭付出了很多。
  Fùmǔ wèi jiātíng fùchū le hěn duō.
  The parents have done so much for their family.

1. Expressing purpose with "weile" (B1), page 291

- 你不 为 自己的孩子 担心 吗?
  Nǐ bù wèi zìjǐ de háizi dānxīn ma?
  Aren't you worried for your child?
- 谢谢你 为 我们 提供 这么多资源。
  Xièxie nǐ wèi wǒmen tígōng zhème duō zīyuán.
  Thank you for providing us with so many resources.
- 他 为 公司的发展 贡献 了很多。
  Tā wèi gōngsī de fāzhǎn gòngxiàn le hěn duō.
  He contributed a lot to the development of the company.
- 很多人都在 为 那些孩子 祈祷 。
  Hěn duō rén dōu zài wèi nàxiē háizi qídǎo .
  Lots of people are praying for those children.

Similar to

- Expressing "for" with "gei" (B1), page 139
- Expressing purpose with "weile" (B1), page 291
- Explaining purpose with "wei… er…" (C1)

Expressing "less than" with "budao" (B1)

The word 到 (dào) means "arrive," but it can also mean "to reach" or "to get to" in an abstract sense. So in this pattern, 不到 (bùdào) means "to not reach (the amount of)," or, to put it another way, "to be less than."

Basic Pattern

Structure

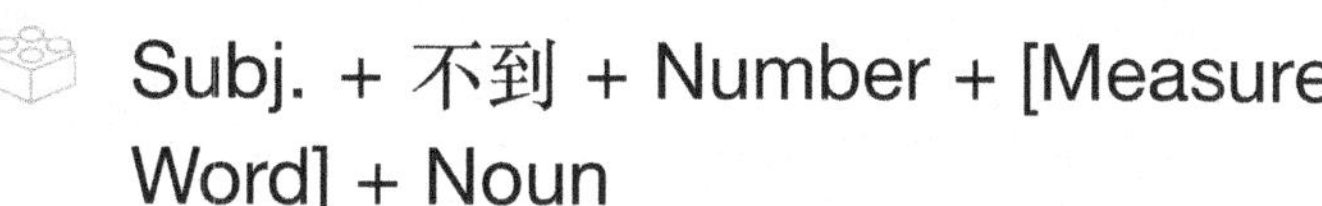

Subj. + 不到 + Number + [Measure Word] + Noun

Examples

- 我女儿 不到 三岁。
  Wǒ nǚ'ér bùdào sān suì.
  My daughter is not yet three years old.
- 我昨天睡了 不到 五个小时。
  Wǒ zuótiān shuì le bùdào wǔ gè xiǎoshí.
  Yesterday I slept for almost five hours.
- 这件衣服花了 不到 一百块。
  Zhè jiàn yīfu huā le bùdào yī bǎi kuài.
  On this piece of clothing I spent less than 100 RMB.
- 我家到公司 不到 五百米。
  Wǒ jiā dào gōngsī bùdào wǔ bǎi mǐ.
  My house is less than 500 meters from the office.
- 在美国，不到 21 岁不能喝酒。
  Zài Měiguó, bùdào èrshí-yī suì, bù néng hējiǔ.
  In the US, if you're under 21 you can't drink alcohol.

Advanced Pattern

Structure

When 不到 (bùdào) is put before a time or a duration of time, it needs to be followed with 就 (jiù). This shows that something (usually referring to the past) has happened earlier than expected.

> Subj. + 不到 + Time + 就 + Predicate + 了

Examples

- 她的病 不到 一个星期 就 好 了 。
  Tā de bìng bùdào yī gè xīngqī jiù hǎo le .
  Her sickness got better in less than a week.
- 他们认识 不到 两个月 就 结婚 了 。
  Tāmen rènshi bùdào liǎng gè yuè jiù jiéhūn le .
  After knowing each other for less than two months they got married.
- 李医生 不到 55 岁 就 退休 了 。
  Lǐ yīshēng bùdào wǔshí-wǔ suì jiù tuìxiū le .
  Dr. Li retired at under the age of 55.
- 爷爷 不到 60 岁 就 去世 了 。
  Yéye bùdào liùshí suì jiù qùshì le .
  My grandpa was less than 60 years old when he died.
- 老板 不到 30 岁 就 有白头发 了 。
  Lǎobǎn bùdào sānshí suì jiù yǒu bái tóufa le .
  My boss is less than 30 years old and already has some gray hair.

For other similar uses of 就, see also expressing earliness with "jiu."[1]

---

1. Expressing earliness with "jiu" (B1), page 69

Expressing "toward" with "wang" (B1)

Although 往 (wǎng) simply means "towards," it's not used as often as certain other prepositions and also has a few special use cases, so it warrants a little extra attention.

Used as "Towards"

往 (wǎng) is a preposition that means "towards" and precedes the verb it modifies.

Used before a Verb

This is the common one used in everyday speech.

Structure

Adding 往 (wǎng) with a location or place word indicates the direction of an action. Remember that the verb comes *after* this 往 phrase.

往 + Direction / Place + Verb

Examples

- 一直往前走。
  Yīzhí wǎng qián zǒu.
  Go straight ahead.
- 往左拐。
  Wǎng zuǒ guǎi.
  Turn left.
- 往上看。
  Wǎng shàng kàn.
  Look up there.
- 那个小偷往东跑了。
  Nàge xiǎotōu wǎng dōng pǎo le.
  That thief ran towards the east.
- 不要往楼下扔垃圾。
  Bùyào wǎng lóuxià rēng lājī.
  Don't throw trash downstairs.
- 不要往小孩嘴巴里塞东西了！
  Bùyào wǎng xiǎohái zuǐba lǐ sāi dōngxi le!
  Stop stuffing food in the kid's mouth!

Used after a Verb

In written language, 往 (wǎng) can also be used *after* a few monosyllabic verbs, which are then followed by location nouns.

Structure

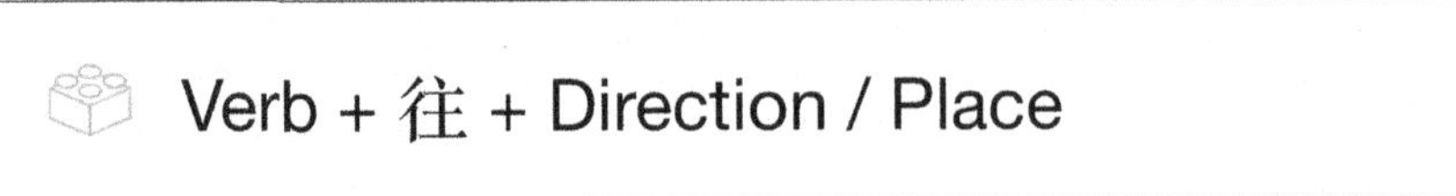

Examples

- 开往北京的火车
  kāi wǎng Běijīng de huǒchē
  the train that goes to Beijing
- 飞往纽约的飞机
  fēi wǎng Niǔyuē de fēijī
  the airplane that flies to New York
- 运往国外的货物
  yùn wǎng guówài de huòwù
  cargo that is shipped overseas

往下 as "Keep Going"

往下 (wǎng xià) expresses "keep going," implying that the process has been interrupted before. The verbs that follow are usually communication or sensory verbs: speak (说), read (读), write (写), watch (看), and listen (听) are common.

Examples

- 往下说。
  Wǎng xià shuō.
  Keep talking.
- 往下读。
  Wǎng xià dú.
  Keep reading.
- 你往下看就知道了。
  Nǐ wǎng xià kàn jiù zhīdào le.
  Keep reading and you'll see.

Similar to

- Expressing "towards" with "xiang" (B1), page 148

- Comparing “chao” “xiang” and “wang” (B2)

Expressing "towards" with "xiang" (B1)

向 (xiàng) is a preposition that means "towards" and is used often with certain verbs. These usages need to be learned together with 向.

Used as "Towards"

Structure

When used as a preposition, 向 indicates an action that is performed towards a reference point but doesn't have any actual motion towards that point.

 向 + Direction / Person + Verb

Examples

- 向东走。
  Xiàng dōng zǒu.
  Walk to the east.
- 向前看。
  Xiàng qián kàn.
  Look forward.
- 向左转。
  Xiàng zuǒ zhuǎn.
  Turn to the left.
- 老师正向我们走来。
  Lǎoshī zhèng xiàng wǒmen zǒu lái.
  The teacher is currently walking towards us.
- 火车已经开了，她还在向我招手。
  Huǒchē yǐjīng kāi le, tā hái zài xiàng wǒ zhāoshǒu.
  The train already departed. She kept waving at me.
- 你必须向他道歉！
  Nǐ bìxū xiàng tā dàoqiàn!
  You must apologize to him!
- 这件事你应该向老板汇报一下。
  Zhè jiàn shì nǐ yīnggāi xiàng lǎobǎn huìbào yīxià.
  You should report this matter to the boss!

Used as "From"

Whereas in English we would say "learn from someone," in Chinese this would be expressed as "learn toward someone," as in the following example (and famous propaganda slogan):

- **向** 雷锋同志学习！
  Xiàng Léi Fēng tóngzhì xuéxí!
  Learn from Comrade Lei Feng!

More examples:

- 我不喜欢 **向** 朋友借钱。
  Wǒ bù xǐhuan **xiàng** péngyou jiè qián.
  I don't like to borrow money from friends.
- 你会 **向** 陌生人求助吗?
  Nǐ huì **xiàng** mòshēngrén qiúzhù ma?
  Would you ask strangers for help?
- 我们都没经验，是来 **向** 你请教的。
  Wǒmen dōu méi jīngyàn, shì lái **xiàng** nǐ qǐngjiào de.
  None of us has experience. We're here to ask you for advice.

Similar to

- Expressing "toward" with "wang" (B1), page 145
- Using "dui" with verbs (B1), page 153
- Verbs followed by "gei" (B1), page 201

Idiomatic phrases with "zai" (B1)

You probably already know how to express location with 在. In this article, we'll go more in depth as to how you can make idiomatic phrases using that construction. This kind of form is actually similar to some that we have in English, so it won't be too difficult.

Used with 上

This construction can be translated as "on the topic of" or "in regards to." It can be used to comment on an idea or concept. The examples below will help.

Structure

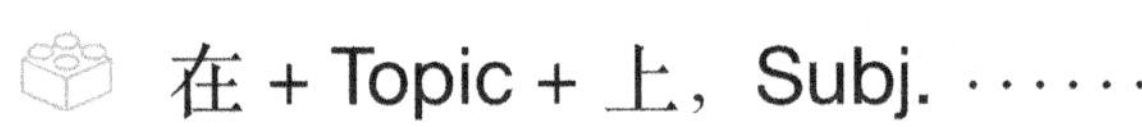

Note that the subject can also be put before 在.

Examples

- 在 这个问题 上 ，我们的看法是一样的。
  Zài zhè gè wèntí shàng , wǒmen de kànfǎ shì yīyàng de.
  In regards to this problem, our opinions are the same.
- 在 美国历史 上 ，谁是最重要的总统？
  Zài Měiguó lìshǐ shàng , shéi shì zuì zhòngyào de zǒngtǒng ?
  In regards to American history, who is the most important president?
- 这个句子 在 语法 上 没什么问题，但是不太自然。
  Zhège jùzi zài yǔfǎ shàng méi shénme wèntí, dànshì bù tài zìrán.
  This sentence is okay to say in terms of grammar, it's just not very natural.
- 南方人和北方人 在 生活习惯 上 有很多差异。
  Nánfāng rén hé běifāng rén zài shēnghuó xíguàn shàng yǒu hěn duō chāyì.
  There are many differences between northern and southern people when it comes to living habits.

Used with 下

This construction can be translated (rather directly) as "under" and expresses conditions that affected the comment that comes after.

Structure

在…… 下，……

Examples

- 在 这样的环境 下 长大，孩子会快乐吗？
  Zài zhèyàng de huánjìng xià zhǎngdà, háizi huì kuàilè ma?
  Do you think kids will be happy growing up in this kind of environment?
- 在 这种情况 下 ，你们会怎么做？
  Zài zhè zhǒng qíngkuàng xià , nǐmen huì zěnme zuò?
  Under these kinds of circumstances, what would you do?
- 在 紧急情况 下 ，你可以这样做。
  Zài jǐnjí qíngkuàng xià , nǐ kěyǐ zhèyàng zuò.
  In an emergency situation, you can do this.
- 在 那么困难的条件 下 ，她还是坚持让孩子们都上学。
  Zài nàme kùnnan de tiáojiàn xià , tā háishì jiānchí ràng háizi men dōu shàngxué.
  Under dire financial conditions, she still insisted that the children should all attend school.

Used with 方面

This construction is similar to the 在…… 上 above, which translates to "in relation to" or "on the topic of."

Structure

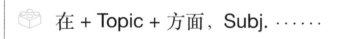

在 + Topic + 方面，Subj. ……

Examples

- 在 事业 方面 ，我老板很成功。
  Zài shìyè fāngmiàn , wǒ lǎobǎn hěn chénggōng.
  With regards to career, my boss is very successful.
- 在 技术 方面 ，他是专家。
  Zài jìshù fāngmiàn , tā shì zhuānjiā.
  When it comes to technology, he's an expert.

- 在 管理 方面 ，你比我有经验。
  Zài guǎnlǐ fāngmiàn , nǐ bǐ wǒ yǒu jīngyàn.
  When it comes to management, you have more experience than I do.
- 中西方文化 在 很多 方面 都有共同点。
  Zhōng-xīfāng wénhuà zài hěn duō fāngmiàn dōu yǒu gòngtóngdiǎn.
  In certain aspects, Chinese and Western culture have a lot in common.

Similar to

- Expressing location with “zai… shang / xia / li” (A2)
- Expressing various aspects with “yi fangmian” (B1), page 329
- Expressing “on the basis of” with “ping” (B2)
- Expressing “within” a period of time using “zai… nei” (B2)

Using "dui" with verbs (B1)

When using 对 (duì) as a preposition, it means "to" or "towards" an object or target. As with all prepositions, you've got to watch out when using this word, as usage of 对 in Chinese doesn't always totally "make sense" or correspond to English at all.

Basic Usage

Structure

 Subj. + 对 + Person + Verb

Note that you shouldn't be plugging in just any old verb here; the ones that work with 对 are limited.

Examples

- 宝宝 对 我 笑了。
  Bǎobao duì wǒ xiào le.
  The baby smiled at me.
- 小狗在 对 你 叫。
  Xiǎogǒu zài duì nǐ jiào.
  The dog is barking at you.
- 你不应该这样 对 父母 说话。
  Nǐ bù yīnggāi zhèyàng duì fùmǔ shuōhuà.
  You shouldn't talk to your parents this way.
- 他总是 对 老师 撒谎。
  Tā zǒngshì duì lǎoshī sāhuǎng.
  He always lies to his teachers.
- 不要 对 孩子 发脾气。
  Bùyào duì háizi fā píqi.
  Don't lose your temper with the child.

Colloquial Expression 对……来说

In English we often start sentences with "to someone" or "for someone" when sharing that person's perspective. In Chinese, the pattern is:

 对 + Person + 来说，……

While this pattern was too common to omit from this page, it's covered in more depth as part of phrases using "laishuo."[1]

Usage with Specific Verbs

Certain verbs, especially psychological verbs, are often used with 对, which means 对 is needed if you want to add an object into the structure. I good example is 对⋯⋯感兴趣 ("to be interested in..."). In this case, 对 means "in," "on," "about," etc., and the object doesn't have to be a person. The short list below will give a few more verbs frequently paired with 对.

Structures

- 对⋯⋯感兴趣 (gǎn xìngqù) to be interested in...
- 对⋯⋯负责 (fùzé) to be responsible for...
- 对⋯⋯满意 (mǎnyì) to feel satisfied with...
- 对⋯⋯失望 (shīwàng) to be disappointed in/with...
- 对⋯⋯好奇 (hàoqí) to be curious about...

Examples

Some example sentences:

- 我儿子 对 学外语很 感兴趣 。
  Wǒ érzi duì xué wàiyǔ hěn gǎn xìngqù .
  My son is very interested in learning foreign languages.
- 你应该 对 自己的工作 负责 。
  Nǐ yīnggāi duì zìjǐ de gōngzuò fùzé .
  You should be responsible for your job.
- 老板 对 你不太 满意 。
  Lǎobǎn duì nǐ bù tài mǎnyì .
  The boss is not very satisfied with you.
- 观众 对 比赛结果非常 失望 。
  Guānzhòng duì bǐsài jiéguǒ fēicháng shīwàng .
  The audience is very disappointed with the result of the game.
- 我的小女儿 对 所有动物都很 好奇 。
  Wǒ de xiǎo nǚ'ér duì suǒyǒu dòngwù dōu hěn hàoqí .
  My younger daughter is curious about all animals.

---

1. Phrases using "laishuo" (B1), page 293

Similar to

- Expressing “for” with “gei” (B1), page 139
- Expressing “toward” with “wang” (B1), page 145
- Expressing “towards” with “xiang” (B1), page 148
- Verbs followed by “gei” (B1), page 201
- Comparing “dui” and “duiyu” (B2)
- Comparing “gen” and “dui” (B2)
- Expressing “for· · ·” with “eryan” (B2)

Appearance with "kanqilai" (B1)

One of the most common ways to express how something "looks" is to use 看起来 (kànqǐlái). This is what we would use if we wanted to express something like "he looks tired."

Used for Judgement

This pattern is most commonly followed by an adjectival phrase. This can include regular adverbs of degree like 很, or negative adverbs like 不.

Structure

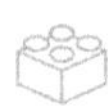 Subj. + 看起来 + Adj.

Examples

- 蛋糕 看起来 很好吃。
  Dàngāo kànqǐlái hěn hǎochī.
  The cake looks really tasty.
- 这家餐厅 看起来 不错。
  Zhè jiā cāntīng kànqǐlái bùcuò.
  This restaurant looks good.
- 你男朋友 看起来 很成熟。
  Nǐ nánpéngyou kànqǐlái hěn chéngshú.
  Your boyfriend looks very mature.
- 老板 看起来 有点不高兴。
  Lǎobǎn kànqǐlái yǒudiǎn bù gāoxìng.
  The boss looks a little unhappy.
- 你们 看起来 差不多高。
  Nǐmen kànqǐlái chàbuduō gāo.
  You look to be about the same height.

Used for Analogy

If you want to state *what* something looks *like*, you'll also need to follow 看起来 with 像 (xiàng), and then the noun phrase.

Structure

Subj. + 看起来 + 像 + Noun Phrase

Examples

- 你妈妈真年轻！看起来 像 你姐姐。
  Nǐ māma zhēn niánqīng! Kànqǐlái xiàng nǐ jiějie.
  Your mother is so young! She looks like your older sister.
- 我 看起来 像 不 像 大老板？
  Wǒ kànqǐlái xiàng bu xiàng dà lǎobǎn.
  Do I look like a big boss?
- 你们俩 看起来 像 情侣。
  Nǐmen liǎ kànqǐlái xiàng qínglǚ.
  You two look like a couple.
- 他们 看起来 不 像 有钱人。
  Tāmen kànqǐlái bù xiàng yǒuqián rén.
  They don't look like rich people.
- 那个喝醉的男人 看起来 像 你老公。
  Nà gè hēzuì de nánrén kànqǐlái xiàng nǐ lǎogōng.
  That drunk guy looks like your husband.

Similar to

- Direction complement "-qilai" (B1), page 217
- Expressing "it seems" with "haoxiang" (B1), page 162
- Advanced uses of direction complement "-qilai" (B2)
- Assessing situations with "kanlai" (B2)
- Expressing "as if" with "sihu" (C1)

Causative verbs (B1)

Causative verbs are used to cause or influence people to do things. In English, these are verbs like "make," "let," "have," and "get," when used in a sentence like "get Billy to eat a live worm."

The most common causative verbs in Chinese are:

- 让 (ràng)
- 叫 (jiào)
- 请 (qǐng)
- 使 (shǐ)

Structure

Subj. + [Causative Verb] + Person + Predicate

The predicate part of the pattern can be a verb or an adjective.

使 (shǐ) and 让 (ràng), when used as causative verbs, basically mean the same thing ("to make"), but 使 (shǐ) is used in more formal or written Chinese, while 让 (ràng) is used more in spoken Chinese.

"Make" vs. "Let"

It's worth noting that 让 is the most common causative verb in spoken Mandarin and is often translated into English as either "make" or "let." It may seem strange to speakers of English that these two very different words are the same word in Chinese. "Make" is kind of like forcing, and "let" is kind of like allowing, right? But in Chinese, the context generally makes clear how willing the object of the causative verb is. It's just something that takes time for learners to get used to.

Examples

- 你为什么不 让 我去?
  Nǐ wèishénme bù ràng wǒ qù?
  Why won't you let me go?
- 这部电影 让 人很感动。
  Zhè bù diànyǐng ràng rén hěn gǎndòng.
  This movie really moves people.

- 那个老人 让 我想到了我爷爷。
  Nàge lǎorén ràng wǒ xiǎng dào le wǒ yéye.
  That old man made me think of my grandpa.
- 他不听话，你 叫 我怎么办？
  Tā bù tīnghuà, nǐ jiào wǒ zěnmebàn?
  He won't listen. What would you have me do?
- 他偷偷约别的女孩，你 叫 我怎么想？
  Tā tōutōu yuē bié de nǚhái, nǐ jiào wǒ zěnme xiǎng?
  He secretly asked other girls out. Tell me what I'm supposed to think.
- 你儿子在学校的表现 叫 老师很头疼。
  Nǐ érzi zài xuéxiào de biǎoxiàn jiào lǎoshī hěn tóuténg.
  Your son's behavior at school gives the teacher quite a headache.
- 我想 请 你帮我一个忙。
  Wǒ xiǎng qǐng nǐ bāng wǒ yī gè máng.
  I want to ask you to do me a favor.
- 能不能 请 你明天照顾一下我的狗？
  Néng bu néng qǐng nǐ míngtiān zhàogù yīxià wǒ de gǒu?
  Can I ask you to look after my dog tomorrow?
- 他的演讲 使 听众们非常激动。
  Tā de yǎnjiǎng shǐ tīngzhòng men fēicháng jīdòng.
  His speech made the audience very excited.
- 经济危机 使 很多公司倒闭了，也 使 很多人失去了工作。
  Jīngjì wēijī shǐ hěn duō gōngsī dǎobì le, yě shǐ hěn duō rén shīqù le gōngzuò.
  The financial crisis caused lot of companies to go out of business and also caused many people to lose their jobs.

Obviously, not every causative verb maps perfectly to an English causative verb. You can see from these examples than in some cases the natural English translation doesn't even need a causative verb.

Similar to

- Using the verb "jiao" (A1)

Expressing “it depends” with “kan” (B1)

Although there are a number of ways to express “it depends” in Chinese, the most common ones in informal spoken Chinese involve the verb 看 (kàn). Some common expressions include 要看 (yào kàn) and 得看 (děi kàn). Both mean “(it) depends (on).” Literally, they would translate as “have to look at,” so the logic is not hard to understand.

Basic Pattern

If you're answering a question with “it depends on...” then this is the pattern you want.

Structure

这 / 那 + 要看 / 得看 + [Unclear Situation]

Examples

Keep in mind that the “answers” below are meant to be an answer to some imaginary question that we don't include.

- 这 得看 你的时间。
  Zhè děi kàn nǐ de shíjiān.
  This depends on when you are available.
- 那 要看 他愿不愿意。
  Nà yào kàn tā yuàn bu yuànyì.
  That depends on whether he is willing or not.
- 这 得看 天气怎么样。
  Zhè děi kàn tiānqì zěnmeyàng.
  It depends on how the weather is.
- 那 要看 老板怎么想。
  Nà yào kàn lǎobǎn zěnme xiǎng.
  It depends on what the boss thinks.
- 那 得看 考试结果。
  Nà děi kàn kǎoshì jiéguǒ.
  That depends on the result of the test.

Advanced Pattern

Structure

If you're going to write a full sentence explaining what "it" depends on, then you're going to need to lead off with some kind of explanation of the "unknown outcome" of what "it depends" on. So you'll start with the "unknown outcome" in the first part of the sentence (*before* 要看 / 得看) and then end up with what "it depends on" (*after* 要看 / 得看).

[Unknown Outcome] + 要看 / 得看 + [Unclear Situation]

The "unknown outcome" normally includes some kind of question word, meaning something like "*whether or not* x happens" or "*what* x does," etc.

Examples

- 去不去 得看 我的心情。
  Qù bu qù děi kàn wǒ de xīnqíng.
  Whether or not I go depends on my mood.
- 什么时候 去 要看 公司的安排。
  Shénme shíhou qù yào kàn gōngsī de ānpái.
  When we go depends on the company's arrangements.
- 学音乐 还是 学画画 要看 孩子的兴趣。
  Xué yīnyuè háishì xué huàhuà yào kàn háizi de xìngqù.
  Whether to study music or drawing depends on your child's interest.
- 能不能 留在中国 要看 我能不能拿到签证。
  Néng bu néng liú zài Zhōngguó yào kàn wǒ néng bu néng nádào qiānzhèng.
  Whether or not I can stay in China depends on whether or not I can get a visa.
- 谁 当总统 得看 大选的结果。
  Shéi dāng zǒngtǒng děi kàn dàxuǎn de jiéguǒ.
  Who the next president will be depends on the result of the election.

If you're looking for more formal language, consider 取决于 (qǔjué yú), "to be determined by."

Expressing "it seems" with "haoxiang" (B1)

To express "seems," the word 好像 (hǎoxiàng) can be used.

Structure

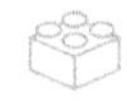 Subj. + 好像……

Examples

- 他 好像 是英国人。
  Tā hǎoxiàng shì Yīngguó rén.
  He seems to be British.
- 你 好像 不是本地人。
  Nǐ hǎoxiàng bù shì běndì rén.
  You don't seem to be a local.
- 她 好像 生病了。
  Tā hǎoxiàng shēngbìng le.
  It seems like she's sick.
- 你 好像 很不喜欢她。
  Nǐ hǎoxiàng hěn bù xǐhuan tā.
  It seems that you dislike her a lot.
- 王先生 好像 很怕他老婆。
  Wáng xiānsheng hǎoxiàng hěn pà tā lǎopo.
  Mr. Wang seems to fear his wife a lot.
- 他一个人坐在那儿，好像 在想事情。
  Tā yī gè rén zuò zài nàr, hǎoxiàng zài xiǎng shìqing.
  He's sitting there all by himself. It seems like he's thinking about something.

Note that if this structure is used without a subject, it has the meaning of "it seems like…" or "it seems that…" in English. This could then be followed by an entire statement.

- 好像 不行。
  Hǎoxiàng bù xíng.
  It seems like it didn't work.

- 好像 要下雨了。
  Hǎoxiàng yào xiàyǔ le.
  It seems like it's going to rain.
- 好像 有人敲门。
  Hǎoxiàng yǒu rén qiāo mén.
  It seems that someone is knocking at the door.
- 好像 有人来过。
  Hǎoxiàng yǒu rén lái guo.
  It seems that someone has been here.

Similar to

- Appearance with "kanqilai" (B1), page 156
- Assessing situations with "kanlai" (B2)
- Expressing "as if" with "sihu" (C1)

Expressing "mistakenly think that" with "yiwei" (B1)

When we talk about mistaken beliefs in English, we just use the word "thought," and the context and the rest of the sentence makes clear that we were wrong. In Chinese, there's a specific verb just for "think mistakenly": 以为 (yǐwéi).

Structure

In English, the verb "to think" can apply to both correct and incorrect notions. Chinese has a specific verb for "to mistakenly think that": 以为 (yǐwéi). Literally, these two characters mean, "take to be," i.e. someone takes one thing to be something else.

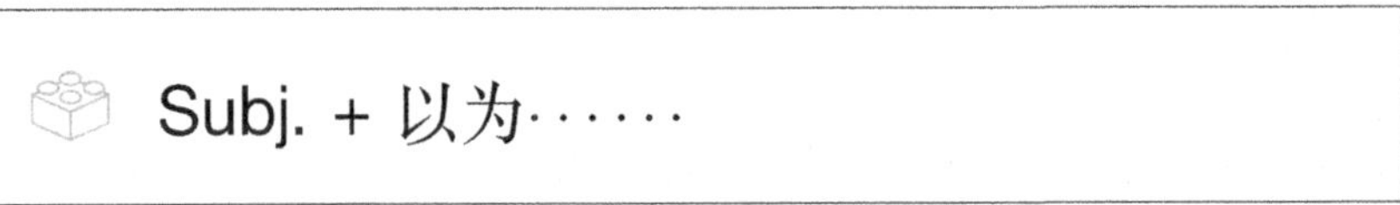

The part that follows 以为 will be a whole phrase that is actually incorrect information. Note that while it's quite common to refer to things that happened in the past, it could also refer to a situation in the present or even the future. It can also be used for commands, usually of the negative "don't think that..." type.

Examples

- 我 以为 他是德国人。
  Wǒ yǐwéi tā shì Déguó rén.
  I thought he was German.
- 我们 以为 你不在家。
  Wǒmen yǐwéi nǐ bù zài jiā .
  We thought you weren't at home.
- 你 以为 你是谁?
  Nǐ yǐwéi nǐ shì shéi?
  Who do you think you are?
- 同事们都 以为 我二十岁。
  Tóngshì men dōu yǐwéi wǒ èrshí suì.
  My colleagues all thought I was twenty.
- 我们都 以为 你生气了。
  Wǒmen dōu yǐwéi nǐ shēngqì le.
  We all thought you were angry.

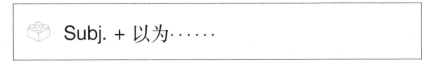

- 老师 以为 学生都听懂了。
  Lǎoshī yǐwéi xuéshēng dōu tīngdǒng le.
  The teacher thought all the students understood.
- 不要 以为 他是你的朋友。
  Bùyào yǐwéi tā shì nǐ de péngyou.
  Don't think that he's your friend.
- 她是你外婆？我 以为 是你妈妈。
  Tā shì nǐ wàipó? Wǒ yǐwéi shì nǐ māma.
  She's your grandma? I thought she was your mother.
- 你去吃四川火锅了？我 以为 你不爱吃辣。
  Nǐ qù chī Sìchuān huǒguō le? Wǒ yǐwéi nǐ bù ài chī là.
  You went to eat Sichuan hotpot? I thought you don't like eating spicy food.
- 你们分手了？我 以为 你们还在一起。
  Nǐmen fēnshǒu le? Wǒ yǐwéi nǐmen hái zài yīqǐ.
  You guys broke up? I thought you were still together.
- 我看到那张照片，以为 你有男朋友了。
  Wǒ kàndào nà zhāng zhàopiàn, yǐwéi nǐ yǒu nánpéngyou le.
  I saw that picture and I thought you had a boyfriend.

Expressing "through" with "jingguo" (B1)

When 经过 (jīngguò) is used as a verb, it means "to pass by." 经过 can be also used as a preposition to describe what experiences or times one went "through."

Used as a Verb

As a verb, 经过 means "to pass by" or "to pass through." It's for saying things like, "I passed through downtown" or "I passed by the shop."

Examples

- 我每天上班都 经过 这里。
  Wǒ měi tiān shàngbān dōu jīngguò zhèlǐ.
  I pass by this place every day on the way to work.
- 我坐火车回老家常常 经过 这个城市。
  Wǒ zuò huǒchē huí lǎojiā chángcháng jīngguò zhège chéngshì.
  I usually pass by this city when I take the train back to my hometown.
- 你 经过 我家门口的时候叫我一下。
  Nǐ jīngguò wǒ jiā ménkǒu de shíhou jiào wǒ yīxià.
  Call me when you pass by my door.
- 她 经过 这个咖啡店的时候就会想到他。
  Tā jīngguò zhège kāfēidiàn de shíhou jiù huì xiǎngdào tā.
  She thinks about him when she walks past this cafe.

Used as a Preposition

As a preposition, 经过 means something like "through" (or "after going through"), and is used to emphasize the process of an experience.

Structure

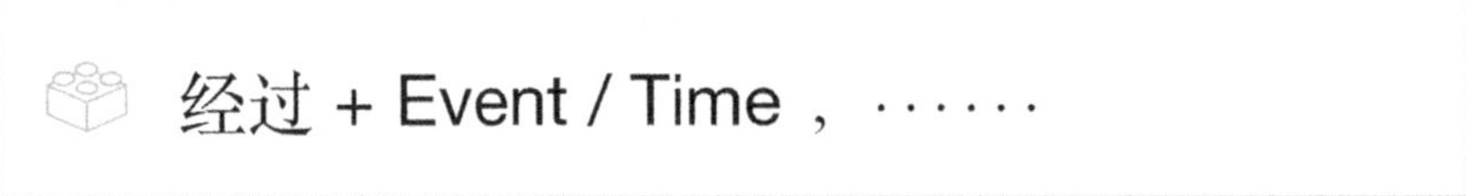

Examples

- 经过 自己的 努力 ，她考上了北京大学。
  Jīngguò zìjǐ de nǔlì , tā kǎoshàng le Běijīng Dàxué.
  Through her own hard work, she was admitted into Peking University.

- 经过 两个月的 准备 ，他顺利地通过了这次面试。
  Jīngguò liǎng gè yuè de zhǔnbèi, tā shùnlì de tōngguò le zhè cì miànshì.
  After two months of preparation, he successfully passed the job interview.
- 经过 这几年的 发展 ，这个城市发生了很大变化。
  Jīngguò zhè jǐ nián de fāzhǎn, zhège chéngshì fāshēng le hěn dà biànhuà.
  After the last few years of development, this city has changed a lot.
- 经过 一个星期的 调查 ，警察认为他没有罪。
  Jīngguò yī gè xīngqī de diàochá, jǐngchá rènwéi tā méiyǒu zuì.
  After one week of investigation, the police believe that he's not guilty.

Similar to

- Expressing “through” with “tongguo” (B1), page 168

Expressing "through" with "tongguo" (B1)

The first meaning of 通过 (tōngguò) used as a verb is "to go through" a certain object, as in penetrating into and coming out of something. The second meaning is "to pass," which means someone goes through effort in order to reach acknowledgment or agreement.

Used as a Verb

Examples

- 从我家到那儿要 通过 两座桥。
  Cóng wǒ jiā dào nàr yào tōngguò liǎng zuò qiáo.
  To get there from my house, you have to cross two bridges.
- 通过 那个红色的大门，左拐就到了。
  Tōngguò nàge hóngsè de dà mén, zuǒ guǎi jiù dào le.
  Go through that red door, turn left and you are there.
- 我 通过 了这个考试。
  Wǒ tōngguò le zhège kǎoshì.
  I passed this test.
- 他没 通过 昨天的面试。
  Tā méi tōngguò zuótiān de miànshì.
  He didn't pass yesterday's job interview.
- 那个穿黑衣服的男人没 通过 机场的安检。
  Nàge chuān hēi yīfu de nánrén méi tōngguò jīchǎng de ānjiǎn.
  That man in black didn't pass the security check at the airport.

Used as a Preposition

As a preposition, 通过 expresses using a certain method to achieve a desired outcome. It emphasizes the manner or method of doing something, and it can be placed before or after the subject.

Structure

通过 + Agent / Method ， Subj. ⋯⋯

Examples

- 我们是 通过 他的朋友 找到他的。
  Wǒmen shì tōngguò tā de péngyou zhǎodào tā de.
  We found him via his friends.
- 通过 这个调查 ，我们发现很多人都支持他。
  Tōngguò zhège diàochá , wǒmen fāxiàn hěn duō rén dōu zhīchí tā.
  Through this survey, we found that many people support him.
- 通过 这个短片 ，我们更了解你们公司了。
  Tōngguò zhège duǎnpiàn , wǒmen gèng liǎojiě nǐmen gōngsī le.
  We've got a better understanding of your company through this short film.
- 通过 他的介绍 ，我认识了我现在的老板。
  Tōngguò tā de jièshào , wǒ rènshi le wǒ xiànzài de lǎobǎn.
  Through his introduction, I met my current boss.
- 通过 每个月的培训 ，我们的员工更专业了。
  Tōngguò měi gè yuè de péixùn , wǒmen de yuángōng gèng zhuānyè le.
  Our employees have become more professional through monthly trainings.

Similar to

- Expressing “through” with “jingguo” (B1), page 166
- Using “lai” to connect two verb phrases (B1), page 107

Expressing "to come from" with "laizi" (B1)

来自 (láizì) is used to express the origin of something or someone. Its meaning is similar to "to come from" in English.

Structure

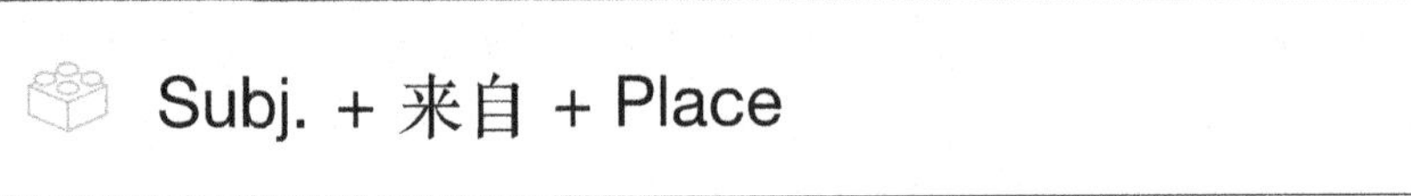

Examples

You can see that in some of the sentences below dealing with ideas and other abstract nouns, a translation like "originate from" may be more appropriate.

- 我 来自 中国。
  Wǒ láizì Zhōngguó.
  I come from China.
- 这些书都 来自 日本。
  Zhèxiē shū dōu láizì Rìběn.
  These books all come from Japan.
- 我们公司的客户 来自 美国。
  Wǒmen gōngsī de kèhù láizì Měiguó.
  Our company's clients come from the USA.
- 我的这个想法 来自 生活。
  Wǒ de zhège xiǎngfǎ láizì shēnghuó.
  This idea of mine originated from daily life.
- 这是 来自 政府的报告。
  Zhè shì láizì zhèngfǔ de bàogào.
  This is a report from the government.
- 有些坏习惯 来自 迷信。
  Yǒu xiē huài xíguàn láizì míxìn.
  There are some bad habits that originate from superstition.
- 小明的成功 来自 他的努力和认真。
  Xiǎo Míng de chénggōng láizì tā de nǔlì hé rènzhēn.
  Xiao Ming's success stems from his hard work and earnestness.

- 听了 来自 教授的建议，我决定去上海。
  Tīng le láizì jiàoshòu de jiànyì, wǒ juédìng qù Shànghǎi.
  After listening to the suggestion from the professor, I decided to go to Shanghai.
- 我和 Tom 虽然 来自 不同的国家，但是我们是好朋友。
  Wǒ hé Tom suīrán láizì bùtóng de guójiā, dànshì wǒmen shì hǎo péngyou.
  Although Tom and I come from different countries, we're good friends.
- 我设计的这副作品 来自 小王的启发。
  Wǒ shèjì de zhè fù zuòpǐn láizì Xiǎo Wáng de qǐfā.
  This piece I designed was inspired by Xiao Wang.

Similar to

- Expressing "from… to…" with "cong… dao…" (A2)

Making judgments with "suan" (B1)

The word 算 (suàn) has a number of uses which can be translated in a number of ways. The common theme is that 算 indicates some kind of judgment and may be thought of as "counts as" or "is considered to be."

Used with a Noun

This essentially expresses that one "considers" something to be something else, as in, "I consider her a genius."

Structure

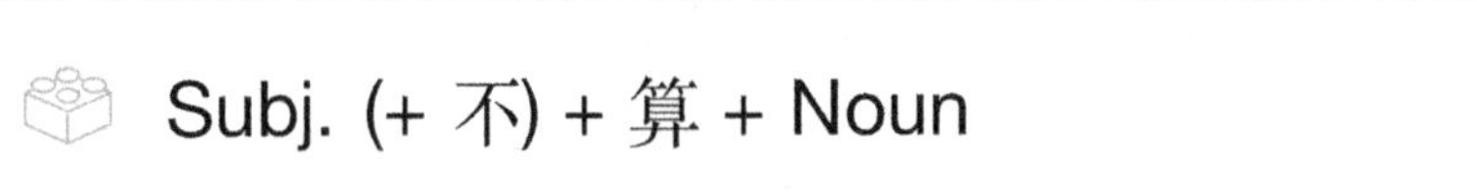

Subj. (+ 不) + 算 + Noun

Examples

- 她 算 天才。
  Tā suàn tiāncái.
  She is considered a genius.
- 这 算 秘密吗?
  Zhè suàn mìmì ma?
  Is this considered a secret?
- 她 算 不 算 你女朋友?
  Tā suàn bu suàn nǐ nǚpéngyou?
  Can she be considered your girlfriend or not?
- 美国的中国菜 算 中国菜吗?
  Měiguó de Zhōngguó cài suàn Zhōngguó cài ma?
  Can American Chinese food be considered Chinese food?
- 我们认识，但是不 算 朋友。
  Wǒmen rènshi, dànshì bù suàn péngyou.
  We know each other, but can't be considered friends.

Used with an Adjective

Affirmative Form

算 can also be used with an adjective. It adds a sense of "comparatively speaking," as in, "in the grand scheme of things, this counts as...."

Structure

Subj. + 算 + Adj. + 的

Examples

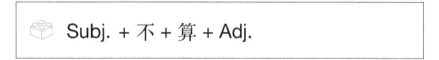

- 这家店的东西 算 便宜 的 。
  Zhè jiā diàn de dōngxi suàn piányi de .
  The things in this shop are pretty cheap.
- 我女儿 算 听话 的 。
  Wǒ nǚér suàn tīnghuà de .
  My daughter pretty much does what she's told.
- 在我们公司，我 算 年轻 的 。
  Zài wǒmen gōngsī, wǒ suàn niánqīng de .
  I'm considered young in our company.
- 你老板 算 大方 的 ，我老板更小气。
  Nǐ lǎobǎn suàn dàfang de , wǒ lǎobǎn gèng xiǎoqì.
  Your boss could be said to be generous. My boss is even stingier.

Negative Form

This is essentially a straight negation of the affirmative form, but because it's so commonly used, it's worth giving providing extra examples.

Structure

Subj. + 不 + 算 + Adj.

Note that you don't need add a 的 here.

Examples

- 这次考试 不算 难。
  Zhè cì kǎoshì bù suàn nán.
  This exam isn't that difficult.
- 三十岁结婚 不算 晚。
  Sānshí suì jiéhūn bù suàn wǎn.
  Getting married when you're 30 can't be considered late.

- 他才一米七五，不算高。
  Tā cái yī mǐ qī wǔ, bù suàn gāo.
  He's only 1.75 meters tall. He can't be considered very tall.
- 剪个头发五十块，不算贵。
  Jiǎn gè tóufa wǔshí kuài, bù suàn guì.
  Fifty kuai for a haircut. It can't be considered expensive.

Adding a Tone of Reluctance with 算是

For both the noun and adjective patterns above, the "judgment" indicated by 算 can be made more reluctant by following 算 immediately with a 是.

✔ 他算天才。
  Tā suàn tiāncái.
  He is considered a genius.

✔ 他算是天才。
  Tā suàn shì tiāncái.
  You could say he's a genius (I guess).

Colloquial Sayings

A few common examples:

- 算你狠！
  Suàn nǐ hěn!
  Well aren't you tough!
- 你算老几?
  Nǐ suàn lǎojǐ?
  So you think you're some kind of big shot?
- 这不算什么。
  Zhè bù suàn shénme.
  It's no big deal.

Using "lai" as a dummy verb (B1)

The verb 来 (lái) can be used as a "dummy verb," similar to the way "do" is used in English. To illustrate the point, imagine a bottle of pickles that you want to open but can't because the lid is so tight. You start passing it around to see who can open it, and no one is able to, until your beefy friend comes in and says, "我来!" He is saying, "Let me do it!"

Structure

The structure for using 来 as a dummy verb is very basic. Usually it is a very short phrase, kind of like "your turn!" or "let me give it a shot!" or "you do it!" in English. Usually it is used with 你 or 我 as the subject, and it ends with the 来. Sometimes it can end with a 吧.

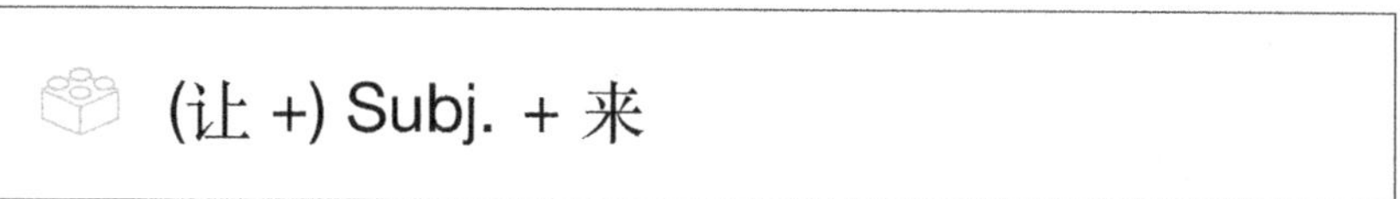

The point of calling 来 a "dummy verb" is that it does't have the original meaning of "to come." It just takes the place of whatever the verb would be in the context.

Examples

- 你来！
  Nǐ lái!
  You do it!
- 我来吧。
  Wǒ lái ba.
  Let me do it.
- 让他自己来。
  Ràng tā zìjǐ lái.
  Let him do it himself.
- 还是你们自己来吧。
  Háishì nǐmen zìjǐ lái ba.
  It's better that you do it by yourselves.
- 你写得好看，你来吧。
  Nǐ xiě de hǎokàn, nǐ lái ba.
  You write well. You write it.

A few example dialogs to provide clearer context:

A: 谁能读一下这段话？
Shéi néng dú yīxià zhè duàn huà?
Who can read this passage?

B: 老师，我 来 。
Lāoshī, wǒ lái.
Teacher, let me read it.

A: 你怎么做得这么慢？
Nǐ zěnme zuò de zhème màn?
How come you do it so slowly?

B: 你觉得我慢？你 来 ！
Nǐ juéde wǒ màn? Nǐ lái!
You think I'm slow? You do it!

A: 这个箱子真重！
Zhège xiāngzi zhēn zhòng!
This box is so heavy!

B: 我 来 吧。
Wǒ lái ba.
Let me help.

Expressing "don't need to" with "buyong" (B1)

In Chinese, 要 (yào) has many meanings, one of which is "need to." However, when you want to express "don't need to," you actually use 不用 (bùyòng), not 不要 (bùyào).

Structure

 Subj. + 不用 + [Verb Phrase]

Examples

- 不用 谢。
  Bùyòng xiè.
  You don't need to thank me.
- 不用 担心。
  Bùyòng dānxīn.
  You don't need to worry.
- 孩子 不用 买票。
  Háizi bùyòng mǎi piào.
  Kids don't need to buy tickets.
- 你 不用 过去，她会过来的。
  Nǐ bùyòng guòqù, tā huì guòlái de.
  You don't need to go over there. She will come here.
- 今天 不用 加班。
  Jīntiān bùyòng jiābān.
  We don't need to work overtime today.
- 这件事 不用 跟他说。
  Zhè jiàn shì bùyòng gēn tā shuō.
  You don't need to tell him about this.
- 告诉他明天 不用 来了。
  Gàosu tā míngtiān bùyòng lái le.
  Tell him that he doesn't need to come tomorrow.
- 买吧，不用 考虑价钱。
  Mǎi ba, bùyòng kǎolǜ jiàqián.
  Buy it. You don't need to consider the price.

- 今天人少，不用排队。
  Jīntiān rén shǎo, bùyòng páiduì.
  There aren't many people today. We don't need to wait in line.
- 你们不用都来，我们不需要这么多人。
  Nǐmen bùyòng dōu lái, wǒmen bù xūyào zhème duō rén.
  Not all of you need to come. We don't need this many people.

Colloquial Saying

In spoken Chinese, the rhetorical question, "这还用说吗？" indicates the speaker believes that the statement is obvious. It is equivalent to the speaker saying, "does that even need to be said?" or "is that seriously a question?" This 用 is the direct opposite of the 不用 in this grammar point, but you don't hear it a lot.

Similar to

- Auxiliary verb "yao" and its multiple meanings (A2)
- Negative commands with "bie" (A2)
- Expressing "must" with "dei" (B1), page 179

Expressing "must" with "dei" (B1)

The auxiliary verb 得 (děi) means "must." Yes, it's annoying that the same character can also be pronounced "de," but at least when you use 得 (děi), there's no ambiguity like with the word 要 (yào).

Structure

Normally, when you see 得, it's a particle and is pronounced "de." However, it can also be an auxiliary verb. In this case it's pronounced "děi" and means "must."

Subj. + 得 + [Verb Phrase]

Examples

- 我们 得 走了。
  Wǒmen děi zǒu le.
  We have to leave now.
- 时间不早了，我 得 回家了。
  Shíjiān bù zǎo le, wǒ děi huíjiā le.
  It's getting late. I have to go home.
- 他是你弟弟，你 得 帮他。
  Tā shì nǐ dìdi, nǐ děi bāng tā.
  He is your younger brother. You must help him.
- 不好意思，你 得 马上离开。
  Bù hǎoyìsi, nǐ děi mǎshàng líkāi.
  Excuse me, but you have to leave here right now.
- 在学校就 得 听老师的话。
  Zài xuéxiào jiù děi tīng lǎoshī de huà.
  You have to listen to the teacher at school.
- 你 得 先付钱再进去。
  Nǐ děi xiān fù qián zài jìnqù.
  You need to pay before you go in.
- 是你的错，你 得 道歉。
  Shì nǐ de cuò, nǐ děi dàoqiàn.
  It's your fault. You must apologize.

- 他没有经验，你 得 教教他。

  Tā méiyǒu jīngyàn, nǐ děi jiāojiao tā.

  He doesn't have experience. You must teach him.

- 明天去面试，你 得 穿得正式一点。

  Míngtiān qù miànshì, nǐ děi chuān de zhèngshì yīdiǎn.

  You must wear something more formal for tomorrow's job interview.

- 你病得太厉害了，得 去看医生。

  Nǐ bìng de tài lìhai le, děi qù kàn yīshēng.

  You are really sick. You must go see a doctor.

Similar to

- Wanting to do something with "yao" (A1)
- Expressing "should" with "yinggai" (A2)
- Expressing "would like to" with "xiang" (A2)
- Expressing "don't need to" with "buyong" (B1), page 177
- Expressing "had better" with "zuihao" (B1), page 57
- Declaring the only option with "zhihao" (B2)
- Expressing "have to" with budebu (B2)
- Adding emphasis with "fei....buke" (C1)
- Expressing "must" with "feidei" (C1)

Doing something less with "shao" (B1)

The word 少 (shǎo) can mean "few," but when when placed before a verb, in takes on the meaning of "less" as in "to do less (of something)." It is often heard when scolding or giving advice (like when parents talk to children). What's not intuitive to learners is that the word 少 should come *before the verb*.

Structure

Just as you can use 多 to talk about doing something more[1], you can use 少 to talk about doing something *less*.

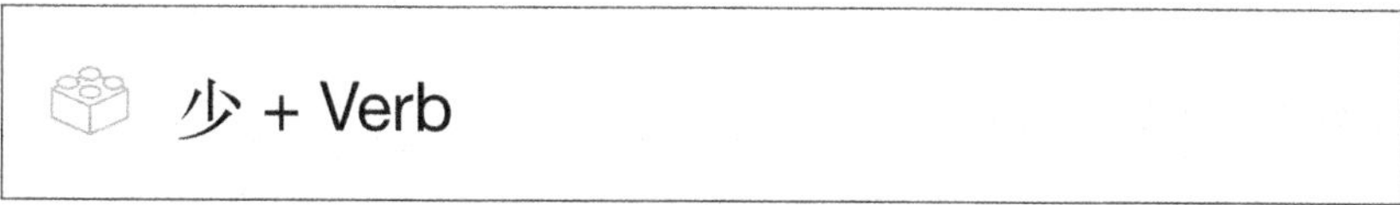

少 + Verb

Note that in English, we don't use the word "less" very much. For example, rather than saying "drink less water," we might say "don't drink so much water." In Chinese, though, using 少 is quite natural and common. Avoiding the negative command (telling someone *not* to do something) is also a subtle way of sounding less bossy and annoying in Chinese.

Examples

- 请 少 放点盐。
  Qǐng shǎo fàng diǎn yán.
  Use less salt, please.
- 少 吃垃圾食品。
  Shǎo chī lājī shípǐn.
  Eat less junk food.
- 少 买点，吃不完会坏的。
  Shǎo mǎi diǎn, chī bu wán huì huài de.
  Don't buy too much. It will go bad if we can't finish eating it all.
- 你能不能 少 抽点烟？
  Nǐ néng bu néng shǎo chōu diǎn yān?
  Can you smoke less?
- 快期中考试了， 少 玩点游戏吧。
  Kuài qīzhōng kǎoshì le, shǎo wán diǎn yóuxì ba.
  The mid-term exams are coming up. Go easy on the video games.

1. Doing something more with "duo" (B1), page 183

- 少 喝点，明天还要上班呢。
  Shǎo hē diǎn, míngtiān háiyào shàngbān ne.
  Don't drink so much. You need go to work tomorrow.
- 少 看点电视，多看书。
  Shǎo kàn diǎn diànshì, duō kànshū.
  Watch less TV. Read more books.
- 少 吃点肉，多吃点蔬菜。
  Shǎo chī diǎn ròu, duō chī diǎn shūcài.
  Eat less meat and eat more vegetables.

Colloquial Sayings

These set phrases are worth special note, because although they follow the grammar pattern, they might not make sense to you without a little extra explanation, just like the meaning of "come on" might not make sense at first to someone learning English.

- 少 来！
  Shǎo lái!
  Come on!
  Lit. "come less"
- 少 说废话！
  Shǎo shuō fèihuà!
  Quit your babbling!
  Lit. "speak less nonsense talk"
- 少 管闲事。
  Shǎo guǎn xiánshì.
  Stay out of other people's business.
  Lit. "get involved less in others' affairs"

Similar to

- Doing something more with "duo" (B1), page 183

Doing something more with "duo" (B1)

In China, you often hear you should do this or that more (eat more, drink more water, wear more warm clothing, etc.), and they often use the word 多 (duō). What's not intuitive to learners is that the word 多 should come *before the verb.*

Structure

This structure is often used in commands or suggestions. Note the position of 多:

多 + Verb

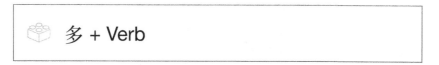

This structure is not used exclusively as a command, so you could also include a subject if you needed to.

Examples

In English we like to say things like "eat *more*," "drink *more* beer," and "I need to exercise *more*." Notice that in every one of these cases, the word "more" (equivalent to this use of 多) comes *after* the verb in English. In Chinese, it's more natural to put the 多 *before* the verb.

- 多吃点。
  Duō chī diǎn.
  Eat a little more.
- 多放点辣。
  Duō fàng diǎn là.
  Add a little more spiciness.
- 多拿一点。
  Duō ná yīdiǎn.
  Take more.
- 爷爷，你要多出去走走。
  Yéye, nǐ yào duō chūqù zǒuzou.
  Gramps, you need to go out and take walks more often.
- 多给他点时间吧。
  Duō gěi tā diǎn shíjiān ba.
  Give him a little more time.
- 我想多陪陪家人。
  Wǒ xiǎng duō péipei jiārén.
  I want to spend more time with my family.

- 感冒的时候要 多 喝水。

  Gǎnmào de shíhou yào duō hē shuǐ.

  Drink more water when you have a cold.

- 医生让我 多 运动。

  Yīshēng ràng wǒ duō yùndòng.

  The doctor told me to exercise more.

- 他比你有经验，你应该 多 向他学习。

  Tā bǐ nǐ yǒu jīngyàn, nǐ yīnggāi duō xiàng tā xuéxí.

  He's more experienced than you. You should learn from him more.

- 想提高汉语口语，就要 多 练习。

  Xiǎng tígāo Hànyǔ kǒuyǔ, jiùyào duō liànxí.

  If you want to improve your spoken Chinese, you need to practice more.

Counter-Examples

Just to be completely clear, the following uses of 多 are not as natural as the ones above. They'll be understood, and they might not be technically *wrong*, but you can do better!

⚠ 吃 多 点。

Chī duō diǎn.

⚠ 我要回家 多 点！

Wǒ yào huíjiā duō diǎn!

⚠ 我应该运动 多 点。

Wǒ yīnggāi yùndòng duō diǎn.

The opposite of 多 is, of course, 少. It is further explained in the article doing something less with "shao"[1].

Similar to

- Asking about degree with "duo" (A2)
- Expressing "really" with "zhen" (A2)
- Intensifying with "duo" (A2)
- Doing something less with "shao" (B1), page 181
- Indicating a number in excess (B1), page 120

1. Doing something less with "shao" (B1), page 181

Expressing "not often" with "bu zenme" (B1)

You might be tempted to conclude that 不怎么 (bù zěnme) seems to mean "not how," but it actually means "not often" when used together with a verb.

Structure

When 不怎么 is used with a verb, it means that one does not put a lot of time or energy into doing it. In other words, the action is done "not often." When the verb is used with an object, it also means that the number (or quantity) is really small.

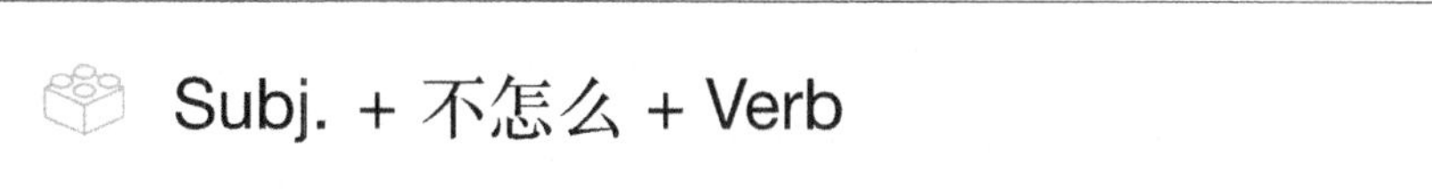

Examples

- 他 不怎么 爱说话。
  Tā bù zěnme ài shuōhuà.
  He doesn't like to talk much.
- 我老公 不怎么 运动。
  Wǒ lǎogōng bù zěnme yùndòng.
  My husband doesn't exercise much.
- 我们在家 不怎么 看电视。
  Wǒmen zài jiā bù zěnme kàn diànshì.
  We don't watch a lot of television at home.
- 我儿子 不怎么 吃零食。
  Wǒ érzi bù zěnme chī língshí.
  My son doesn't snack much.
- 老板 不怎么 来办公室。
  Lǎobǎn bù zěnme lái bàngōngshì.
  My boss doesn't come to the office very often.
- 我 不怎么 在网上买东西。
  Wǒ bù zěnme zài wǎngshàng mǎi dóngxi.
  I don't online shop very often.
- 他们 不怎么 跟朋友出去玩。
  Tāmen bù zěnme gēn péngyou chūqù wán.
  They don't often go out with friends.

Usage of 没怎么

Note that the examples below use 没 instead of 不. This is because the verb uses or implies 有 and thus it uses the same the 有 negation rules.

- 我 没怎么 复习。
  Wǒ méi zěnme fùxí.
  I didn't review much.
- 我 没怎么 想过这个问题。
  Wǒ méi zěnme xiǎng guo zhège wèntí.
  I didn't really think about this before.
- 昨天我肚子不舒服，没怎么 吃东西。
  Zuótiān wǒ dùzi bù shūfu, méi zěnme chī dōngxi.
  My stomach didn't feel well yesterday, so I didn't eat much.

Lastly, make sure to use 不怎么 with a verb if you want it to mean "not often." Using it with an adjective gives it a different meaning.

Similar to

- How to do something with "zenme" (A1)
- Asking why with "zenme" (A2)
- Expressing "not very" with "bu zenme" (B1), page 6

Expressing "until" with "dao" (B1)

One kind of complement in Chinese involves putting 到 (dào) after the verb, followed by a time or other event. This 到 works much like the English word "until."

Basic Pattern

Structure

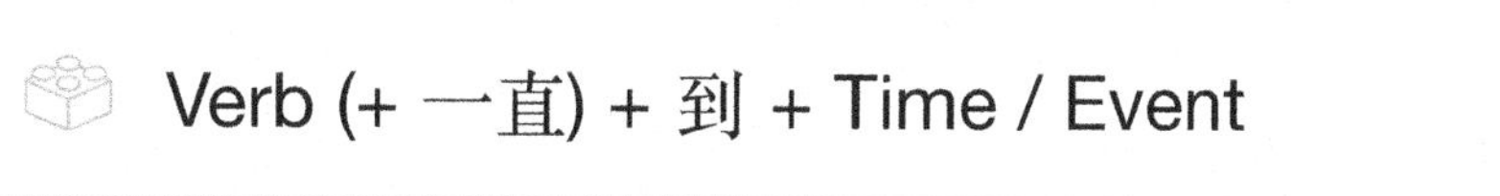

You will sometimes see 一直 (yīzhí) proceeding 到, which serves the purpose of the emphasis on the "ongoing duration."

Note that the verbs are mostly single-syllable.

Examples

- 你们要玩 到 几点?
  Nǐmen yào wán dào jǐ diǎn?
  When will you be done playing?
- 我们在酒吧 一直 聊 到 半夜。
  Wǒmen zài jiǔbā yīzhí liáo dào bànyè.
  We were chatting in the bar until midnight.
- 你弟弟要在我们家住 到 什么时候?
  Nǐ dìdi yào zài wǒmen jiā zhù dào shénme shíhou?
  Your younger brother is going to stay in our house until when?
- 昨天的会 一直 开 到 晚上九点。
  Zuótiān de huì yīzhí kāi dào wǎnshang jiǔ diǎn.
  Yesterday's meeting lasted until 9 pm.
- 我邻居今天吵架了, 一直 吵 到 警察过来。
  Wǒ línjū jīntiān chǎojià le, yīzhí chǎo dào jǐngchá guòlái.
  My neighbors had a fight today, which lasted until the police came.
- 我们晚上去吃火锅了, 一直 吃 到 火锅店关门。
  Wǒmen wǎnshang qù chī huǒguō le, yīzhí chī dào huǒguō diàn guānmén.
  We went to eat hotpot tonight, and we didn't finish until the place was closed.

- 他昨天一天都在打游戏，一直 打 到 他妈妈回家。
  Tā zuótiān yī tiān dōu zài dǎ yóuxì, yīzhí dǎ dào tā māma huí jiā.
  He was playing computer games all day yesterday. He didn't stop until his mother came home.

Pattern with Repeating Verb

Structure

If there is a verb phrase proceeding 到, use this structure:

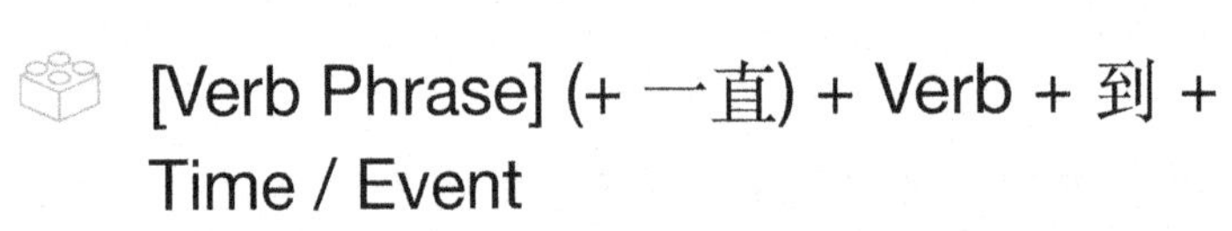

[Verb Phrase] (+ 一直) + Verb + 到 + Time / Event

Note that in this pattern, the verb is going to repeat.

Examples

- 你知不知道我们 等你 等 到 半夜？
  Nǐ zhī bu zhīdào wǒmen děng nǐ děng dào bànyè?
  Do you know we waited for you until midnight?
- 我女儿昨天晚上 写作业 写 到 十二点半。
  Wǒ nǚ'ér zuótiān wǎnshang xiě zuòyè xiě dào shí'èr diǎn bàn.
  My daughter didn't finish her homework until 12:30 last night.
- 她给男朋友 打电话 打 到 手机没电。
  Tā gěi nánpéngyou dǎ diànhuà dǎ dào shǒujī méi diàn.
  She called her boyfriend and they kept talking until her phone was out of battery.

Similar to

- Using "dao" to mean "to go to" (A2)

Expressing actions in progress (full form) (B1)

You may have learned that 在 (zài) and 正在 (zhèngzài) can be used before verbs to express that an action is *ongoing* or *in progress*. They are used to create the Mandarin equivalent of *present continuous* in English. But that pattern is actually a part of a longer, fuller pattern. It's rarely used in its full form, but bits and pieces of it are frequently used in everyday speech, so it's important to know the full form, even if you don't use it regularly yourself.

Structure

Subj. + 正在 / 正 / 在 + Verb + 呢

If it's a Separable verb[1], you need to put the 着 between the verb and the object, or you can just leave 着 out.

Subj. (+ 正) + Verb + 着 + Obj. + 呢

Subj. + Verb + Obj. + 呢

It's important to remember that **virtually every part of the above pattern is *optional***, so you're going to see all sorts of variations of it (and rarely the full form). The most common variation is just the "在 + V" pattern that you probably already learned long ago. Another common variation is "正 + V" pattern.

Examples

- 我 正在 吃饭。
  Wǒ zhèngzài chīfàn.
- 我 正 吃 着 饭 呢 。
  Wǒ zhèng chī zhe fàn ne .

1. Separable verb (B1), page 194

- 我吃饭 呢 。
  Wǒ chīfàn ne .
  I'm eating now.
- 爷爷 正在 看报纸，别打扰他。
  Yéye zhèngzài kàn bàozhǐ, bié dǎrǎo tā.
- 爷爷 在 看报纸 呢 ，别打扰他。
  Yéye zài kàn bàozhǐ ne , bié dǎrǎo tā.
- 爷爷看报纸 呢 ，别打扰他。
  Yéye kàn bàozhǐ ne , bié dǎrǎo tā.
  Grandpa is reading newspapers now. Don't disturb him.
- 他 在 上厕所。
  Tā zài shàng cèsuǒ.
- 他 正 上厕所 呢 。
  Tā zhèng shàng cèsuǒ ne .
- 他上厕所 呢 。
  Tā shàng cèsuǒ ne .
  He's using the bathroom now.
- 我们 在 上汉语课。
  Wǒmen zài shàng Hànyǔ kè.
- 我们 正 上汉语课 呢 。
  Wǒmen zhèng shàng Hànyǔ kè ne .
- 我们上 着 汉语课 呢 。
  Wǒmen shàng zhe Hànyǔ kè ne .
  We're having a Chinese lesson now.
- 老板 在 开会，不方便接电话。
  Lǎobǎn zài kāihuì, bù fāngbiàn jiē diànhuà.
- 老板 正 开 着 会，不方便接电话。
  Lǎobǎn zhèng kāi zhe huì, bù fāngbiàn jiē diànhuà.
- 老板开 着 会 呢 ，不方便接电话。
  Lǎobǎn kāi zhe huì ne , bù fāngbiàn jiē diànhuà.
  The boss is in the middle of a meeting. It's not convenient for him to talk on the phone.

Similar to

- Expressing actions in progress with “zai” (A2)
- Alternative existential sentences (B1), page 264
- Aspect particle “zhe” (B1), page 125

Measure words for verbs (B1)

Also known as: 动量词 (dòng liàngcí), verbal measure word and verbal classifier.

When a verb is done more than once, it also requires a measure word to accompany it. This way the measure word is acting as a way to count the frequency or re-occurrence of an action. The most basic one you probably already know is 次 (cì).

Structure

 Verb + Number + Measure Word

The grammar pattern is very similar to English. For example, "看三次" and "saw three times" mirror each other in structure. In Chinese sentences, these measure words come after the verb. You should also know that, like nouns, some verbs have special measure words to go with them. The basic verbal measure word, however, is 次, as in the number of "times" something is done or happens.

Common verb measure words include 次 (cì), 遍 (biàn), and 下 (xià).

Examples

- 再说一 遍 。
  Zài shuō yī biàn.
  Say it again.
- 你能再读一 遍 吗?
  Nǐ néng zài dú yī biàn ma?
  Could you please read it again?
- 这个电影我看过两 遍 。
  Zhège diànyǐng wǒ kàn guo liǎng biàn.
  I've seen this movie twice.
- 这个故事我听她说过一百多 遍 了。
  Zhège gùshi wǒ tīng tā shuō guo yī bǎi duō biàn le.
  I've heard her tell this story more than one hundred times.
- 我们去过两 次 。
  Wǒme qù guo liǎng cì.
  We've been there twice.
- 我问了他很多 次 ，可是他不告诉我。
  Wǒ wèn le tā hěn duō cì, kěshì tā bù gàosu wǒ.
  I've asked him about it many times, but he won't tell me.

- 这个问题我们讨论过几 次 。
  Zhège wèntí wǒmen tǎolùn guo jǐ cì.
  We've discussed this issue a few times.
- 那个红头发的男孩打了我三 下 。
  Nàge hóng tóufa de nánhái dǎ le wǒ sān xià.
  That red-haired boy hit me three times.
- 他轻轻地拍了我两 下 。
  Tā qīngqīng de pāi le wǒ liǎng xià.
  He very lightly pat me a few times.
- 你没听见吗？我敲了好几 下 。
  Nǐ méi tīngjiàn ma? Wǒ qiāo le hǎo jǐ xià.
  Did you not hear the door? I knocked quite a few times.

Similar to

- Expressing “every” with “mei” (A2)
- Measure words for counting (A2)
- Measure words in quantity questions (A2)
- Measure words with “this” and “that” (A2)

Separable verb (B1)

Also known as: 离合词 (líhécí) and verb-object phrase.

"Separable verbs" get their name from their ability to "separate" into two parts (a verb part and an object part), with other words in between. In fact, you could also simply call separable verbs "verb-object phrases."

What Are Separable Verbs?

Separable verbs are "verb-object phrases." They consist of two characters: the first is the verb, and the second is the object. Very often, these two will appear together, seemingly acting as a single verb, as in 吃饭, "to eat," 见面, "to meet," or 睡觉, "to sleep." But the two can also separate, and the verb can also be used without the object.

Structure

The Typical Learner Mistake

Let's look at a typical example in Chinese, using the verb 见面, meaning "to meet." 见 is the verb; 面 is the object, which literally means "face," but is never translated as such. The mistake everyone makes is to put an object after 见面. You can't do this, though, because 见面 *already has its own object*.

✔ 我没有时间 见面 。
Wǒ méiyǒu shíjiān jiànmiàn.
I don't have time to meet.
It may seem like it has no object, but 面 is the object.
✔ 我没有时间 见 你 。
Wǒ méiyǒu shíjiān jiàn nǐ.
I don't have time to meet you.
Here, 见 is the verb and 你 is the object.
✘ 我没有时间 见面 你 。
Wǒ méiyǒu shíjiān jiànmiàn nǐ.
面 is the object, so adding 你 after it is wrong.

The key features of separable verbs are:

- Many separable verbs can't be easily translated into other languages in a way that makes both the verb and the object part clear. For instance, 见面 ("to meet"),

睡觉 ("to sleep"), and 游泳 ("to swim") are such examples. In these examples, it's just not easy to think of the objects as a separate word.

- The relationship between the verb and the object in a separable verb pair is very close; adding the object to the verb is sort of the "default form" of the verb, even if the verb part can be used without the object.
- Separable verbs are a source of frequent errors from learners of Chinese because you can't add an object after a separable verb. Many learners don't know if a verb is a regular two-character verb like 工作 or a verb-object construct like 开会. *If you don't know, you're sure to use it wrong.*

The key to using separable verbs correctly is to remember that they are "Verb + Object" constructs. The verb alone must be treated as a verb, and the object cannot be treated as part of the verb.

How to Use Separable Verbs

The first step in mastering separable verbs is knowing which verbs are actually separable verbs.

Some of the more common separable verbs you should already know include: 吃饭 (chīfàn), 出差 (chūchāi), 读书 (dúshū), 过年 (guònián), 见面 (jiànmiàn), 讲话 (jiǎnghuà), 开车 (kāichē), 开会 (kāihuì), 看病 (kànbìng), 聊天 (liáotiān), 生气 (shēngqì), 谈话 (tánhuà), 洗澡 (xǐzǎo), 游泳 (yóuyǒng).

Slightly less common (but still useful for intermediate learners) separable verbs include: 帮忙 (bāngmáng), 分手 (fēnshǒu), 结婚 (jiéhūn), 请假 (qǐngjià), 离婚 (líhūn), 跑步 (pǎobù), 报名 (bàomíng), 道歉 (dàoqiàn), 散步 (sànbù), 排队 (páiduì).

Perhaps the most common examples of separable verbs that beginners first struggle with are 见面 and 睡觉. What makes them especially hard is that the "object" part of each word seem to have no counterpart in English. "Meet face?" "Sleep a sleep?" It all feels very odd.

Below we will introduce separable verbs in more detail, provide more examples, and also offer more specific cases which can trip up learners.

Using 跟 with Separable Verbs

A few verbs allow you to effectively add an additional object by using a 跟 (or 和) phrase before the verb.

Structure

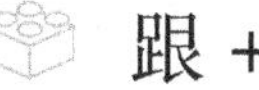

跟 + Person + Verb + Object

In this pattern, the verb-object construct remains unseparated.

Examples

- 我明天跟他见面。
  Wǒ míngtiān gēn tā jiànmiàn.
  I'll meet him tomorrow.
- 我不要跟她结婚。
  Wǒ bùyào gēn tā jiéhūn.
  I don't want to marry her.
- 你还没有跟我道歉。
  Nǐ hái méiyǒu 跟 wǒ dàoqiàn.
  You still haven't apologized to me.

You'll have to learn which separable verbs allow this pattern on a case-by-case basis.

Where to put 了, 过, 着 with Separable Verbs

Hint: they go after the verb, *not* the object.

Structure

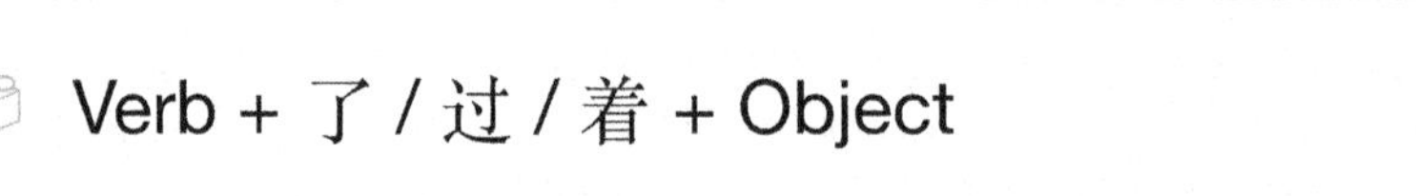

Verb + 了 / 过 / 着 + Object

Examples

见面 (jiànmiàn)

- 我们昨天见了面。 *separated, 了 inserted*
  Wǒmen zuótiān jiàn le miàn.
  We met yesterday.
- 我们见过面。 *separated, 过 inserted*
  Wǒmen jiàn guo miàn.
  We've met.

开会 (kāihuì)

- 我们早上开了会。
  Wǒmen zǎoshang kāi le huì.
  We had a meeting in the morning.
- 你们开过会了吗?
  Nǐmen kāi guo huì le ma?
  Have you had the meeting yet?

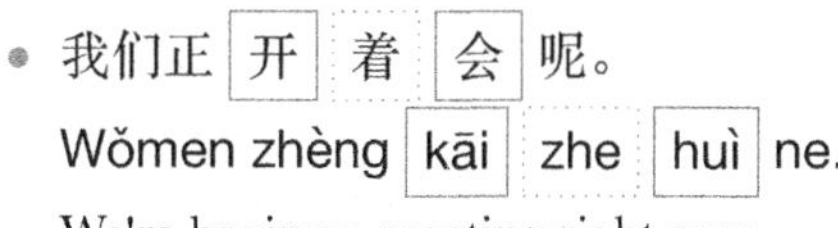

- 我们正 开 着 会 呢。
  Wǒmen zhèng kāi zhe huì ne.
  We're having a meeting right now.

吃饭 (chīfàn)

- 他昨天来我家了，还 吃 了 饭 。
  Tā zuótiān lái wǒ jiā le, hái chī le fàn.
  He came to my house yesterday and he ate a meal with us.
- 他 吃 过 饭 了吗?
  Tā chī guo fàn le ma?
  Has he eaten yet?
- 他正 吃 着 饭 呢。
  Tā zhèng chī zhe fàn ne.
  He's eating a meal right now.

Note: unlike the particles 过 and 着, the particle 了 is especially tricky, and it can also appear after the object. So it can be correct in multiple places.

Where to Put Measure Words with Separable Verbs

You guessed it: they go after the verb, *not* the object.

Structure

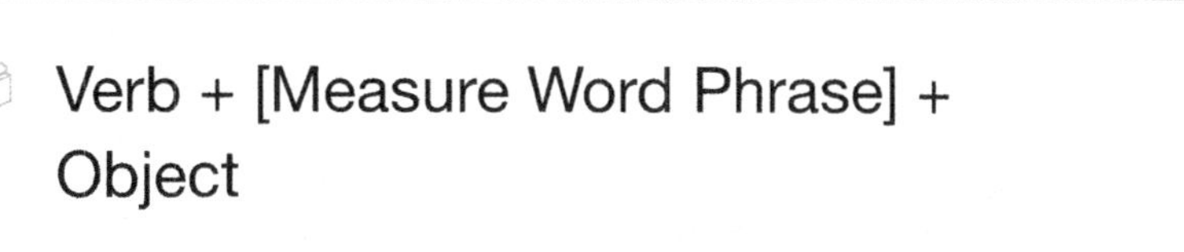
Verb + [Measure Word Phrase] +
Object

Examples

见面 (jiànmiàn)

- 我们 见 个 面 吧。
  Wǒmen jiàn gè miàn ba.
  Let's meet.
- 我们 见 过 几次 面 。
  Wǒmen jiàn guo jǐ cì miàn.
  We've met a few times.

吃饭 (chīfàn)

- 我们一起 吃 过 几次 饭 。
  Wǒmen yīqǐ chī guo jǐ cì fàn.
  We've had several meals together.

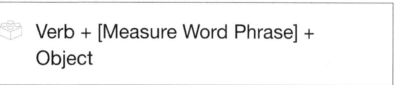

- 老板请大家 吃 了 一顿 饭 。
  Lǎobǎn qǐng dàjiā chī le yī dùn fàn.
  The boss treated everyone to dinner.

睡觉 (shuìjiào)

- 晚安！睡 个 好觉 。
  Wǎn'ān! Shuì gè hǎo jiào.
  Good night! I hope you have a good sleep.
- 昨晚我只 睡 了 两个小时 觉 。
  Zuówǎn wǒ zhǐ shuì le liǎng gè xiǎoshí jiào.
  I only slept two hours last night.

How to Reduplicate Separable Verbs

Reduplication is a way to express the casual nature of a verb or that it happens only briefly. When it comes to separable verbs, *only the verb part reduplicates.*

Structure

Examples

✔ 见 见 面
jiàn jian miàn

✔ 吃 吃 饭
chī chi fàn

✔ 聊 聊 天
liáo liao tiān

✖ 吃 饭 吃饭
chī fàn chīfàn

饭 is the object; it should not be repeated.

✖ 聊 天 聊天
liáo tiān liáotiān

天 is the object; it should not be repeated.

Note that you can't put 一下 after separable verbs to express that it happened briefly.

✖ 见面 一下
jiànmiàn yīxià

Common Examples and Common Mistakes with Separable Verbs

帮忙 (bāngmáng) to help; to do a favor. 帮 is the verb; 忙 is the object, meaning "a favor."

✘ 我们可以 帮忙 你。
Wǒmen kěyǐ bāngmáng nǐ.

✔ 我们可以 帮你 。
Wǒmen kěyǐ bāng nǐ.
We can help you.

✔ 我们可以 帮忙 。
Wǒmen kěyǐ bāngmáng.
We can do (you) this favor.

If you want to ask someone to do you a favor, check this out:

✔ 你可以 帮 我 一个忙 吗?
Nǐ kěyǐ bāng wǒ yī gè máng ma?
Can you do me a favor?

结婚 (jiéhūn) to get married. 结 is the verb; 婚 acts as the object, meaning "marriage." However, 婚 cannot typically be used as a noun by itself.

✘ 我想 结婚 她。
Wǒ xiǎng jiéhūn tā.

✔ 我想 跟 她 结婚 。
Wǒ xiǎng gēn tā jiéhūn.
I want to get married to her.

the prepositional phrase, literally "with her," comes before the verb

聊天 (liáotiān) to chat; to talk (about things in general). 聊 is the verb; 天 acts as the object.

✘ 他很喜欢 聊天 女生。
Tā hěn xǐhuan liáotiān nǚshēng.

✔ 他很喜欢 聊 女生。
Tā hěn xǐhuan liáotiān nǚshēng.
He loves talking about girls.

✔ 他很喜欢 跟 女生 聊天 。
Tā hěn xǐhuan gēn nǚshēng liáotiān.
He loves talking with girls.

the prepositional phrase, literally "with you," comes before the verb

Literally, 天 doesn't mean anything. The object needs to be something specific if you mean to be clear.

- ✘ 爸爸不喜欢 聊天 他的工作。
  Bàba bù xǐhuan liáotiān tā de gōngzuò.
- ✔ 爸爸不喜欢 聊 他的工作。
  Bàba bù xǐhuan liáo tā de gōngzuò.
  My father doesn't like to talk about his work.

Why Use Them

If separable verbs are simply verb-object phrases, then why the special name? It's because there are some special features of Chinese verb-object phrases worth special attention, and the name "separable verbs" helps call attention to this. Mastering separable verbs can be a little tricky and is an essential objective of the intermediate (B1) level learner of Chinese.

Separable verbs are just one of those things you can't avoid. Many extremely common verbs, such as "to sleep" (睡觉) or "to meet" (见面) are separable verbs, and until you understand which verbs are separable verbs and how they work, you'll forever be making mistakes with these words, even in very basic sentences. In addition, you will continue to encounter new separable verbs, and being already familiar with the concept makes mastering new words much easier.

Academic debate

There is some debate as to how useful the concept of separable verbs really is. For our purposes, we're only concerned with whether or not separable verbs are a useful concept *for the student of Mandarin Chinese*. Many learners do, in fact, find the concept to be quite useful in helping them speak more natural Chinese.

Verbs followed by “gei” (B1)

Although it’s standard practice to put a word or phrase that modifies a verb *before* the verb, there are, of course, exceptions. 给 (gěi) is one of those exceptions; it sometimes comes before the verb[1] and sometimes after. This article is about when it comes after.

Basic Pattern

Structure

Note that the verbs that fit into this pattern are normally single-syllable verbs.

Subj. + Verb + 给 + Recipient + Obj.

or

Obj. + Subj. + Verb + 给 + Recipient

Examples

- 昨天有人 送给 我一束花。
  Zuótiān yǒu rén sòng gěi wǒ yī shù huā.
  Yesterday someone gave me a bouquet of flowers.
- 请 递给 我一盒纸巾。
  Qǐng dì gěi wǒ yī hé zhǐjīn.
  Please pass me a box of tissues.
- 这是我们 送给 你的生日礼物。
  Zhè shì wǒmen sòng gěi nǐ de shēngrì lǐwù.
  This is your birthday present from us.
- 这本书是谁 借给 你的？
  Zhè běn shū shì shéi jiè gěi nǐ de?
  Who lent you this book?
- 邮件我已经 发给 你了。
  Yóujiàn wǒ yǐjīng fā gěi nǐ le.
  I sent you that email already.

---

1. Verbs preceded by “gei” (B1), page 204

Advanced Pattern

Structure

Additionally, you can add 把[1] into this structure. This does not change the meaning of the sentence and when used in context can even add emphasis to what's being done and given.

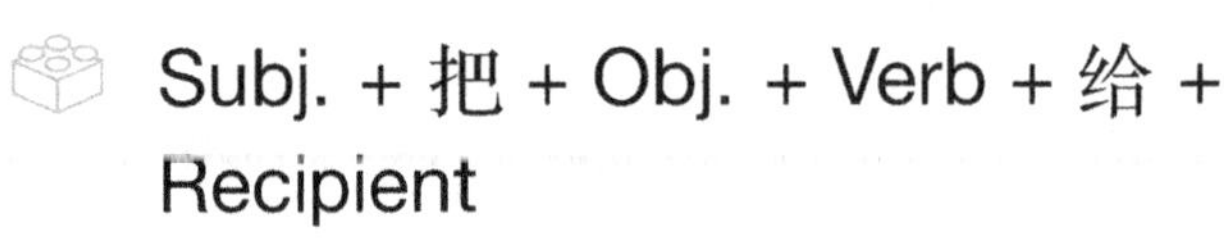
Subj. + 把 + Obj. + Verb + 给 + Recipient

Examples

- 你想 把 这个礼物 送给 谁?
  Nǐ xiǎng bǎ zhège lǐwù sòng gěi shéi?
  Who are you going to give this present to?
- 请 把 那些照片都 发给 我。
  Qǐng bǎ nàxiē zhàopiàn dōu fā gěi wǒ.
  Please send all of those pictures to me.
- 我已经 把 车 卖给 了一个朋友。
  Wǒ yǐjīng bǎ chē mài gěi le yī gè péngyou.
  I've already sold my car to a friend of mine.
- 请 把 盐 递给 我，谢谢。
  Qǐng bǎ yán dì gěi wǒ, xièxie.
  Please pass me the salt. Thanks.
- 可以 把 这本书 借给 我吗?
  Kěyǐ bǎ zhè běn shū jiè gěi wǒ ma?
  Could you please lend me this book?

Note that the verb 嫁 (jià) cannot fit into the 把 pattern above; it's an exception.

- 她 嫁给 了一个有钱的老头。
  Tā jià gěi le yī gè yǒuqián de lǎotóu.
  She married a rich old man.

1. Using "ba" sentences (B1), page 253

If you really want to make a 把 sentence, though, you can do it in this sexist way:

- 她爸爸 把 她 嫁给 了一个有钱的老头。
  Tā bàba bǎ tā jià gěi le yī gè yǒuqián de lǎotóu.
  Her father married her off to a rich old man.

Academic Debate

Although 给 phrases should normally precede a verb like any other prepositional phrase, they sometimes come after. Why have it both ways? There is some academic debate over whether this 给 is actually a preposition, a type of verb (often called a "co-verb"), or even a type of complement. This type of discussion is outside the scope of this article, however.

Similar to

- Expressing "for" with "gei" (B1), page 139
- Using "dui" with verbs (B1), page 153
- Verbs preceded by "gei" (B1), page 204

Verbs preceded by "gei" (B1)

The word 给 (gěi) literally means "to give" but is frequently used in Chinese to indicate the *target* of a verb. The target is who or what the verb is aimed or directed at.

Structure

 Subj. + 给 + Target + [Verb Phrase]

Examples

- 现在不要给他打电话。
  Xiànzài bùyào gěi tā dǎ diànhuà.
  Don't give him a phone call now.
- 请快点给我回邮件。
  Qǐng kuàidiǎn gěi wǒ huí yóujiàn.
  Please hurry up and reply to my email.
- 他说他会给我写信的。
  Tā shuō tā huì gěi wǒ xiě xìn de.
  He said he would write letters to me.
- 你可以给大家读一下吗?
  Nǐ kěyǐ gěi dàjiā dú yīxià ma?
  Could you please read it for everybody?
- 我给你发短信了，你怎么不回?
  Wǒ gěi nǐ fā duǎnxìn le. Nǐ zěnme bù huí?
  I sent you a text. Why didn't you reply?
- 她的粉丝常常给她寄礼物。
  Tā de fěnsī chángcháng gěi tā jì lǐwù.
  Her fans often send her gifts.
- 小时候，妈妈每天都给我讲故事。
  Xiǎo shíhou, māma měi tiān dōu gěi wǒ jiǎng gùshi.
  When I was young, my mother would tell me stories every day.
- 爸爸应该给儿子道歉。
  Bàba yīnggāi gěi érzi dàoqiàn.
  The father should apologize to his son.

- 谁能 给 我 解释一下 ？

  Shéi néng gěi wǒ jiěshì yīxià ?

  Who can explain this to me?

- 老板让我明天 给 客户 介绍我们的新产品 。

  Lǎobǎn ràng wǒ míngtiān gěi kèhù jièshào wǒmen de xīn chǎnpǐn .

  My boss asked to present our new product to the client tomorrow.

Chinese speakers use 给 in some interesting ways, similar to how English speakers use "to give," as in "to give someone a phone call" or "to give someone a reply."

Alternative Structure

Although the structure above is the best one to learn first, some verbs frequently use 给 but have the 给 coming after the verb, rather than before. It's best to think of these as exceptions to the rule above, and you can learn more about these exceptions by reading about verbs followed by "gei"[1].

Similar to

- Expressing "for" with "gei" (B1), page 139
- Using "dui" with verbs (B1), page 153
- Verbs followed by "gei" (B1), page 201

1. Verbs followed by "gei" (B1), page 201

Degree complement (B1)

Also known as: 程度补语 (chéngdù bǔyǔ) and complement of degree.

While most complements follow verbs, degree complements can follow both verbs and adjectives. These complements intensify or modify the degree of expression of the verb or adjective.

When to use it

Until now, you may have been getting by just fine modifying your verbs with adverbs. You can use 非常 to say "very" and all that. Great. But once you learn to use degree complements, a whole new layer of expressiveness is infused into your language. You will be able to express **degree** of verbs and adjectives with much more precision and color. But how do you know *when to use* the degree complement? Here are the main reasons to use it:

1. To express **how** a verb happened or assess its quality
2. To express **to what extent** (or degree) an adjective is true

For the first case, the most typical examples would be describing *how well* an action is done, or in *asking* how well an action is done, which are sometimes also classified as descriptive complements and state complements.

- 你们觉得我画 [得怎么样] ？
  Nǐmen juéde wǒ huà [de zěnmeyàng]?
  The complement is used to ask "how well I draw."
- 我们觉得你画 [得很好] 。
  Wǒmen juéde nǐ huà [de hěn hǎo].
  The complement tells us that "you draw very well."
- 他英语说 [得怎么样] ？
  Tā Yīngyǔ shuō [de zěnmeyàng]?
  The complement is used to ask "how well he speaks English."
- 他英语说 [得一般] 。
  Tā Yīngyǔ shuō [de yībān].
  The complement tells us that "His English is average."

Basic Pattern Following Verbs

We can use all kinds of degree complements to add some color to our verbs.

Structure

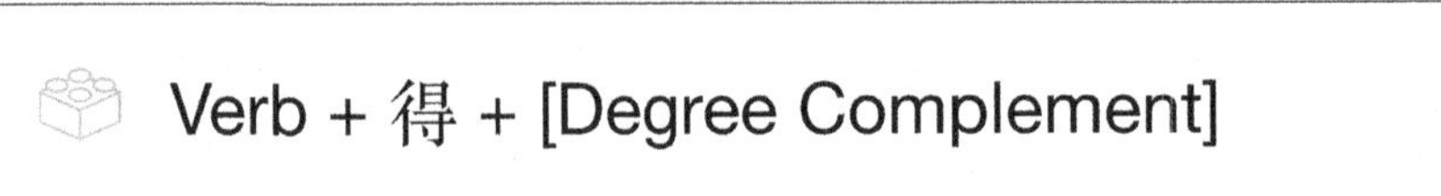

Verb + 得 + [Degree Complement]

Examples

- 你做 得不错 。
  Nǐ zuò de bùcuò.
  You're doing a great job.
- 孩子们学 得挺快的 。
  Háizi men xué de tǐng kuài de.
  The kids are learning fast.
- 我吃 得太饱了 。
  Wǒ chī de tài bǎo le.
  I'm stuffed.
- 你们谈 得顺利 吗?
  Nǐmen tán de shùnlì ma?
  Did your conversation go well?
- 她长 得还可以 。
  Tā zhǎng de hái kěyǐ.
  She is all right-looking.

Degree Complements with Objects

Both adding a complement to a verb with an object and adding an objective to a verb with a complement complicate a sentence in Mandarin, because *a single verb cannot be followed by both an object and a complement*. In order to get all three pieces of information into a grammatically correct Chinese sentence, there are two approaches to take:

Approach #1: Repeat the Verb

✔ 你 说 中文 说 得很好 。
Nǐ shuō Zhōngwén shuō de hěn hǎo.
You speak Chinese well. (lit. You speak Chinese speak it well.)

Just like little kids, objects and complements don't know how to share. Make sure each gets its own (identical) verb. Also make sure that the object comes after the first instance of the verb, and the complement after the second.

Approach #2: Move the Object to the Front

✔ 你的 中文 说 得很好 。
Nǐ de Zhōngwén shuō de hěn hǎo.
You speak Chinese well. (lit. You Chinese speak well.)

Note: the 你的中文 in the sentence above can also be 你中文 (without the 的). When it makes sense to include the 的, it often sounds better.

Just to be completely clear, the following sentences are both *incorrect*:

✕ 你说中文**很好**。

Nǐ shuō Zhōngwén **hěn hǎo**.

✕ 你说中文**得很好**。

Nǐ shuō Zhōngwén **de hěn hǎo**.

A few more examples:

- 你做菜做得很好。

  Nǐ zuò cài zuò de hěn hǎo.

  You cook very well.

- 你的菜做得很好。

  Nǐ de cài zuò de hěn hǎo.

  You cook very well.

- 你写字写得很漂亮。

  Nǐ xiě zì xiě de hěn piàoliang.

  Your handwriting is beautiful.

- 你的字写得很漂亮。

  Nǐ de zì xiě de hěn piàoliang.

  Your handwriting is beautiful.

Degree Complements Following Adjectives

Common Patterns

There are three especially common degree complements which can follow adjectives immediately and are *not* preceded by a 得:

- 极了[1] often comes after adjectives with positive connotations (often 好), indicating an extremely high degree.
- 死了 usually comes after adjectives with negative connotations (like 忙, 累, 臭, 难看) and are commonly used to exaggerate the degree of how bad something is. In recent years, however, 死了 also comes after adjectives with positive connotations.
- 坏了 is a bit like the complement 死了 and can be used to mean "extremely" in either a positive or a negative sense.

Examples

- 味道好极了。

  Wèidào hǎo jíle.

  The taste is amazing.

---

1. Adjectives with "-ji le" (B1), page 4

- 这里的天气 舒服 极了 。

  Zhèlǐ de tiānqì shūfu jíle.

  The weather here is so comfortable.

- 他的袜子 臭 死了 。

  Tā de wàzi chòu sǐle.

  His socks totally reek.

- 小狗 可爱 死了 。

  Xiǎogǒu kě'ài sǐle.

  The puppy is so adorable!

- 老师说今天没有作业，我们都 高兴 坏了 。

  Lǎoshī shuō jīntiān méiyǒu zuòyè, wǒmen dōu gāoxìng huàile.

  The teacher said there's no homework for today, which thrilled us all.

- 找不到孩子，妈妈 急 坏了 。

  Zhǎo bu dào háizi, māma jí huàile.

  Having not found the child, the mother was an anxious wreck.

Note that 死 can also act as a result complement in verb phrases such as 打死 (literally, "beat to death"). In the examples above, however, it merely indicates an extreme degree (no actual deaths involved!).

Compared with Potential Complements

Some sentences that contain adjective complements may be indistinguishable as degree or potential complements when they are taken out of context. The following table explains different meanings that one complement phrase could have as either a degree complement or potential complement.

- 她说得清楚

  tā shuō de qīngchu

  she speaks clearly (Degree Complement Translation)

  she is able to speak clearly (Potential Complement Translation)

- 他们做得好

  tāmen zuò de hǎo

  they do it well (Degree Complement Translation)

  they are able to do it well (Potential Complement Translation)

- 他跑得快

  tā pǎo de kuài

  he runs fast (Degree Complement Translation)

  he is able to run fast (Potential Complement Translation)

Degree complements are commonly directly preceded by an adverb like 很. For example: 她说得很清楚. This serves to distinguish them from potential complements, which are never directly preceded by an adverb.

Descriptive and State Complements

Not every aspect of Chinese grammar is agreed upon in the world of academia, and this is the case with degree complements, descriptive complements, and state complements. Some scholars hold that the three are distinct, while others posit they're all just types of degree complements. Still, others maintain that degree complements are one, and descriptive complements and state complements are also one.

Here's how a professor of Chinese at Yale puts it:

> *Generally speaking, the complement of degree is a grammatical unit that describes the main verb of the sentence. Specifically, the complement of degree is an assessment of an action or a description of the consequential state of an action. It may also be a description of the degree of a state.*

Okayyy, so it sounds like descriptions and states are all degree complements? That's one of the views on the issue.

None of these classifications truly matters though: the key is *understanding* them and *using* complements correctly to express yourself in Chinese. (This is already difficult without adding in unnecessary academic distinctions!)

Similar to

- Direction complement (B1), page 211
- Advanced degree complements (B2)

Direction complement (B1)

Also known as: 趋向补语 (qūxiàng bǔyǔ), directional complement and complement of direction.

A direction complement is a complement used to describe the direction of a verb. Verbs often already have some inherent movement implied, but by adding a direction complement, it becomes clearer where, exactly, that action is going.

Simple Direction Complement

The most basic (and common) form of direction complement is formed by a verb and 来 or 去.

Structure

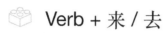

The most important thing to consider with direction complements is **the position of the speaker**. If the action moves towards the speaker or comes closer in any way, use 来. If the action moves away from the speaker or becomes more distant in any way, use 去.

Verb	+ Complement	Explanation
下	下来 xiàlái	The movement is down towards the speaker: "come down"
下	下去 xiàqù	The movement is down away from the speaker: "go down"
上	上来 shànglái	The movement is up towards the speaker: "come up"
上	上去 shàngqù	The movement is up and away from the speaker: "go up"
出	出来 chūlái	The movement is out and towards the speaker: "come out"
出	出去 chūqù	The movement is out and away from the speaker: "go out"
进	进来 jìnlái	The movement is in and towards the speaker: "come in"
进	进去 jìnqù	The movement is in and away from the speaker: "go in"

回	回来 huílái	The movement is towards the speaker: “come back”
回	回去 huíqù	The movement is away from the speaker: “go back”

You might be wondering how the directional distinction between 来 and 去 works when you're talking about yourself moving. You can't move away from or towards yourself, so should it be 来 or 去? The answer is to look at the context of the movement you're talking about. Are you telling someone you'll see them tomorrow? Similar to English, in Chinese you'd say something like “I'll come and see you tomorrow.”

Examples

You can use these simple compounds in a huge variety of situations. Here are some example dialogs to provide a little more context:

A: 我在楼上，你 上来 。

Wǒ zài lóushàng, nǐ shànglái.

I'm on the upper floor. Come up to me.

B: 你在楼上等我一下。我一会儿就 上去 。

Nǐ zài lóushàng děng wǒ yīxià. Wǒ yīhuìr jiù shàngqù.

Please wait a moment on the upper floor. I'll come up in a few minutes.

A: 出来 玩吧，我们在酒吧等你。

Chūlái wán ba, wǒmen zài jiǔbā děng nǐ.

Come and hang out with us. We'll be waiting in the bar.

B: 我妈不让我 出去 。

Wǒ mā bù ràng wǒ chūqù.

My mother won't let me go out.

A: 这是我家， 进来 吧，随便坐。

Zhè shì wǒ jiā, jìnlái ba, suíbiàn zuò.

This is my house. Please come inside. Feel free to take a seat.

B: 那是你的卧室吗？我能 进去 吗？

Nà shì nǐ de wòshì ma? Wǒ néng jìnqù ma?

Is that your bedroom? Can I go in?

A: 你下班了吗？几点 回来 吃饭？

Nǐ xiàbān le ma? Jǐ diǎn huílái chīfàn?

Are you off work now? When are you coming back for dinner?

B: 我今天不 回去 吃饭。

Wǒ jīntiān bù huíqù chīfàn.

I'm not going back home for dinner today.

Compound Direction Complements

Direction complements can be more complex than just 来 or 去.

Forming Compound Direction Complements

You can form compound direction complements in the following way:

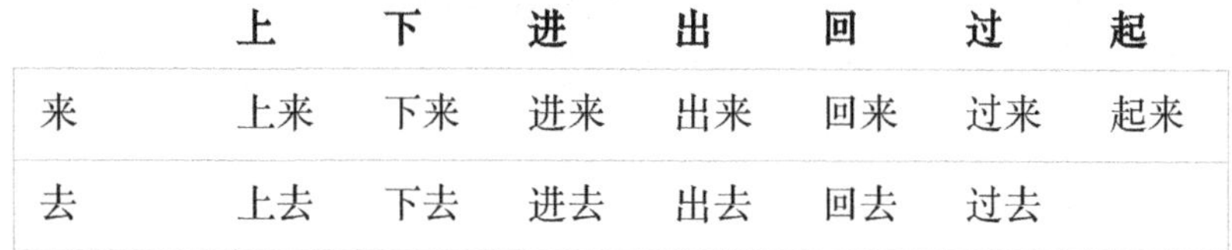

	上	下	进	出	回	过	起
来	上来	下来	进来	出来	回来	过来	起来
去	上去	下去	进去	出去	回去	过去	

These compounds can then be used in much the same way as 来 and 去. Attach them to verbs to give detail about the direction of the action.

Structure

Verb + [Compound Direction Complement]

Examples

- 请站 起来 。

  Qǐng zhàn qǐlái.

  Please stand up.

- 不要让它跑 出去 。

  Bùyào ràng tā pǎo chūqù.

  Don't let it run out.

- 从我家走 过来 要半个小时。

  Cóng wǒ jiā zǒu guòlái yào bàn gè xiǎoshí.

  It took me half an hour to walk here from my place.

- 你包里的东西都拿 出来 了吗?

  Nǐ bāo lǐ de dōngxi dōu ná chūlái le ma?

  Did you take all your stuff out of your bag?

Direction Complements with Objects

Direction complements are not only used to describe the movement of people. Moving objects can also be described with direction complements. Again, the direction of the movement relative to the speaker (or at least to the context of the conversation) is important when deciding what complement to use.

The verbs that commonly appear in this construction include 拿, 送, and 带.

Structure

Verb + Object + Complement

Examples

Some examples:

- 服务员，请再拿 几个碗 来 。
  Fúwùyuán, qǐng zài ná jǐ gè wǎn lái.
  Waiter, please bring a few more bowls.
- 快点送 孩子 去 吧，别迟到了。
  Kuàidiǎn sòng háizi qù ba, bié chídào le.
  Hurry up, send the kids off. Don't be late.
- 师傅，送 两桶水 来 。
  Shīfu, sòng liǎng tǒng shuǐ lái.
  Shifu, please deliver two buckets of water.
- 可以带 朋友 过来 吗?
  Kěyǐ dài péngyou guòlái ma?
  Can I bring some friends over?
- 他们带了 一些礼物 回去 。
  Tāmen dài le yīxiē lǐwù huíqù.
  They took some presents back with them.

Common Mistakes

Although 回来 and 回去 can be compound complements, they can each also just be the verb 回 with a simple direction complement. Many Chinese learners make the following mistakes:

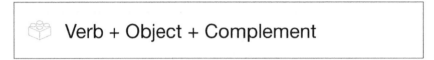

✗ 回来中国

huílai Zhōngguó

✓ 回中国来

huí Zhōngguó lái

come back to China

✗ 回去美国

huíqu Měiguó

✓ 回美国去

huí Měiguó qù

go back to the USA

You can't say 回来中国 because 回 is the verb, 来 is the complement, and 中国 is the object. You can't put both a complement and an object after a single verb, but it's OK to put just a 来 or 去 after the object. In spoken language, if the context is clear, people often omit 来 or 去 and only say 回美国 or 回中国.

Direction Complements with 把

Direction complements work very well in 把 sentences, as they can be used to describe the disposal of an object (what happened to it in the end). Because of this, it's very common to see direction complements and 把 appearing together.

Structure

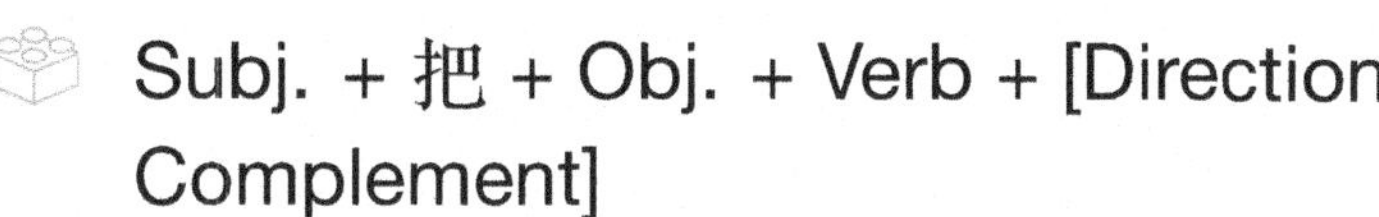

Subj. + 把 + Obj. + Verb + [Direction Complement]

Examples

- 把 书 拿出来 。
  Bǎ shū ná chūlái.
  Take out your book.
- 把 手 举起来 。
  Bǎ shǒu jǔ qǐlái.
  Raise your hands.
- 帮我 把 这个箱子 搬过去 。
  Bāng wǒ bǎ zhège xiāngzi bān guòqù.
  Help me move this suitcase over there.

See also: 把 sentences

Converting to Potential Complement

Adding 得 to directional complements makes the phrase an affirmative potential complement. Adding 不 makes the phrase a negative potential complement.

Direction Complement	Aff. Potential Complement	Neg. Potential Complement
回去	回得去	回不去
过来	过得来	过不来
站起来	站得起来	站不起来
走上去	走得上去	走不上去
开进去	开得进去	开不进去
拿出来	拿得出来	拿不出来

Additional Meanings

A lot of direction complements, particularly compound direction complements, have additional idiomatic meanings beyond literally describing the direction of an action. The most common of these are:

- 起来[1]
- 出来
- 下去[2]

Similar to

- Directional verbs "lai" and "qu" (A2)
- Direction complement "-qilai" (B1), page 217
- Result complement "-xiaqu" (B1), page 224
- Using "bei" sentences (B1), page 259
- Advanced uses of "ba" (B2)
- Advanced uses of direction complement "-qilai" (B2)

1. Direction complement "-qilai" (B1), page 217
2. Result complement "-xiaqu" (B1), page 224

Direction complement "-qilai" (B1)

起来 (qǐlái) comes up very frequently in Chinese and can be used both literally and figuratively. This is a little like the usage of "up" in English, which can be used literally, as in "stand up," or figuratively, as in "add up." When used figuratively, 起来 often serves as a direction complement[1].

Basic Meaning

Structure

起来 can be used to express an upward movement like "up," as in the English examples of "stand up" or "pick up."

Examples

- 请大家站起来。
  Qǐng dàjiā zhàn qǐlái.
  Everyone, please stand up.
- 捡起来。
  Jiǎn qǐlái.
  Pick it up (from the floor).
- 头抬起来。
  Tóu tái qǐlái.
  Raise your head.
- 别动！把手举起来。
  Bié dòng! Bǎ shǒu jǔ qǐlái.
  Don't move! Put your hands up.

Used for Initiation of an Action

Structure

起来 can also be used to show that an action or state has started and is ongoing:

---

1. Direction complement (B1), page 211

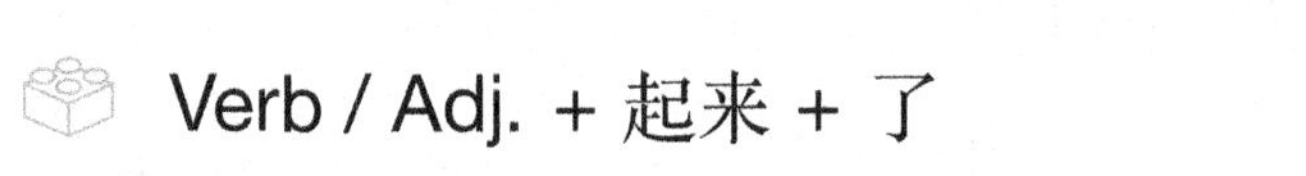

Examples

- 小鸟飞 起来 了 。
  Xiǎoniǎo fēi qǐlái le .
  The birds started flying.
- 宝宝哭 起来 了 。
  Bǎobao kū qǐlái le .
  The baby started crying.
- 两个大妈吵 起来 了 。
  Liǎng gè dàmā chǎo qǐlái le .
  Two middle-aged ladies started arguing.
- 天气热 起来 了 。
  Tiānqì rè qǐlái le .
  It's getting hot.
- 结婚以后，她胖 起来 了 。
  Jiéhūn yǐhòu, tā pàng qǐlái le .
  After she got married, she has started to gain weight.
- 爷爷的身体好 起来 了 。
  Yéye de shēntǐ hǎo qǐlái le .
  Grandpa's health is getting better.

When used like this, 起来 is only used with spontaneous actions, like 唱 (chàng), 跳 (tiào), 聊 (liáo), or with states like 热 (rè), 冷 (lěng), or 好 (hǎo) etc. It cannot be used with planned actions.

✗ 我们 做饭 起来 吧。
Wǒmen zuòfàn qǐlái ba.
✓ 我们 开始 做饭 吧。
Wǒmen kāishǐ zuòfàn ba.

Let's start cooking.

It can also used as a way to encourage people to start doing something immediately:

- 大家 唱 起来 ， 跳 起来 ！
  Dàjiā chàng qǐlái, tiào qǐlái !
  Let's sing and dance!

Used for an Initial Judgement

起来 is used here to express that the speaker has only just initiated an action, and based on that, has made a preliminary judgment. It is used in the following structure:

Structure

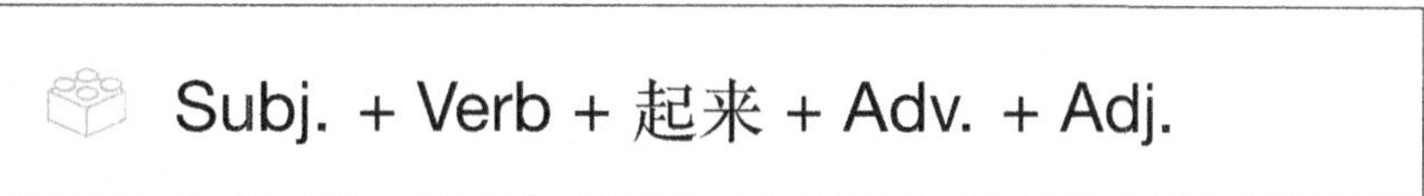

Subj. + Verb + 起来 + Adv. + Adj.

This expresses that the subject seems *adjective* when the action of the verb is performed. This structure is frequently used with perception verbs such as 看, 听, 闻, 摸, etc.

Examples

- 他 看起来 很友好 。
  Tā kàn qǐlái hěn yǒuhǎo .
  He looks very friendly.
- 你的头发 闻起来 很香 。
  Nǐ de tóufa wén qǐlái hěn xiāng .
  Your hair smells good.
- 这件事情 听起来 有点复杂 。
  Zhè jiàn shìqing tīng qǐlái yǒudiǎn fùzá .
  This matter sounds a little bit complex.
- 这些菜 尝起来 都 不错 。
  Zhèxiē cài cháng qǐlái dōu bùcuò .
  These foods all taste good.
- 你的床 摸起来 很舒服 。
  Nǐ de chuáng mō qǐlái hěn shūfu .
  Your bed feels very comfortable.

Similar to

- Result complements "-dao" and "-jian" (A2)
- Appearance with "kanqilai" (B1), page 156

- Direction complement (B1), page 211
- Result complement "-xiaqu" (B1), page 224
- Result complements (B1), page 227
- Advanced uses of direction complement "-qilai" (B2)

Potential complement (B1)

Verbs can take potential complements to indicate whether or not an action is possible. Potential complements contain a 的 (de) or a 不 (bu) immediate after the verb being modified, and are quite common in everyday spoken Mandarin.

Affirmative Form

Structurally, potential complements are closely related to both result complements and direction complements[1], so it helps to be familiar with those first. The most important and commonly used potential complements are derived from other complements such as the following:

- Verb + 见 e.g. 看见, 听见 (result complements)
- Verb + 懂 e.g. 看懂, 听懂 (result complements)
- Verb + 完 e.g. 吃完, 做完, 用完, 花完 (result complements)
- Verb + Adj. e.g. 看清楚, 听明白, 洗干净 (result complements)
- Verb + 到 e.g. 找到, 买到, 收到 (result complements)
- Verb + Direction e.g. 上来, 下去, 进去, 起来, 走过去, 爬上去 (direction complements[1])

These forms will be our starting point for forming potential complements.

Structure

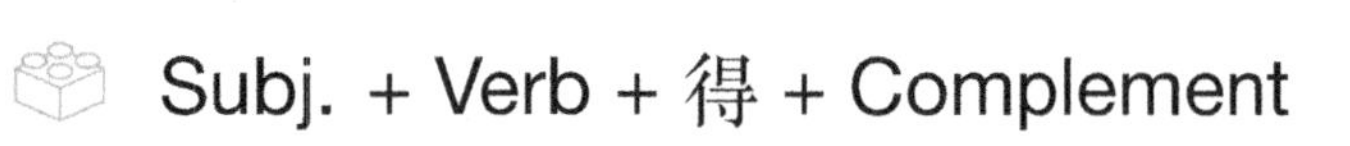
Subj. + Verb + 得 + Complement

Examples

- 你没戴眼镜，看 得 清楚 吗?
  Nǐ méi dài yǎnjìng, kàn de qīngchu ma?
  You didn't wear glasses. Can you see clearly?
- 他这么粗心，做 得 好 吗?
  Tā zhème cūxīn, zuò de hǎo ma?
  He'a so careless. Can he do it well?
- 你这么聪明，肯定学 得 会 。
  Nǐ zhème cōngming, kěndìng xué de huì .
  You're so smart. You can definitely learn this.

1. Direction complement (B1), page 211

- 早上五点出发，孩子们起 得 来 吗?
  Zǎoshang wǔdiǎn chūfā, háizi men qǐ de lái ma?
  We're leaving at five a.m.. Will the kids be able to get up?
- 这么高的山，你爬 得 上去 吗?
  Zhème gāo de shān, nǐ pá de shàngqù ma?
  The mountain is so high. Can you climb to the top?

Negative Form

The only difference between the affirmative and negative forms is swapping a 得 for a 不.

Structure

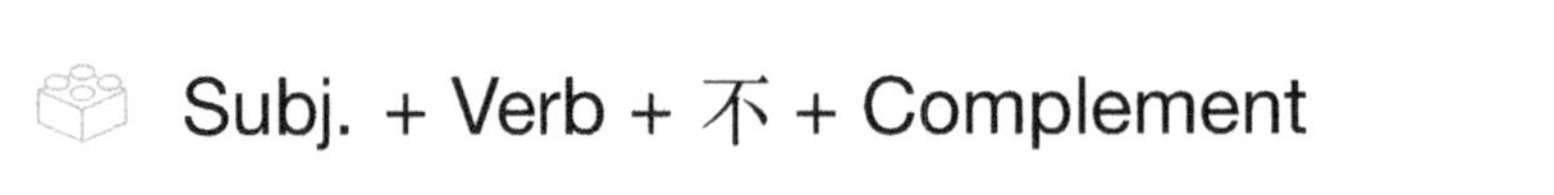

Examples

- 你的声音太小了，我们听 不 见 。
  Nǐ de shēngyīn tài xiǎo le, wǒmen tīng bu jiàn .
  Your voice is too soft. We can't hear you.
- 这里太暗了，我看 不 清楚 。
  Zhèlǐ tài àn le, wǒ kàn bu qīngchu .
  It's too dim here. I can't see clearly.
- 这个自行车太破了，谁都修 不 好 。
  Zhège zìxíngchē tài pò le, shéi dōu xiū bu hǎo .
  This bike is so beaten up. Nobody can fix it.
- 她的腿受伤了，站 不 起来 了。
  Tā de tuǐ shòushāng le, zhàn bu qǐlái le.
  Her leg is injured. She can't stand.
- 包太小了，手机放 不 进去 。
  Bāo tài xiǎo le, shǒujī fàng bu jìnqù .
  The bag is too small. I can't fit the cell phone in it.

Potential Complement with Objects

Objects in sentences with potential complements can occur either after the complement or at the beginning of a sentence.

A few examples:

- 你听 得 懂 上海话吗?
  Nǐ tīng de dǒng Shànghǎi-huà ma?
  Can you understand Shanghai dialect?
- 她这么小，看 得 懂 这本书吗?
  Tā zhème xiǎo, kàn de dǒng zhè běn shū ma?
  She's so young. Can she really understand this book?
- 我怕我做 不 好 这份工作。
  Wǒ pà wǒ zuò bu hǎo zhè fèn gōngzuò.
  I'm afraid that I can't do this job well.
- 这种手机现在买 不 到 了。
  Zhè zhǒng shǒujī xiànzài mǎi bu dào le.
  You can't buy this type of cell phone now.
- 这本书我一个星期肯定看 得 完 。
  Zhè běn shū wǒ yī gè xīngiqī kěndìng kàn de wán .
  I can definitely finish reading this book within one week.

Advanced Potential Complements

There are actually quite a few potential complements out there, and this article touches on some of the simplest and most common ones. Be aware that there are many more, but they all follow the same basic pattern outlined here. You can also refer to our article on advanced potential complements.

Similar to

- Potential complement "-bu dong" for not understanding (A2)
- Direction complement (B1), page 211
- Advanced potential complements (B2)
- Advanced result complements (B2)
- Using "zhao" as complement (B2)

Result complement "-xiaqu" (B1)

下去 (xiàqù) can be used as a result complement to talk about things *continuing* or *carrying on*. Think of it as a figurative way of "keeping the ball rolling" (downhill).

Affirmative Form

Structure-wise, this pattern is the same as other result complements.

Structure

Examples

- 说 下去 。
  Shuō xiàqù.
  Keep talking.
- 这本书你一定要认真地 看 下去 。
  Zhè běn shū nǐ yīdìng yào rènzhēn de kàn xiàqù.
  You must keep reading this book carefully.
- 这样做很有意义，你应该 做 下去 。
  Zhèyàng zuò hěn yǒu yìyì, nǐ yīnggāi zuò xiàqù.
  It's very meaningful to do this. You should keep doing it.
- 他走了，因为他没脸 待 下去 了。
  Tā zǒu le, yīnwèi tā méiliǎn dāi xiàqù le.
  He left because he felt shame if he stayed.
- 你不能这样 生活 下去 了。
  Nǐ bù néng zhèyàng shēnghuó xiàqù le.
  You can't keep living like this.

Negative Form

Strictly speaking, simply adding 不 in front of the main verb is all it takes to create the negative form. But it's actually more common to use this negative potential complement[1] form. So it's not just "not go on" (doing something), but actually *"can't* go on" (doing something).

1. Potential complement (B1), page 221

Structure

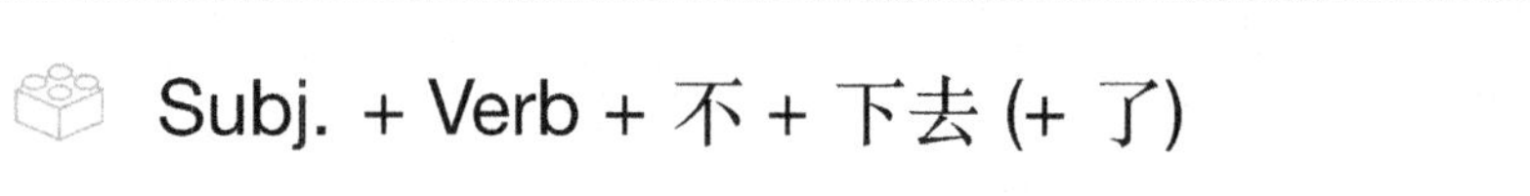

Subj. + Verb + 不 + 下去 (+ 了)

Note that 了 is often used when it's negated.

Examples

- 这个故事太无聊了，我听 不下去 了 。
  Zhège gùshi tài wúliáo le, wǒ tīng bu xiàqù le .
  This story is too boring, I can't keep listening.
- 这个电影太暴力了，我看 不下去 了 。
  Zhège diànyǐng tài bàolì le, wǒ kàn bu xiàqù le .
  This movie is too violent. I can't keep watching it.
- 你说话太恶心了，我吃 不下去 了 。
  Nǐ shuōhuà tài ěxīn le, wǒ chī bu xiàqù le .
  The way you talk is so disgusting. I can't continue eating my food.
- 这个宾馆太脏了，我待 不下去 了 。
  Zhège bīnguǎn tài zāng le, wǒ dāi bu xiàqù le .
  This hotel is too dirty. I can't stay here any longer.
- 我跟他过 不下去 了 ，我要离婚。
  Wǒ gēn tā guò bu xiàqù le , wǒ yào líhūn.
  I can't go on like this with him. I want a divorce.

Used with 再

When the adverb 再 comes before the verb, there's an implication that if "things keep going on this way," then something bad is going to happen.

A few examples:

- 你 再 赌 下去 会 输光的。
  Nǐ zài dǔ xiàqù huì shūguāng de.
  If you keep gambling, you're going to lose all your money.
- 你 再 喝 下去 就 醉了。
  Nǐ zài hē xiàqù jiù zuì le.
  If you keep drinking you're going to get drunk.

Similar to

- Direction complement "-qilai" (B1), page 217
- Advanced result complements (B2)
- Advanced uses of direction complement "-qilai" (B2)

Result complements (B1)

Result complements come immediately after verbs to indicate that an action has led to a certain result and make that result clear to the listener. Often the complement is simply an adjective like 好 (hǎo) or a single syllable like 完 (wán).

Using Adjectives

好 (hǎo) implies that something is done to *completion* or done *well*. Forming a result complement with 好 has a very similar meaning to forming one with 完. It expresses that the action has been completed successfully.

错 (cuò) is used to express that an action has been performed incorrectly in some way, resulting in a mistake (错). This pattern covers what is often expressed with the adverb "incorrectly" in English.

Other adjectives commonly used as result complements include: 晚 (wǎn), 饱 (bǎo), 坏 (huài), 清楚 (qīngchu), 干净 (gānjìng), 破 (pò).

Structure

For the basic structure, you'll almost always see a 了 after the complement:

Subj. + Verb + Adj. + 了 (+ Obj.)

To negate a result complement, use 没 instead of 不:

Subj. + 没 + Verb + Adj. (+ Obj.)

Examples

- 你吃好了吗?
  Nǐ chī hǎo le ma?
  Are you done eating?
- 对不起，我记错了时间。
  Duìbuqǐ, wǒ jì cuò le shíjiān.
  Sorry, I misremembered the time.
- 你来晚了，我们已经关门了。
  Nǐ lái wǎn le, wǒmen yǐjīng guānmén le.
  You came too late. We're already closed.

- 他玩 坏 了 哥哥的玩具。
  Tā wán huài le gēge de wánjù.
  He broke his older brother's toy.
- 我 没 吃 饱 。
  Wǒ méi chī bǎo.
  I didn't get full.
- 他还 没 想 好 。
  Tā hái méi xiǎng hǎo.
  He hasn't thought it through yet.
- 我们 没 听 清楚 ，请再说一遍。
  Wǒmen méi tīng qīngchu, qǐng zài shuō yī biàn.
  We didn't hear it clearly. Please say it again.

When using result complements, it's very common to make the object a topic[1]. This means the object is moved to the beginning of the sentence and the subject is often omitted.

Some examples:

- 这个字 写 错 了。
  Zhège zì xiě cuò le.
  You wrote this character wrong.
- 杯子 摔 坏 了。
  Bēizi shuāi huài le.
  The cup is broken.
- 房间 打扫 干净 了吗?
  Fángjiān dǎsǎo gānjìng le ma?
  Is your room all cleaned up?

Using One-Syllable Verbs

Besides adjectives, there are a few single-syllable verbs which can also be used as result complements. Some examples include 到 (dào), 见 (jiàn), 懂 (dǒng), 会 (huì), 走 (zǒu), 掉 (diào). There really aren't a lot of these, which is part of the reason why these are usually seen as one verb instead of a verb-complement structure.

Structure

For the basic structure, you'll often see a 了 after the complement:

---

1. Topic-comment sentences (B1), page 251

Subj. + Verb + [One-syllable Verb] + 了 (+ Obj.)

Examples

- 你们都 听懂 了吗?
  Nǐmen dōu tīng dǒng le ma?
  Do you all understand?
- 我看了，但是没 看懂 。
  Wǒ kàn le, dànshì méi kàn dǒng.
  I read it, but I didn't really understand it.
- 你 踩到 了我的脚。
  Nǐ cǎi dào le wǒ de jiǎo.
  You're stepping on my foot.
- 我不小心 撞到 了墙。
  Wǒ bù xiǎoxīn zhuàng dào le qiáng.
  I hit the wall by accident.
- 我女儿 学会 了数数。
  Wǒ nǚ'ér xué huì le shǔ shù.
  My daughter has learned how to count.
- 我爸爸还没 学会 用智能手机。
  Wǒ bàba hái méi xué huì yòng zhìnéng shǒujī.
  My father hasn't learned how to use a smartphone yet.
- 老师 拿走 了我的 iPad 。
  Lǎoshī ná zǒu le wǒ de iPad.
  The teacher took away my iPad.
- 小偷 偷走 了我的钱包。
  Xiǎotōu tōu zǒu le wǒ de qiánbāo.
  The thief stole my wallet.
- 他不小心 推倒 了一个老人。
  Tā bù xiǎoxīn tuī dǎo le yī gè lǎorén.
  He pushed over an old person by accident.

- 你 撞倒 了我的自行车。
  Nǐ zhuàng dǎo le wǒ de zìxíngchē.
  You knocked over my bike.
- 谁 扔掉 了我的袜子?
  Shéi rēng diào le wǒ de wàzi?
  Who threw away my socks?
- 我 卖掉 了我的旧手机。
  Wǒ mài diào le wǒ de jiù shǒujī.
  I sold my old cell phone.

Compared with Potential Complements

Result Complement	Aff. Potential Complement	Neg. Potential Complement
做完	做 得 完	做 不 完
听懂	听 得 懂	听 不 懂
看清楚	看 得 清楚	看 不 清楚
洗干净	洗 得 干净	洗 不 干净

Used in 把 Sentences

Although we have avoided 把 sentences in this article for the sake of simplicity, you may have noticed that sentences which feature result complements often also use 把. This is because 把 sentences and result complements work particularly well together, as they both deal with the result of an action or the "disposal" of an object. Apart from result complements involving perception and psychological verbs, most result compounds work nicely in 把 sentences.

- 我 把 杯子 摔坏 了。
  Wǒ bǎ bēizi shuāi huài le .
  I broke the glass.
- 他 把 我的电脑 修好 了。
  Tā bǎ wǒ de diànnǎo xiū hǎo le .
  He fixed my computer.
- 小偷 把 我的钱包 偷走 了。
  Xiǎotōu bǎ wǒ de qiánbāo tōu zǒu le .
  The thief made off with my wallet.

- 我们 把 房间 打扫干净 了。
  Wǒmen bǎ fángjiān dǎsǎo gānjìng le .
  We've cleaned the room.

Similar to

- Result complement "-wan" for finishing (A2)
- Expressing not knowing how to do something using "hao" (B1), page 289
- Using "bei" sentences (B1), page 259

Expressing "all" with "suoyou" (B1)

You can use 所有 (suǒyǒu) to say "all of" something. It's what you use to say phrases like "all the money in the world" or "all of my friends."

Basic Pattern

Structure

This pattern is used to refer to "all" of a noun, with the quantity of said noun usually being fairly large. You may notice that the 的 after 所有 is occasionally omitted.

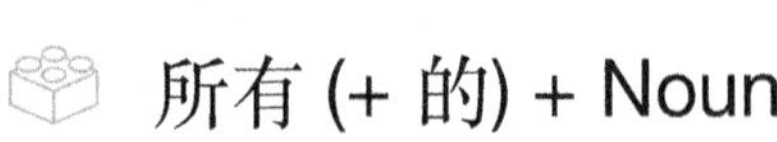

所有 (+ 的) + Noun

Examples

- 你买了她 所有的 书?
  Nǐ mǎi le tā suǒyǒu de shū?
  You've bought all her books?
- 我喜欢 所有 我妈妈做的菜。
  Wǒ xǐhuan suǒyǒu wǒ māma zuò de cài.
  I like all the food my mom cooks.
- 他记得 所有 朋友的生日。
  Tā jìde suǒyǒu péngyou de shēngrì.
  He remembers all of his friends' birthdays.
- 我的孩子看过 所有 的迪斯尼动画片。
  Wǒ de háizi kàn guo suǒyǒu de Dísīní dònghuàpiàn.
  My child has seen all of the Disney animated films.

Full Sentence Pattern

When you make 所有 part of the subject, you're typically going to need 都 before the predicate.

Structure

所有 (+ 的) + Noun + 都 + Predicate

The predicate part of the pattern can be a verb or an adjective.

Examples

- 所有 人 都 走了吗?
  Suǒyǒu rén dōu zǒu le ma?
  Did all the people leave?
- 所有的 学校 都 放假了。
  Suǒyǒu de xuéxiào dōu fàngjià le.
  All the schools are out for the holiday.
- 我们学校 所有的 老师 都 会说英文。
  Wǒmen xuéxiào suǒyǒu de lǎoshī dōu huì shuō Yīngwén.
  All the teachers in our school can speak English.
- 我们公司 所有 人 都 参加了这个会议。
  Wǒmen gōngsī suǒyǒu rén dōu cānjiā le zhège huìyì.
  All people in our company attended this meeting.

"Not All" with 不是所有的

Take note that you use 不是 rather than just 不 to negate 所有.

Structure

不是 + 所有 (+ 的) + Noun + 都 + Predicate

Examples

- 不是 所有的 美国人 都 爱喝咖啡。
  Bù shì suǒyǒu de Měiguó rén dōu ài hē kāfēi.
  Not all Americans like drinking coffee.
- 不是 所有 问题 都 能用钱来解决。
  Bù shì suǒyǒu wèntí dōu néng yòng qián lái jiějué.
  Not all problems can be solved with money.
- 不是 所有 朋友 都 愿意帮他。
  Bù shì suǒyǒu péngyou dōu yuànyì bāng tā.
  Not all of his friends are willing to help him.

- 不是 所有的 公司 都 给员工提供培训。
  Bù shì suǒyǒu de gōngsī dōu gěi yuángōng tígōng péixùn.
  Not all companies provide their employees with training.

Similar to

- Emphasizing quantity with "dou" (A2)
- Expressing "everything" with "shenme dou" (A2)
- Expressing "double negation" (B1), page 268
- Expressing "every time" with "mei" and "dou" (B1), page 273
- Expressing "every" with question words (B1), page 275
- Expressing "less than" with "budao" (B1), page 143
- Indicating the whole with "quan" (B1), page 8
- Expressing "any" with "renhe" (B2)
- Expressing "no exception" with "yilu" (C1)

Expressing "one of" with "zhiyi" (B1)

之一 (zhīyī) is a simple phrase which means "one of." Although it uses the somewhat archaic word 之 (zhī), it's quite common in spoken Chinese, and is even commonly used in jokes.

Structure

In order to express "one of" in Chinese, 之一 (zhī yī) can be used at the end of a noun phrase, which is often modified with 最 (zuì), meaning "the most."

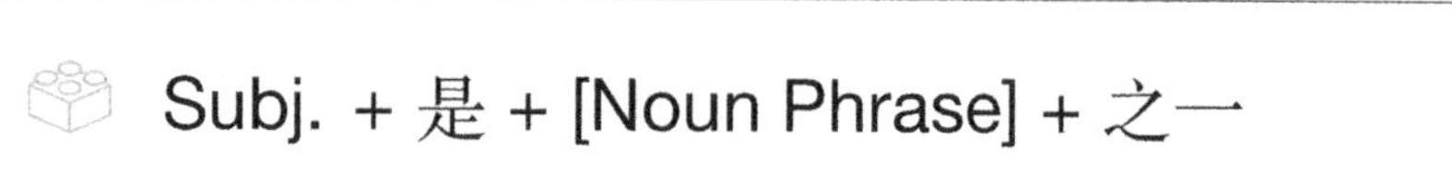
Subj. + 是 + [Noun Phrase] + 之一

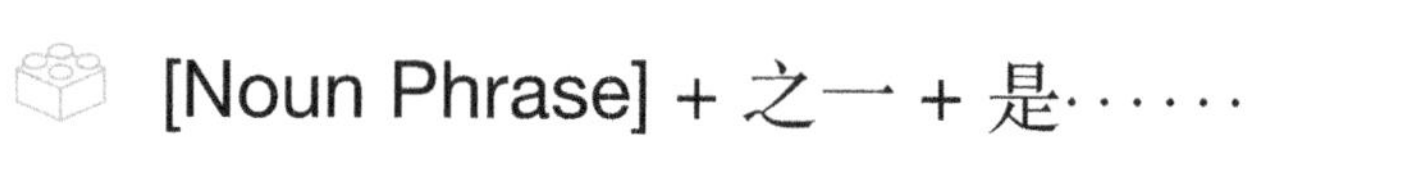
[Noun Phrase] + 之一 + 是……

Examples

- 她是我最好的朋友之一。
  Tā shì wǒ zuì hǎo de péngyou zhī yī.
  She is one of my best friends.
- Frozen 是我最喜欢的迪斯尼电影之一。
  Frozen shì wǒ zuì xǐhuan de Dísīní diànyǐng zhī yī.
  Frozen is one of my favorite Disney movies.
- 纽约是世界上最国际化的城市之一。
  Niǔyuē shì shìjiè shàng zuì guójìhuà de chéngshì zhī yī.
  New York is the one of the most international cities in the world.
- 他是这个公司的创始人之一。
  Tā shì zhège gōngsī de chuàngshǐ rén zhī yī.
  He is one of the founders of this company.
- 成龙是最有名的中国明星之一。
  Chéng Lóng shì zuì yǒumíng de Zhōngguó míngxīng zhī yī.
  Jackie Chan is one of the most famous Chinese movie stars.
- 我想离开北京的原因之一是空气污染。
  Wǒ xiǎng líkāi Běijīng de yuányīn zhī yī shì kōngqì wūrǎn.
  One of the reasons why I want to leave Beijing is the air pollution.

- 中秋节是中国重要的传统节日 之一 。

  Zhōngqiūjié shì Zhōngguó zhòngyào de chuántǒng jiérì zhī yī.

  Mid-autumn Day is one of the most important traditional festivals in China.

The Common 之一 Joke

A joke you'll hear a lot in Chinese involves using 最… but then pausing before saying 之一. This can leave the impression that you're saying someone or something is "the best," but really you're saying "*one of* the best," which can make a big difference (and is not nearly as complimentary).

- 她是我 最好 的朋友…… 之一 。

  Tā shì wǒ zuì hǎo de péngyou… zhī yī.

  She is my best friend… well, one of them.

- 你是我 最喜欢 的老师…… 之一 。

  Nǐ shì wǒ zuì xǐhuan de lǎoshī… zhī yī.

  You are my favorite teacher… well, one of them.

- 中国是我 最爱 的地方…… 之一 。

  Zhōngguó shì wǒ zuì ài de dìfang… zhī yī.

  China is my favorite place… well, one of them.

Expressing “the other” with “lingwai” (B1)

另外 (lìngwài) or 另 (lìng) is often used as a pronoun to denote “the other.” There is no need to add 的 after 另外, but it's often followed by 一个.

Structure

另外 + Number + [Measure Word] + Noun

另 can be used instead of 另外 when the following noun is singular (frequently as part of the phrase “另一个”).

Examples

- 我有两个手机，一个是小米，另一个是 iPhone 。
  Wǒ yǒu liǎng gè shǒujī, yī gè shì Xiǎomǐ, lìng yī gè shì iPhone.
  I have two cell phones. One is a Xiaomi, and the other is an iPhone.
- 她有两套房子，一套自己住，另一套租给别人了。
  Tā yǒu liǎng tào fángzi, yī tào zìjǐ zhù, lìng yī tào zū gěi biérén le.
  She has two houses. She lives in one and rents the other one to other people.
- 我买了三张票，一张是我的，另外两张是给朋友的。
  Wǒ mǎi le sān zhāng piào, yī zhāng shì wǒ de, lìngwài liǎng zhāng shì gěi péngyou de.
  I bought three tickets. One is for myself, and the other two are for my friends.
- 这几本书我今天拿走，另外几本下次再拿。
  Zhè jǐ běn shū wǒ jīntiān názǒu, lìngwài jǐ běn xià cì zài ná.
  I will take these books today. I can get the others next time.
- 这个蛋糕一半是你的，另一半是妹妹的。
  Zhège dàngāo yībàn shì nǐ de, lìng yībàn shì mèimei de.
  Half of this cake is yours. The other half is your little sister's.
- 跟他一起去的另外两个人已经死了。
  Gēn tā yīqǐ qù de lìngwài liǎng gè rén yǐjīng sǐ le.
  The other two people who went with him already died.

- 她打算在北京待五天。三天出去玩，另外两天去看朋友。

  Tā dǎsuàn zài Běijīng dāi wǔ tiān. Sān tiān chūqù wán, lìngwài liǎng tiān qù kàn péngyou.

  She plans to stay in Beijing for five days. Three of the days are for going out and having fun. The other two days for visiting friends.

- 我们公司和另外两家公司共用一个办公室。

  Wǒmen gōngsī hé lìngwài liǎng jiā gōngsī gòngyòng yī gè bàngōngshì.

  Our company shares the office with two other companies.

- 他的两个女儿一个嫁给了法国人，另一个嫁给了德国人。

  Tā de liǎng gè nǚ'ér yī gè jià gěi le Fǎguó rén, lìng yī gè jià gěi le Déguó rén.

  He has two daughters, one of which married a French guy and the other married a German guy.

- 一些人总是对另外一些人有偏见。

  Yīxiē rén zǒngshì duì lìngwài yīxiē rén yǒu piānjiàn.

  Some people always have prejudices against other people.

The "shi... de" construction for emphasizing details (B1)

Also known as: 是……的结构 (shì... de jiégòu), 是……的 sentence and 是……的 pattern.

The 是……的 (shì... de) construction is used to draw attention to certain information in a sentence. It's often used to ask questions that seek specific information, or to explain a situation by emphasizing a particular detail. While not strictly tied to any "tense," the 是……的 construction is frequently used when asking or telling *details* about the past.

This use of 是……的 (shì... de) is usually emphasized in textbooks over other uses, and therefore is sometimes called the "classic" 是……的 construction.

When to Use It

Even if you understand that 了 is not used to mark "past tense" in Chinese, it's possible that you incorrectly use it that way sometimes. For example, what if you want to ask a question about something that happened in the past? Would you ever say one of the following sentences?

- ✘ 你昨天 几点 到 了 ?
  Nǐ zuótiān jǐ diǎn dào le?
  What time did you arrive yesterday?
- ✘ 你跟 谁 去 了 ?
  Nǐ gēn shéi qù le?
  Who did you go with?
- ✘ 他 用什么 打你 了 ?
  Tā yòng shénme dǎ nǐ le?
  What did he use to hit you?

In each of these sentences above, 了 is not the right choice, because you're not asking if an event happened or not. You're asking about details of past events. When you are singling out details for emphasis–in a question or a statement–you need to use the 是……的 construction.

A 是……的 construction can pick out any detail that's related to a past event. Whatever comes immediately after 是 is emphasized. Check out this example:

A: 昨天我去杭州了。
Zuótiān wǒ qù Hángzhōu le.
I went to Hangzhou yesterday.

B: 你 是 怎么 去 的 ?
Nǐ shì zěnme qù de?
How did you get there?

A: 我 是 坐火车 去 的 。
Wǒ shì zuò huǒchē qù de.
I went by train.

Now let's revisit those other three sentences and ask the questions correctly with 是……的:

- ✔ 你昨天 是 几点 到 的 ?
  Nǐ zuótiān shì jǐ diǎn dào de?
  What time did you arrive yesterday?
- ✔ 你 是 跟谁 去 的 ?
  Nǐ shì gēn shéi qù de?
  Who did you go with?
- ✔ 他 是 用什么 打你 的 ?
  Tā shì yòng shénme dǎ nǐ de?
  What did he use to hit you?

Affirmative Form

是……的 is not generally used for reporting new information but for adding important details that make the information clearer. You could think of 是……的 as being equivalent to saying one of the following in English:

- "The situation is that…"
- "It's that… "
- "It was… that… "

Structure

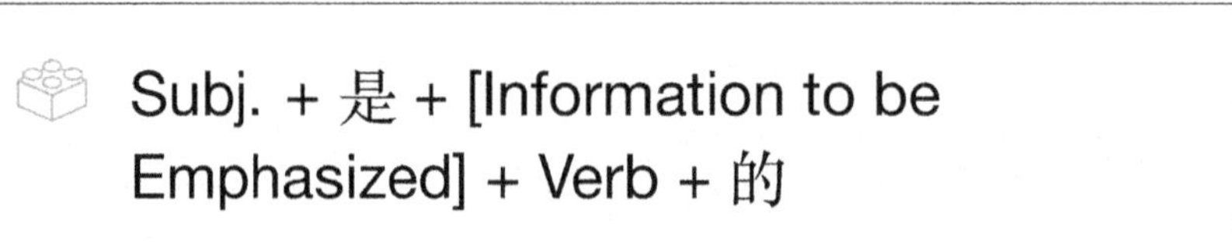
Subj. + 是 + [Information to be Emphasized] + Verb + 的

This structure can be used to emphasize any detail, but most commonly it emphasizes **time**, **manner**, or **place**. Don't worry if this still seems a little confusing; lots of helpful examples are coming up!

Examples

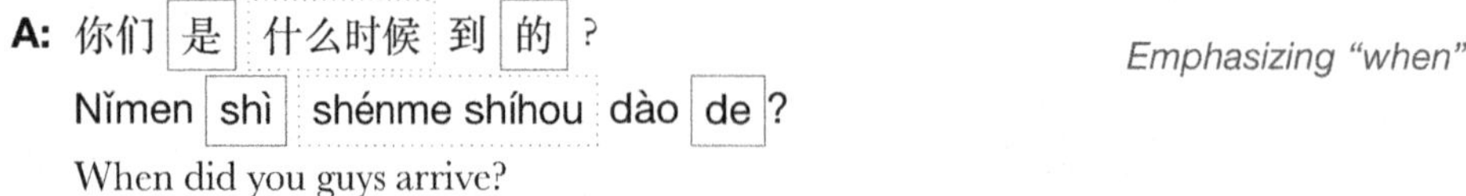

A: 你们 是 什么时候 到 的 ?
Nǐmen shì shénme shíhou dào de?
When did you guys arrive?

Emphasizing "when"

B: 我们 是 昨天 到 的 。
Wǒmen shì zuótiān dào de.
We arrived yesterday.
"Yesterday" is emphasized.

A: 你 是 在哪儿 出生 的 ?
Nǐ shì zài nǎr chūshēng de?
Where were you born?
"Where" is emphasized.

B: 我 是 在香港 出生 的 。
Wǒ shì zài Xiānggǎng chūshēng de.
I was born in Hong Kong.
"In Hong Kong" is emphasized.

Although this structure is called the 是⋯⋯的 construction, the 是 is nearly always optional. You will often hear this structure with 是 omitted, so be aware. The only time 是 is required in this construction is when it's being negated. Other than that, 是 is commonly omitted.

A: 你 骑自行车 来 的 吗?
Nǐ qí zìxíngchē lái de ma?
Did you come by bike?
Emphasizing "by bike"

B: 我 走 来 的 。
Wǒ zǒu lái de.
I came by foot.
Emphasizing "by foot"

A: 谁 告诉你 的 ?
Shéi gàosu nǐ de?
Who told you?
Emphasizing "who"

B: 一个同事 告诉我 的 。
Yī gè tóngshì gàosu wǒ de.
A colleague told me.
Emphasizing "a colleague"

You might be wondering, "can I still say the same thing without the 是 and the 的?" The answer is that in most cases, *no, not really*. While the 是 can sometimes be dropped, these examples sound weird without the 的. It's just a part of learning to ask questions naturally in Mandarin. You don't have to learn a "past tense," but you do have to learn this way of asking for details about the past sooner or later.

Negative Form

是⋯⋯的 sentences can only be negated with 不, as 没 can not be used to negate 是. Remember that you need *both* the 不 *and* the 是 together to make the correct negative form.

Some examples:

- ✔ 他们 不是 在网上 认识 的 。
  Tāmen bù shì zài wǎngshàng rènshi de.
  They didn't meet online.
- ✔ 他 不是 跟我们一起 去 的 。
  Tā bù shì gēn wǒmen yīqǐ qù de.
  He didn't go with us.
- ✘ 我 不 坐地铁 来 的 。 *The 是 is missing*
  Wǒ bù zuò dìtiě lái de.
  I didn't come by metro.
- ✘ 我 不 在中国 出生 的 。 *The 是 is missing*
  Wǒ bù zài Zhōngguó chūshēng de.
  I wasn't born in China.

Note that negating a 是……的 construction creates the implication that the action in the sentence *was* carried out, and only the detail emphasized by 是……的 is being denied. So, in the second sentence, the implication is that 他 didn't go with 我们, but *did* go out with *someone*. So negative 是……的 constructions would work nicely in the final scenes of detective dramas.

Used in a Question

是……的 constructions can be made into questions in the usual three ways to form questions in Chinese:

- With a question particle
- Within affirmative-negative questions
- With a question word

Some examples:

- 她 用邮件 回复 的 吗? *吗 is a question particle*
  Tā yòng yóujiàn huífù de ma?
  Did she reply by email?
- 你们 是不是 去年 认识 的 ? *是不是 is an affirmative-negative pattern*
  Nǐmen shì bu shì qùnián rènshi de?
  Did you meet each other last year?
- 这个东西 多少钱 买 的 ? *多少 is a question word*
  Zhège dōngxi duōshao qián mǎi de?
  How much did you buy this thing for?

Is 是 always optional?

Generally, 是 can be omitted, and the meaning will not change. However, in a small number of cases, omitting 是 will make it unclear which part of the sentence is being emphasized. In these cases, 是 clearly indicates which words are being emphasized. Take a look at this example:

- 你上周和他去北京的吗?
  Nǐ shàng zhōu hé tā qù Běijīng de ma?
  Did you go to Beijing with him last weekend?

This sentence could emphasize 上周 (time), or 和他 (part of the subject). A simple 是 can make clear which one the speaker is emphasizing.

✔ 你是上周和他去北京的吗?
Nǐ shì shàng zhōu hé tā qù Běijīng de ma?
Was it last week that you went to Beijing with him?
上周 is emphasized

✔ 你上周是和他去北京的吗?
Nǐ shàng zhōu shì hé tā qù Běijīng de ma?
Was it him that you went to Beijing with last week?
和他 is emphasized

Position of 的

Until now we've said that the 的 appears at the end of the sentence in a 是…… 的 construction. This is very often the case. However, it can actually appear in one of two places. Take a look at the examples below:

✔ 我们是用 Skype 开会的。
Wǒmen shì yòng Skype kāi huì de.
We had a meeting by Skype.

✔ 我们是用 Skype 开的会。
Wǒmen shì yòng Skype kāi de huì.
We had a meeting by Skype.

As you can see, when the verb is followed by an object, 的 can go before *or* after the object. Both sentences are grammatically correct, but the first the sentence could be referring to either a specific event in the past or habitual actions.

Take a look at these two sentences which remove the ambiguity by including a bit more information about the timeframe:

- 那次我们是用 Skype 开会的。
  Nà cì wǒmen shì yòng Skype kāi huì de.
  That time we had the meeting by Skype.

- 我们 平时 是 用 Skype 开 会 的 。
  Wǒmen píngshí shì yòng Skype kāi huì de.
  We usually have meetings by Skype.

For the most part, you should be fine regularly putting 的 at the end of your 是……的 sentences. Just be aware that there is some potential for ambiguity in certain situations. If you don't want to move 的 around, then including a bit of extra information about time can keep things clear.

Completed Action

It's important to note that while the 是…… 的 construction also indicates that an action has been completed, this is not the *purpose* of a 是…… 的 construction. The completed action part is more like a *prerequisite* for using 是…… 的. This means you shouldn't use 是…… 的 just to indicate that an action is completed. Use the aspect particle 了 for that. Instead, use 是…… 的 to draw attention to certain details of a completed action.

Similar to

- The "shi... de" construction for indicating purpose (B1), page 245
- The "shi... de" patterns: an overview (B1), page 247
- Using "de" (modal particle) (B1), page 133

The "shi... de" construction for indicating purpose (B1)

There are many ways to explain why you are doing something or what an object is used for. One of the more natural ways just happens to involve 是……的. This is a different usage from the "classic" 是……的 pattern[1].

A Person as Subject

Structure

If the subject is a person, there is often a 来 or 去 after the 是, indicating direction like "coming here" or "going there."

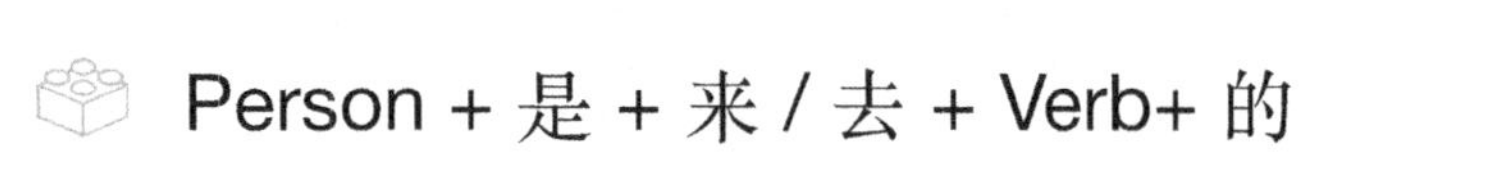

Examples

- 我是来玩的。
  Wǒ shì lái wán de.
  I came for fun.
- 我们都是去出差的。
  Wǒmen dōu shì qù chūchāi de.
  We are all going on business trips.
- 他们都是来实习的。
  Tāmen dōu shì lái shíxí de.
  They all came here to do internships.
- 你真的是来帮我们的吗?
  Nǐ zhēnde shì lái bāng wǒmen de ma?
  Are you really here to help us?
- 我们不是去玩的，是去做调查的。
  Wǒmen bù shì qù wán de, shì qù zuò diàochá de.
  We're not going for fun. We're going to do research.

A Thing as Subject

Structure

If the subject is a thing, 用来 is often used. Look at the examples below for some more

1. The "shi... de" construction for emphasizing details (B1), page 239

clarification.

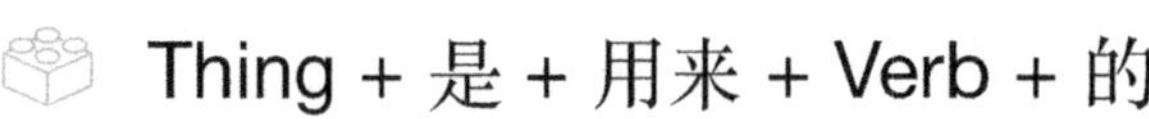
Thing + 是 + 用来 + Verb + 的

or

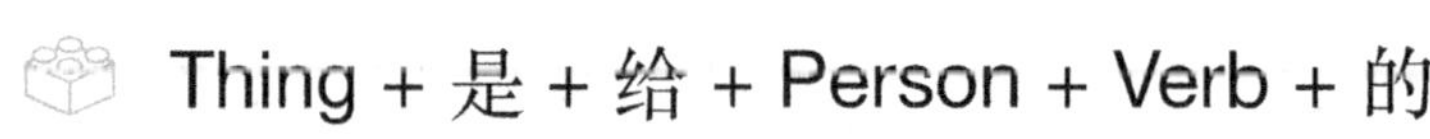
Thing + 是 + 给 + Person + Verb + 的

Examples

- 这种菜 是 用来 做汤 的 。
  Zhè zhǒng cài shì yònglái zuò tāng de.
  This kind of vegetable is for making soup.
- 这个房间 是 给 客人住 的 。
  Zhège fángjiān shì gěi kèrén zhù de.
  This room is for our guest to stay in.
- 这些钱 是 给 孩子上大学 的 。
  Zhèxiē qián shì gěi háizi shàng dàxué de.
  This money is for our child's college education.
- 这些礼物 是 给 客户准备 的 。
  Zhèxiē lǐwù shì gěi kèhù zhǔnbèi de.
  These presents have been prepared for the clients.
- 钱 是 用来 花 的 ，不 是 用来 省 的 。
  Qián shì yònglái huā de, bù shì yònglái shěng de.
  Money is for spending, not for saving.

Similar to

- The "shi… de" construction for emphasizing details (B1), page 239
- The "shi… de" patterns: an overview (B1), page 247

The "shi... de" patterns: an overview (B1)

An intermediate student of Chinese should be aware of the classic "shi... de" construction. It's important to learn and use. But don't be tempted to think that the "official" 是……的 (shì... de) pattern is the only way that 是 and 的 can work together in a sentence! There are multiple ways to use 是 and 的 together, and they can be used for different purposes. This article helps break down the various uses of 是……的 and tackle the confusion head-on.

Omitting a Noun with 的

This is the most simple way to use 是 with 的: you drop the noun and let 的 represent it. This usage requires context; otherwise the other person won't know what noun you are referring to. Having the 的 take the place of the noun is sort of like the way we say "one" or "it" in English. It's a basic substitution, but it's one that is very common and very helpful in everyday Chinese.

A: 你也是大学生？你 是 什么专业 的 ？
Nǐ yě shì dàxuéshēng? Nǐ shì shénme zhuānyè de?
Are you also a college student? What's your major?

B: 我 是 中文专业 的 。
Wǒ shì Zhōngwén zhuānyè de.
My major is Chinese.

Used with Distinguishing Words

If you're a good student, you learned the classic pattern for simple sentences using adjectives long ago (you know, the 你很漂亮 type), and you know that you're ***not*** supposed to use 是 in these sentences. But then you may have later come across some sentence patterns–apparently using adjectives–where you ***have*** to use 是 (and also 的). These are sentences that use a special type of word (you might think of it as a special class of adjectives, if that helps) called distinguishing words.

Structure

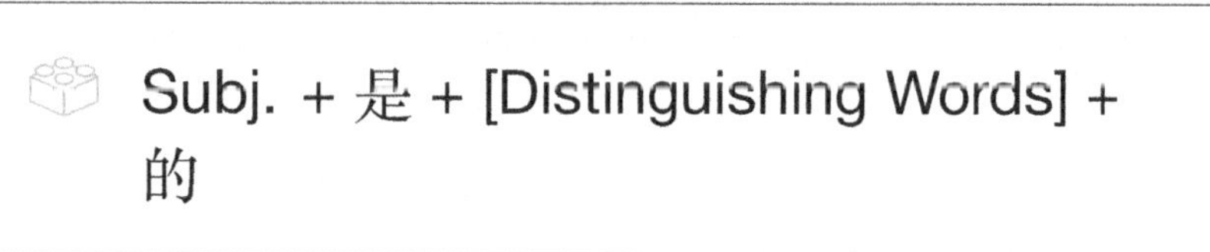

Subj. + 是 + [Distinguishing Words] + 的

Examples

Pay attention to the "distinguishing words" between 是 and 的.

- 这个苹果 是 坏 的 。
  Zhège píngguǒ shì huài de.
  This apple is bad.

- 你错了，那个人 是 女 的 。

  Nǐ cuò le, nàge rén shì nǚ de.

  You are mistaken. That person is a woman.

- 他家的家具都 是 中式 的 。

  Tā jiā de jiājù dōu shì Zhōng shì de.

  The furniture in his house is all in Chinese style.

Other "distinguishing words" include colors, materials, sexes, and other categories that can have no degree.

The Classic Construction

Structure

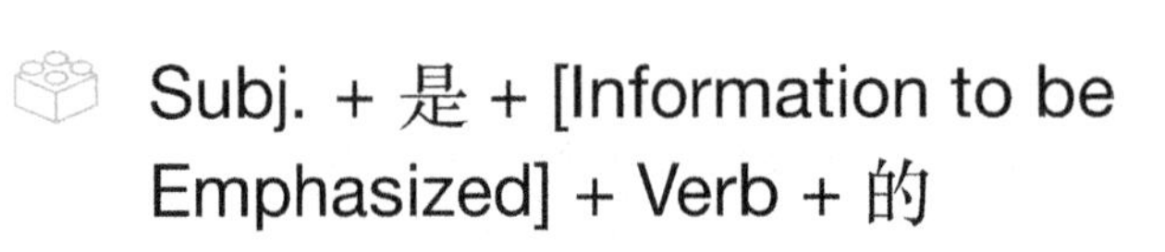

Subj. + 是 + [Information to be Emphasized] + Verb + 的

This classic pattern is the one for emphasizing certain *details* about events in the *past*. It's often used to ask pointed questions about past events, and then to answer those questions. Usually, the situation is already established, and the speakers are trying to get more specific clarification, such as when, where, or how the action took place. When this is the case, the phrase that follows the 是 is the part of the situation that is being emphasized.

It is also important to know that you can't use 了 in this type of sentence. 了 only tells you that the action is completed, not any of the other details that this construction is looking for. Since it is already understood that the action took place, the 了 is unhelpful and inappropriate. A more complete explanation of this particular usage can be found in the article on 是……的 for emphasizing details[1].

Examples

The examples below share the theme: 我在上海学了两年中文. Each sentence has a different aspect of the situation being emphasized.

A: 你 是 什么时候 开始学中文 的 ?

Nǐ shì shénme shíhou kāishǐ xué Zhōngwén de?

A: When was it that you started studying Chinese?

B: 我 是 两年前 开始学中文 的 。

Wǒ shì liǎng nián qián kāishǐ xué Zhōngwén de.

It was two years ago that I started studying Chinese.

1. The "shi... de" construction for emphasizing details (B1), page 239

A: 你是在哪里学的中文?

Nǐ shì zài nǎlǐ xué de Zhōngwén?

Where is it that you study Chinese?

B: 我是在上海学的中文。

Wǒ shì zài Shànghǎi xué de Zhōngwén.

It's in Shanghai that I study Chinese.

In the example above, you might have noticed something funny with the object of the verb. In this construction, if the verb is transitive (it takes an object), then the object can be placed either before or after the 的 without affecting the meaning. Take a look at the example below:

A: 昨天你是怎么回的家?

Zuótiān nǐ shì zěnme huí de jiā?

How did you come back yesterday?

B: 昨天我是打车回家的。

Zuótiān wǒ shì dǎchē huíjiā de.

I went home by taxi yesterday.

It's correct to put the 的 before *or* after the 家 in both of those sentences.

Used for Indicating Purpose or Intent

Structure

When explaining "what you came for" or "what you want to do," it's common to use yet another type of 是……的 construction.

Person + 是 + 来 / 去 + Verb + 的

When expressing a purpose, 是 and 的 are often used together with 用来, especially when the subject is a thing.

Examples

- 我是来实习的。

  Wǒ shì lái shíxí de.

  I came here to do an internship.

- 钱 是 用来 花 的 ，不 是 用来 省 的 。
  Qián shì yònglái huā de, bù shì yònglái shěng de.
  Money is for spending, not for saving.

Used for Talking about What People Do

This pattern can also be used to talk about what kind of work people do:

A: 我 是 教汉语 的 。你 是 做什么 的 ？
Wǒ shì jiāo Hànyǔ de. Nǐ shì zuò shénme de?
I teach Chinese. What kind of work do you do?

B: 我 是 送外卖 的 。
Wǒ shì sòng wàimài de.
I'm a take-out delivery guy.

Used for a Tone of Strong Affirmation

Sometimes you can use 的 to really add a kick to your responses, making them stronger. You might even hear Chinese people reply with just 是的 which means "That's right." This usage is similar to the way that English speakers might stress the word "is" in sentences like "It *is* my food." When used to express affirmation, 会, 能, and 可以 are often used as well. Again, the 是 is optional.

- 这个东西 是 可以 吃 的 。
  Zhège dōngxi shì kěyǐ chī de.
  This thing is edible.
- 我 会 去 的 。
  Wǒ huì qù de.
  I will go.
- 我们 能 做到 的 。
  Wǒmen néng zuòdào de.
  We can do it.

Similar to

- The "shi… de" construction for emphasizing details (B1), page 239
- The "shi… de" construction for indicating purpose (B1), page 245
- Using "de" (modal particle) (B1), page 133

Topic-comment sentences (B1)

In a topic-comment sentence, the usual word order is rearranged a bit, in order to emphasize a certain part of a sentence. The part that is to be emphasized becomes the topic and moves to the beginning of the sentence, with the comment on the topic coming after the topic has been stated.

Structure

Topic , Comment

Examples

Just make sure to put a comma after the topic if you are writing the sentence down!

- 水果，我最爱吃草莓。
  Shuǐguǒ, wǒ zuì ài chī cǎoméi.
  Fruit, I like strawberries best.
- 不好意思，咖啡，我都喝完了。
  Bù hǎoyìsi, kāfēi, wǒ dōu hē wán le.
  I'm sorry. I finished all the coffee.
- 你好，票，还有吗？
  Nǐhǎo, piào, háiyǒu ma?
  Hello. Are there any tickets left?
- 这个问题，你一个人没办法解决。
  Zhège wèntí, nǐ yīgèrén méi bànfǎ jiějué.
  There is no way that you can solve this problem all by yourself.
- 那部电影，看过的人都喜欢。
  Nà bù diànyǐng, kàn guo de rén dōu xǐhuan.
  All the people that have watched that movie like it.
- 这个新项目，公司打算让我来负责。
  Zhège xīn xiàngmù, gōngsī dǎsuàn ràng wǒ lái fùzé.
  The company plans to let me take charge of this new project.
- 你借我的钱，还没还吧？
  Nǐ jiè wǒ de qián, hái méi huán ba?
  You haven't returned the money you borrowed from me, right?

- 他的事，我不想管那么多。
  Tā de shì, wǒ bù xiǎng guǎn nàme duō.
  I don't want to be so involved in his business.
- 明天下午要开会，你记得吧?
  Míngtiān xiàwǔ yào kāi huì, nǐ jìde ba?
  You have a meeting tomorrow afternoon. You remember, don't you?
- 我的笔，弟弟弄坏了。
  Wǒ de bǐ, dìdi nòng huài le.
  My younger brother broke my pen.

Similar to

- Marking a topic with “de hua” (B2)
- Marking a topic with “ma” (B2)

Using “ba” sentences (B1)

Also known as: 把字句 (“bǎ”zìjù), 把 construction, preposition 把, disposal construction and pre-transitive 把.

The 把 (bǎ) sentence is a useful structure for constructing longer sentences which focus on the result or influence of an action. One of its key features is that it brings the object of the verb closer to the front of the sentence and precedes it with a 把. It's really common in Mandarin but can feel a bit awkward at first for English speakers.

What is a 把 sentence?

A basic sentence in Mandarin is formed with a subject-verb-object (SVO) word order, as in English:

 Subj. + [Verb Phrase] + Obj.

A 把 sentence shakes things up a bit, and you get this structure:

 Subj. + 把 + Obj. + [Verb Phrase]

Note that the **object has moved**, and is preceded by 把. You now have SOV word order.

This is all well and good, but most students of Chinese, on learning about 把 sentences for the first time, have the same reaction: *“Why the heck would I ever use this structure? The SVO word order always works just fine, right?”* The answer is: well, no... not always. It's true that 把 sentences are often used to achieve somewhat subtle differences in emphasis, but there are also very good reasons to use 把 sentences when a regular sentence just won't do. Take this sentence for example:

- 把 书 放 在 桌子 上 。
  Bǎ shū fàng zài zhuōzi shàng .
  Put the book on the table.

How would you say this without the 把 construction? You might try this:

✘ 放 书 在桌子 上 。
Fàng shū zài zhuōzi shàng .

The problem is that the above Chinese sentence is not grammatical. *You can't put an object right after a verb, and then put other modifiers of the verb after the object.* Here are other examples of how to successfully use 把 and 放 in the same sentence.

- 她 把 我的手机 放 在 她的包 里 了。

  Tā bǎ wǒ de shǒujī fàng zài tā de bāo lǐ le.

  She put my cell phone in her bag.

- 他 把 脏衣服 放 在 床 下面 了。

  Tā bǎ zāng yīfu fàng zài chuáng xiàmiàn le.

  He put his dirty laundry under the bed.

- 你是不是 把 护照 放 在 行李箱 里 了?

  Nǐ shì bu shì bǎ hùzhào fàng zài xínglixiāng lǐ le?

  Did you put your passport in your suitcase?

For each of these, the sentence would be ungrammatical if you tried to do away with the 把 and put the object right after the verb.

Key Things to Keep in Mind When Using 把

- The object should be known. So it has already been mentioned or discussed previously.
- 把字句 are most often used to describe what happened to the object in some detail. The verb is not just "bare"; there's "more stuff" after it. Often the "stuff" is related to some kind of manipulation of the object.
- 把字句 are not tied to any particular time. You can use them when talking about events in the past, or for making a request.

把 Sentences with Two Objects

The usual structure for 把 sentences, as described above, puts the object right after 把. For certain verbs, however, you can have two objects in a 把 sentence. Their use in a 把 sentence will also involve prepositions.

They use the following structure:

> Subj. + 把 + Obj. 1 + Verb + 给 + Obj. 2

Common verbs that take two objects include: 送 (sòng), 拿 (ná), 递 (dì), 卖 (mài), 借 (jiè), 还 (huán), 介绍 (jièshào).

Subject	把	Object 1	Verb	Preposition	Object 2		
我们	把	礼物	送	给	客人	了	。
	把	盐	递	给	我		。
他	把	房子	卖	给	谁	了	?
我	把	他	介绍	给	我老板	了	。

把 Sentences with Complements

Because 把 sentences are all about "doing stuff" to the object, and complements in Mandarin often handle this issue, it's good to be aware of how these two grammar features interact.

Result complements work particularly well in 把 sentences. When you consider that both structures deal with the result or outcome of an action, this makes sense. The majority of result complements (except for perception verbs) fit in very well in a 把 construction. For example:

- 我把作业做完了。
  Wǒ bǎ zuòyè zuò wán le.
  I finished doing my homework.
- 老师把我的名字读错了。
  Lǎoshī bǎ wǒ de míngzì dú cuò le.
  The teacher read my name wrong.

Direction complements[1] also work well in 把 constructions, for similar reasons. For example:

- 请把客人带进去。
  Qǐng bǎ kèrén dài jìnqù.
  Please take the guests inside.
- 把我的眼镜拿过来。
  Bǎ wǒ de yǎnjìng ná guòlái.
  Please bring my glasses over here.

Note that potential complements[2] do not appear in 把 sentences. This is because they are hypothetical, whereas a 把 sentence must describe what actually happens.

---

1. Direction complement (B1), page 211
2. Potential complement (B1), page 221

Forming 把 Sentences

Since the basic structure has already been given above, we can jump right into some more exciting patterns!

Negating 把 Sentences

To negate a 把 sentence, insert 不要 or 别 (present or future) or 没有 (past) directly in front of 把. You can't put it after 把, 'inside' the 把 construction, as this would break the rule about describing what actually happened to the object. It would be like saying "What happened to… was nothing." It doesn't sound natural.

Subject	Negative	把	Object	Verb Phrase	
阿姨	没有	把	房间	打扫干净	。
我	没	把	钱	借给他	。
你们	不要	把	这件事	告诉她	。

Question Forms of 把 Sentences

You can make 把 sentences into questions in the usual three ways to form questions in Mandarin:

- With a question particle
- With a question word
- With positive-negative verbs

Some examples:

- 你们 把 那个问题 解决了吗?
  Nǐmen bǎ nàge wèntí jiějué le ma?
  Did you solve that problem?
- 你 把 我手机 放在哪儿了?
  Nǐ bǎ wǒ shǒujī fàng zài nǎr le?
  Where did you put my cell phone?
- 他 把 钱 借给谁了?
  Tā bǎ qián jiè gěi shéi le?
  Who did he lend the money to?
- 你能不能 把 你房间 打扫干净?
  Nǐ néng bu néng bǎ nǐ fángjiān dǎsǎo gānjìng?
  Can you clean your room or not?

Be careful how you form questions with 把 sentences though. Remember that you have to have a definite object, and you have to describe what was done to that object. A question form could easily get in the way of one of these conditions.

Adverbs in 把 Sentences

Adverbs can usually be placed before 把 or before the verb (the exception is negative adverbs, as described above). Adverbs in each of these positions can change the meaning in slightly different ways, as demonstrated with 都 in the examples below.

Subj.	Adv.	把	Object	Adv.	Verb Phrase	
我们	都	把	作业		做完了	。
他		把	咖啡	都	喝完了	。
他	已经	把	钱		还给我了	。
我	可能	把	手机		忘在朋友家了	。

In the first sentence, 都 modifies 我们 to express "we all finished the homework." In the second sentence, 都 modifies 咖啡 to express "he finished all the coffee".

把 Sentences and Quantity Phrases

As mentioned above, the object of a 把 sentence must be something specific and definite. This might involve noun measure words, which will come after the 把 and before the object.

Subject	把	Quantity Phrase	Noun	Verb Phrase	
我	把	那两件	脏衣服	洗干净了	。
他	把	最后三块	蛋糕	吃完了	。
你	把	这几句	话	读一下	。

Verb measure words are frequently used in 把 sentences and come at the end of a 把 sentence.

Subject	把	Object	Verb	Quantity Phrase	
	把	课文	读	一遍	。
她	把	这个字	写了	十遍	。

Note that in all of these sentences, the object is something specific and definite.

Verbs for 把 Sentences

Some verbs generally can't indicate what happened *to* the object. They only describe what the subject did. Below are some examples of verbs that do not generally work in 把 sentences.

Psychological verbs: 爱 (ài) "to love," 喜欢 (xǐhuan) "to like," 想 (xiǎng) "to miss," 了解 (liǎojiě) "to know well," 害怕 (hàipà) "to fear," 恨 (hèn) "to hate."

Perception verbs: 看 (kàn) "to look at," 听 (tīng) "to listen to," 闻 (wén) "to smell," 像 (xiàng) "to resemble."

Other Uses of 把

It's important to note that 把 is a word with other uses. The most common is as a measure word for things with handles, or things that you hold. Examples include 一把伞 ("an umbrella"), 一把枪 ("a gun"), and 一把椅子 ("a chair"). So, you've got to look at how 把 is being used in a sentence before you can understand its meaning.

To demonstrate the difference, here's a sentence with both kinds of 把:

- 请你把那把伞拿给我。
  Qǐng nǐ bǎ nà bǎ sǎn ná gěi wǒ.
  Please give me that umbrella.

Similar to

- Direction complement (B1), page 211
- Using "bei" sentences (B1), page 259
- Advanced uses of "ba" (B2)
- Using "jiang" as a formal "ba" (B2)

Using "bei" sentences (B1)

被 (bèi) sentences, which are called 被字句 (bèizìjù) in Chinese, are a key way to express the passive voice in modern Mandarin Chinese. In passive sentences, the *object* of an action becomes the subject of the sentence, and the "doer" of the action, which would have been the subject of the normal (active voice) sentence, becomes secondary and may or may not be mentioned in the passive sentence.

What is a 被 sentence?

被 (bèi) sentences are simply sentences which use a passive verb and the word 被. 被 sentences are not the only way to create the passive verb form in Chinese, but they are the most common and definitely the type to tackle first.

For the sake of clarity, take these sentences for example:

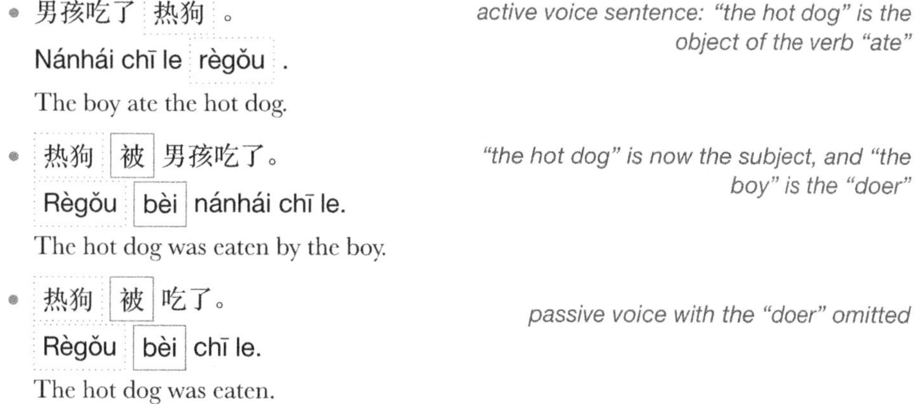

- 男孩吃了 热狗 。
  Nánhái chī le règǒu .
  The boy ate the hot dog.
  active voice sentence: "the hot dog" is the object of the verb "ate"
- 热狗 被 男孩吃了。
  Règǒu bèi nánhái chī le.
  The hot dog was eaten by the boy.
  "the hot dog" is now the subject, and "the boy" is the "doer"
- 热狗 被 吃了。
  Règǒu bèi chī le.
  The hot dog was eaten.
  passive voice with the "doer" omitted

Why use them?

First, passive sentences indicate that one has been negatively affected. For example:

- 他 被 打了。
  Tā bèi dǎ le.
  He was beaten.

Second, passive sentences shift emphasis from the "doer" of the action to the one affected by that action. For example:

- 你 被 公司炒鱿鱼了?
  Nǐ bèi gōngsī chǎo yóuyú le?
  You got fired by the company?

Third, passive sentences allow one to avoid having to mention the "doer" of the action, either because it is unknown, or for other reasons. For example:

- 我的手机 被 偷了。
  Wǒ de shǒujī bèi tōu le.
  My cell phone got stolen.

How to Use 被 Sentences

Normal use of 被 has a few preconditions:

- The verb to be used with 被 needs to have an object (this will become the new subject of the 被 sentence). Verbs that take objects are called transitive verbs.
- If you're going to state *who the verb was done by* (the "doer"), then the subject doing the original action must be known.
- The verb can't be too simple (for example, a one-character verb like 吃). Put simply, *something needs to come after the verb.* That "something" can be a particle like 了, a complement, or sometimes even an additional object.

Structure

Subj. + 被 (+ Doer) + Verb + 了

Examples

被 sentences with a doer:

- 我 被 他 骗 了 。
  Wǒ bèi tā piàn le .
  I was deceived by him.
- 他 被 警察 抓 了 。
  Tā bèi jǐngchá zhuā le .
  He was caught by the police.
- 他 被 父母 骂 了 。
  Tā bèi fùmǔ mà le .
  He was scolded by his parents.

被 sentences without a doer:

- 我的车 被 撞 了 。
  Wǒ de chē bèi zhuàng le .
  My car was hit.
- 他们做的坏事 被 发现 了 。
  Tāmen zuò de huàishì bèi fāxiàn le .
  The bad things they've done were discovered.

Wénjiàn bèi shān le.

The files were deleted.

Common Errors

✗ 咖啡被我喝。

Kāfēi bèi wǒ hē.

Remember: you need SOMEthing after the verb.

✓ 咖啡被我喝了。

Kāfēi bèi wǒ hē le.

The coffee was drunk by me.

✓ 咖啡被我喝完了。

Kāfēi bèi wǒ hē wán le.

The coffee was finished by me.

✗ 他被打。

Tā bèi dǎ.

Remember: you need SOMEthing after the verb.

✓ 他被打了。

Tā bèi dǎ le.

He was beaten.

✓ 他被打伤了。

Tā bèi dǎ shāng le.

He was beaten and wounded.

Forming 被 Sentences

You know the basic pattern already, so it's time to go deeper…

Negating 被 Sentences

There's just one other complication. What if you want to make a sentence in the *negative*? To negate a 被 sentence, you need to insert 没 or 没有 (past) directly in front of 被. For the present and future, use 不.

Doer	Negative	被	Subject	Verb Phrase	
他	没有	被		打伤	。
他	没	被		炒鱿鱼	。
她的想法	不	被	父母	理解	。

Question Forms of 被 Sentences

You can make 被 sentences into questions in the usual three ways to form questions in Mandarin:

- With a question particle
- With a question word
- With positive-negative verbs

Some examples:

- 那些书 被 借 走了 吗?
  Nàxiē shū bèi jiè zǒu le ma?
  Have those books been borrowed?
- 他 被 谁打 的 ?
  Tā bèi shéi dǎ de ?
  Who was he beaten by?
- 你是不是 被 公司炒鱿鱼 了 ?
  Nǐ shì bu shì bèi gōngsī chǎo yóuyú le ?
  Did you get fired by the company or not?

被 Sentences with Aspect Particles

The particles 了 and 过 can both be used with 被 constructions, while 着 cannot. 着 indicates an action is "ongoing," which is not appropriate for a 被 construction, which should refer to an already complete action.

Subject	被	Object	Verb	Aspect particle	
他	被	老师	打	过	。
你	被	他	骗	了	！
我的车	被		撞	过	。
她	被	男朋友	甩	了	。

被 Sentences with Complements

Both result complements and direction complements[1] work well in 被 sentences.

Some examples:

---

1. Direction complement (B1), page 211

- 花瓶 被 摔 碎 了。
  Huāpíng bèi shuāi suì le.
  The vase was broken into pieces.
- 那个人 被 车撞 死 了。
  Nàge rén bèi chē zhuàng sǐ le.
  That man got hit and killed by a car.
- 那个男人 被 警察赶 出去 了。
  Nàge nánrén bèi jǐngchá gǎn chūqù le.
  The man was kicked out by the policeman.
- 孩子 被 他父母送 回去 了。
  Háizi bèi tā fùmǔ sòng huíqù le.
  The child was sent back by his parents.

Sorry if these example sentences all seem like downers, but 被 sentences tend to be negative (or even tragic!).

Adverbs in 被 Sentences

What if you want to include adverbs in your 被 sentence? Where should those go? They go in the same place as the *negative* adverb 没有, above.

Subject	Adv.	被	Doer	Verb Phrase		
他	刚才	被	同学	打	了	。
我们	都	被	老师	骂	了	。
手机	又	被		偷	了	?
小偷	终于	被		抓住	了	!

Similar to

- Direction complement (B1), page 211
- Using "ba" sentences (B1), page 253
- Advanced uses of "ba" (B2)
- Expressing passive voice with "gei" (B2)
- Passive verbs with "shou" (B2)

Alternative existential sentences (B1)

Expressing something's existence in a certain place or location is not just limited to 在 (zài) and 有 (yǒu). The word order may be a little different from what you are used to, but 着 (zhe) and 是 (shì) are also ways to make everyday statements such as, "There is a book lying on the desk."

Pattern with 着

Verbs that are paired with 着 are usually stative verbs. So unlike with action verbs, you're going to be describing an action that is kind of like just sitting there. It could be standing there, lying there, sitting there hanging there… the point is it isn't actively expending energy *doing* anything.

Structure

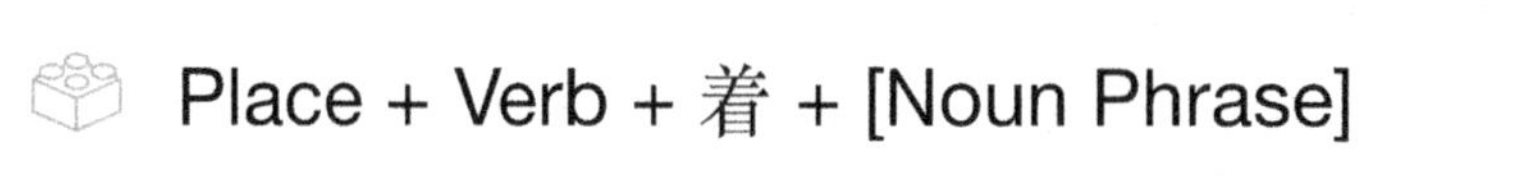

Place + Verb + 着 + [Noun Phrase]

Examples

- 桌子上放 着 一本书。
  Zhuōzi shàng fàng zhe yī běn shū .
  There is a book on the desk.
- 大厅里站 着 一些警察。
  Dàtīng lǐ zhàn zhe yīxiē jǐngchá.
  There are several policemen standing in the hall.
- 教室里坐 着 两百多个学生。
  Jiàoshì lǐ zuò zhe liǎng bǎi duō gè xuéshēng.
  There are more than two hundred students sitting in the classroom.
- 地下室里堆 着 很多旧东西。
  Dìxiàshì lǐ duī zhe hěn duō jiù dōngxi.
  There is lots of old stuff piled up in the basement.
- 楼下停 着 几辆车。
  Lóuxià tíng zhe jǐ liàng chē.
  A few cars are parked downstairs.

Note that in English we sometimes use a verb in its "-ing" form, and sometimes use the passive "-ed" form of the verb.

Pattern with 是

The subject in the 是 sentence pattern indicates the location or area. The object that comes after 是 is the only thing (worth mentioning) in that area. It's worth noting that there's no real time indication for most sentences like this. It could be setting a scene in a story (in the past), or it could be describing the current state of things (in the present).

Structure

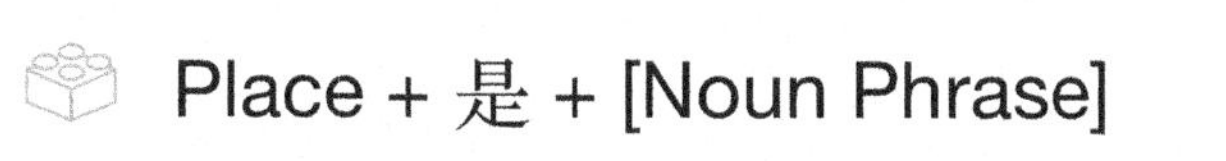
Place + 是 + [Noun Phrase]

Examples

- 洗衣机里 是 一些脏衣服。
  Xǐyījī lǐ shì yīxiē zāng yīfu.
  There are dirty clothes inside the washing machine.
  There is nothing in the washing machine other than the dirty clothes.
- 袋子里 是 我的午饭。
  Dàizi lǐ shì wǒ de wǔfàn.
  My lunch is in the bag.
  The only thing in the bag is my lunch.
- 墙上都 是 他家人的照片。
  Qiáng shàng dōu shì tā jiārén de zhàopiàn.
  His family's photos are hanging on the wall.
  His family's photos are all over the wall, and nothing else is on he wall.
- 盒子里 是 你的礼物。
  Hézi lǐ shì nǐ de lǐwù.
  Your gift is in the box.
  Other than your gift, there is nothing else in the box.
- 桌子上 是 昨天没吃完的菜。
  Zhuōzi shàng shì zuótiān méi chī wán de cài.
  The food that was left over from yesterday is on the table.
  The food that was left over from yesterday is the only thing on the table.

Note that 是 is used to describe a singular object existing somewhere, while 有 can refer to multiple objects/people.

Similar to

- Expressing actions in progress (full form) (B1), page 189

Expressing "as one likes" with "jiu" (B1)

When we want to express "to do something as one pleases," we can use the "想 (xiǎng) *verb* 就 (jiù) *verb*" pattern.

Basic Pattern

This structure is similar to how we would say in English, "whatever I want to eat, I eat" or, "wherever I want to go, I go." The verb that comes after the 想 and the 就 are the same verb.

Structure

Examples

- 想吃就吃。
  Xiǎng chī jiù chī.
  If you want to eat, help yourself.
- 想走就走吧。
  Xiǎng zǒu jiù zǒu ba.
  Leave if you want to.
- 想买就买，不用问我。
  Xiǎng mǎi jiù mǎi, bùyòng wèn wǒ.
  If you want to buy it, go ahead. You don't need to ask me.
- 别害怕，想说就说。
  Bié hàipà, xiǎng shuō jiù shuō.
  Don't be afraid. If you want to say, say it.
- 想做就做，考虑那么多干吗？
  Xiǎng zuò jiù zuò, kǎolǜ nàme duō gànmá?
  If you want to do it, do it. Why do you need to think about it so much?

Advanced Pattern

You can also add in a question word, like 什么, 哪儿, or 怎么. When this is the case, the pronouns don't necessarily refer to anything specific. They can be seen more as words like "whatever" or "wherever." This way, question pronouns (什么, 谁, 什么时候,etc) serve as "indefinite references."

Structure

想 + Verb + [Question Word] + 就 + Verb + [Question Word]

Examples

- 想去哪儿就去哪儿。
  Xiǎng qù nǎr jiù qù nǎr.
  You can go wherever you'd like to go.
- 想请谁就请谁。
  Xiǎng qǐng shéi jiù qǐng shéi.
  You can invite whoever you like.
- 想什么时候来就什么时候来。
  Xiǎng shénme shíhou lái jiù shénme shíhou lái.
  You can come whenever you like.
- 想点什么就点什么，我请客。
  Xiǎng diǎn shénme jiù diǎn shénme, wǒ qǐngkè.
  You can order whatever you like. I'm buying.
- 这些钱我想怎么花就怎么花。
  Zhèxiē qián wǒ xiǎng zěnme huā jiù zěnme huā.
  I will spend this money however I like.

Similar to

- Conditions with “yao” and “jiu” (B2)

Expressing "double negation" (B1)

There are two main methods for double negation. The simpler method is to use a double negative with modal verbs like 会 or 能. The more complicated method is to negate both the subject and the predicate.

Negation Before a Negative Word

Structure

This pattern just uses 不是 right before a negated predicate:

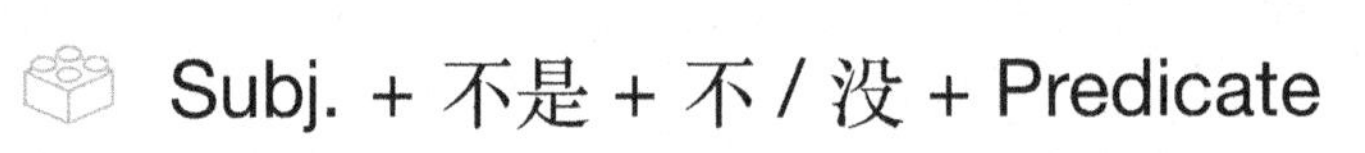

This pattern uses modal verbs like 会, 能, or 可能, which are negated before a negated predicate:

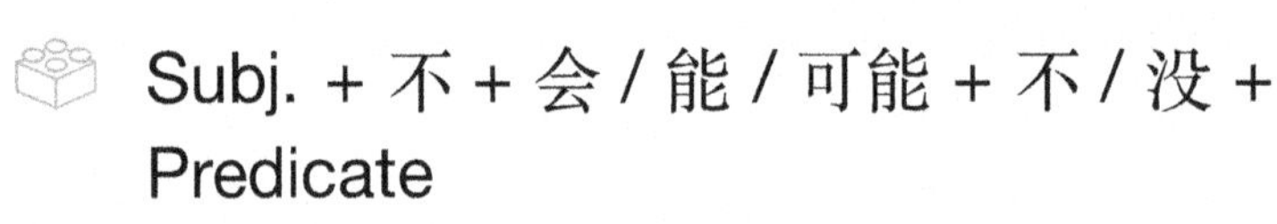

The predicate part of either pattern can be a verb or an adjective.

Examples

- 他不会不来的。
  Tā bù huì bù lái de.
  There is no way he's not coming.
- 她不可能不知道。
  Tā bù kěnéng bù zhīdào.
  There is no way she doesn't know about this.
- 她太害羞了，不是不礼貌。
  Tā tài hàixiū le, bù shì bù lǐmào.
  She's too shy; It's not that she's not polite.
- 他不是没有钱，是不想乱花钱。
  Tā bù shì méiyǒu qián, shì bù xiǎng luàn huā qián.
  It's not that he doesn't have money; it's just he doesn't want to spend it recklessly.

- 我知道你想减肥，但是不能不吃早饭。
  Wǒ zhīdào nǐ xiǎng jiǎnféi, dànshì bù néng bù chī zǎofàn.
  I know you want to lose weight, but you can't not eat breakfast.

Negation Before a Singular Noun

This structure is used for saying things like "not a single one," often with topic comments[1]. 没有一个人 ("not a single person") is equivalent to 没有谁 ("not anyone").

Structure

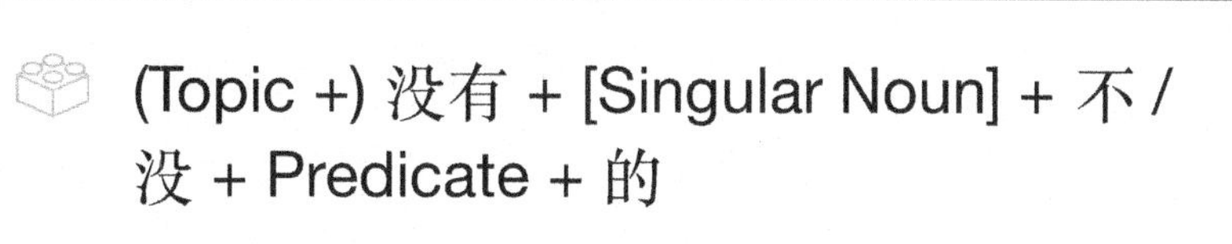
(Topic +) 没有 + [Singular Noun] + 不 / 没 + Predicate + 的

Examples

- 没有一个人不讨厌他的。
  Méiyǒu yī gè rén bù tǎoyàn tā de.
  There is not one person who doesn't dislike him.
- 这些菜没有一个不辣的。
  Zhèxiē cài méiyǒu yī gè bù là de.
  There is no single one that is not spicy among these dishes.
- 我们公司的员工没有一个不会说英语的。
  Wǒmen gōngsī de yuángōng méiyǒu yī gè bù huì shuō Yīngyǔ de.
  Our company doesn't have a single employee who can't speak English.
- 他的女朋友没有一个不漂亮的。
  Tā de nǚpéngyou méiyǒu yī gè bù piàoliang de.
  None of his girlfriends were not beautiful.
- 我们学校的学生没有一个没参加高考的。
  Wǒmen xuéxiào de xuéshēng méiyǒu yī gè méi cānjiā gāokǎo de.
  In our school there wasn't a single student who didn't take the national college entrance exam.

---

1. Topic-comment sentences (B1), page 251

Expressing "even" with "lian" and "dou" (B1)

连……都……(lián... dōu...) is used similarly to how *even* is used in English and can emphasize certain surprising pieces of information. The tricky part about using it is that you have to remember to use *both* parts of the pattern (rather than just throwing in one word, like "even" in English).

Used Before the Subject

Structure

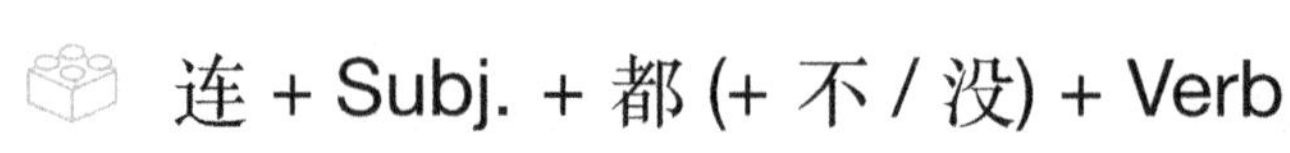
连 + Subj. + 都 (+ 不 / 没) + Verb

Sometimes 也 (yě) is used instead of 都 (dōu), and the two are interchangeable for this pattern, but 都 is more commonly used with 连 (lián), so it's the one we'll use exclusively here.

Examples

- 这个问题太简单了，连三岁小孩都知道。
  Zhège wèntí tài jiǎndān le, lián sān suì xiǎohái dōu zhīdào.
  This question is so easy that even a three-year-old kid knows the answer.
- 这个汉字太难了，连我的中文老师都不认识。
  Zhège Hànzì tài nán le, lián wǒ de Zhōngwén lǎoshī dōu bù rènshi.
  This Chinese character is so difficult that even my Chinese teacher doesn't know it.
- 他很可怜，连他妈妈都不管他。
  Tā hěn kělián, lián tā māma dōu bù guǎn tā.
  The poor child. Even his mother doesn't care about him.
- 她什么都放辣，连汤都是辣的。
  Tā shénme dōu fàng là, lián tāng dōu shì là de.
  She put spice in everything. Even the soup is spicy.
- 你们算什么好朋友？他连结婚都没请你。
  Nǐmen suàn shénme hǎo péngyou, tā lián jiéhūn dōu méi qǐng nǐ.
  What kind of "good friend" are you to him? He didn't even invite you to his wedding.

Note that 都 can't be omitted in any of these sentences. You really need *both parts of the pattern*.

- ✘ 这个问题太简单了，连三岁小孩知道。
  Zhège wèntí tài jiǎndān le, lián sān suì xiǎohái zhīdào.

× 你们算什么好朋友？他 连 结婚 没 请你。

Nǐmen suàn shénme hǎo péngyou? Tā lián jiéhūn méi qǐng nǐ.

Used Before the Object

Note that for this pattern, the object moves to the front of the sentence instead of coming after the verb as it normally does. After you move the object to the front of the sentence, you can use 连 before the object and 都 before the verb or verb phrase.

Structure

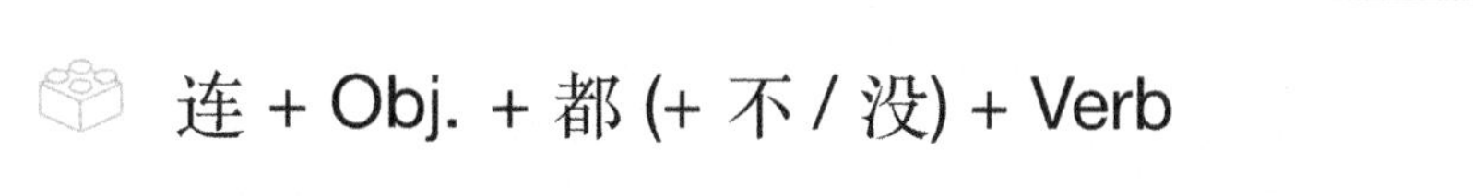

连 + Obj. + 都 (+ 不 / 没) + Verb

Examples

- 他什么都吃，连 狗肉 都 吃。

  Tā shénme dōu chī, lián gǒu ròu dōu chī.

  He eats everything, even dog meat.

- 你 连 你最好的朋友 都 不 相信？

  Nǐ lián nǐ zuìhǎo de péngyou dōu bù xiāngxìn?

  You don't even trust your best friend?

- 你 连 麦当劳 都 吃不起吗？

  Nǐ lián Màidāngláo dōu chī bu qǐ ma?

  You can't even afford a meal at McDonald's?

If the object the comes after 连 is a whole sentence, there must be a specific interrogative pronoun (a "question word") in the sentence.

- 你 连 她叫 什么 都 没 问？

  Nǐ lián tā jiào shénme dōu méi wèn?

  You didn't even ask what her name is?

- 你怎么了？连 你住 在哪儿 都 不 记得了？

  Nǐ zěnme le? Lián nǐ zhù zàinǎr dōu bù jìde le?

  Are you OK? You can't even remember where you live?

- 她是你女朋友？你 连 人家姓 什么 都 不 知道。

  Tā shì nǐ nǚpéngyou? Nǐ lián rénjia xìng shénme dōu bù zhīdào.

  She's your girlfriend? You don't even know what her last name is.

Avoidance

If you're an intermediate learner and find yourself *never* using this pattern, you're not alone. That's fairly typical. And the truth is that you *can* get away with not actively using it for a pretty long time. Eventually you'll get more comfortable with it, but it probably won't come as naturally as some other patterns.

Similar to

- Expressing "even" with "shenzhi" (B2)
- Expressing "let alone" with "bie shuo" (B2)
- Expressing "let alone" with "geng buyong shuo" (B2)
- Expressing "not even one" (B2)

Expressing "every time" with "mei" and "dou" (B1)

每次……都……(měi cì... dōu...) is a pattern used to express "every time." Translating from English, you might feel that the only part really needed is 每次 (měi cì), since it literally means "every time." This is incorrect! Not only is the adverb 都 (dōu) *required*, but it's arguably more vital than the 每次 (měi cì)! So it's important to get used to using both parts.

Structure

This pattern actually builds on the basic 每……都…… pattern, which you should already know. In this grammar structure, we go beyond just saying things like "every person" or "every day," and focus on what happens ***every time** a certain action is done.*

每次 + Event 1 + 都 + Event 2

Examples

- 她 每次 来我家 都 带花。
  Tā měi cì lái wǒ jiā dōu dài huā.
  She brings flowers every time she visits me.
- 为什么 每次 我来他 都 不在?
  Wèishénme měi cì wǒ lái tā dōu bù zài?
  How come he's not here every time I come?
- 我 每次 玩这个游戏 都 输。
  Wǒ měi cì wán zhège yóuxì dōu shū.
  Every time I play this game, I lose.
- 你怎么 每次 吃火锅 都 拉肚子?
  Nǐ zěnme měicì chī huǒguō dōu lādùzi?
  How come you have diarrhea every time you eat hotpot?
- 他 每次 迟到 都 说因为堵车。
  Tā měicì chídào dōu shuō yīnwèi dǔchē.
  Every time he's late, he says it's because of bad traffic.
- 我 每次 经过这家店 都 会进去看看。
  Wǒ měi cì jīngguò zhè jiā diàn dōu huì jìnqù kànkan.
  Every time I pass this shop, I go inside and take a look.

- 我妹妹 每次 打针 都 哭。
  Wǒ mèimei měicì dǎzhēn dōu kū.
  My little sister cries every time she has to get a shot.
- 每次 遇到生词他 都 要查字典。
  Měi cì yùdào shēngcí tā dōu yào chá zìdiǎn.
  Every time he comes across a new word, he looks it up in the dictionary.
- 每次 编辑 都 要保存。
  Měi cì biānjí dōu yào bǎocún.
  Every time you edit, you need to save it.
- 爸爸 每次 出差 都 给我买礼物。
  Bàba měi cì chūchāi dōu gěi wǒ mǎi lǐwù.
  Dad buys presents for me every time he goes on business trips.

Similar to

- The "all" adverb "dou" (A1)
- Emphasizing quantity with "dou" (A2)
- Expressing "every" with "mei" (A2)
- Expressing "all" with "suoyou" (B1), page 232
- Indicating the whole with "quan" (B1), page 8
- Measure words for verbs (B1), page 192

Expressing "every" with question words (B1)

This grammar point is not about how to use 每 (měi) to mean "every," but rather how to combine question words with 都 (dōu) to make words and phrases like "everywhere" or "everyone." You may have learned this same pattern for expressing "everything," but now it's time to extend it.

"Everyone" with 谁都

谁都 (shéi dōu) is a pattern used to express "everyone" (or possibly "anyone") in Chinese. The placement of the question word 谁 is very similar to the way 什么 (shénme) can be used to express "every", along with other question words like 哪儿 (nǎr) and 多少 (duōshao).

Structure

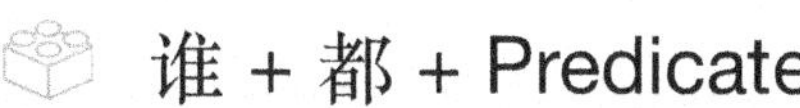

谁 + 都 + Predicate

The predicate part of the pattern can be a verb or an adjective.

Examples

- 谁 都 喜欢美食。
  Shéi dōu xǐhuan měishí.
  Everyone likes delicious food.
- 谁 都 可以进。
  Shéi dōu kěyǐ jìn.
  Everyone can come in.
- 谁 都 不相信他说的话。
  Shéi dōu bù xiāngxìn tā shuō de huà.
  No one believes what he said.

"Everywhere" with 哪儿都

This pattern works with both 哪儿 (nǎr) and 哪里 (nǎlǐ).

Structure

哪儿 / 哪里 (+ Verb) + 都 + Predicate

Examples

- 他的房间里 哪儿 都 是脏衣服。
  Tā de fángjiān lǐ nǎr dōu shì zāng yīfu.
  His dirty laundry is all over his room.
- 我太累了，哪儿 都 不想去。
  Wǒ tài lèi le, nǎr dōu bù xiǎng qù.
  I'm too tired. I don't want to go anywhere.
- 在 哪里 见面 都 行。
  Zài nǎlǐ jiànmiàn dōu xíng.
  I'm fine with meeting anywhere.

"Whenever" with 什么时候都

什么时候 (shénme shíhou) combines with 都 (dōu) to mean "whenever" or "anytime."

Structure

什么时候 (+ Verb) + 都 + Predicate

Examples

- 什么时候 都 可以。
  Shénme shíhou dōu kěyǐ.
  Anytime is fine.
- 你 什么时候 来 都 欢迎。
  Nǐ shénme shíhou lái dōu huānyíng.
  You're welcome to come anytime.
- 什么时候 开始 都 不晚。
  Shénme shíhou kāishǐ dōu bù wǎn.
  It's never too late to start.

"However Much" with 多少都

多少 (duōshao) also works with 都 in this case.

Structure

Verb + 多少 + 都 + Predicate

Examples

- 你想吃 多少 都 可以。
  Nǐ xiǎng chī duōshao dōu kěyǐ.
  You can eat however much you want.
- 这些是免费的，我们拿 多少 都 没问题。
  Zhèxiē shì miǎnfèi de, wǒmen ná duōshao dōu méi wèntí.
  These are all free. We can take as much as we want.
- 我跟他说 多少 遍 都 没有用。
  Wǒ gēn tā shuō duōshao biàn dōu méiyǒu yòng.
  It doesn't matter how many times I tell him.

"However" with 怎么都

怎么 (zěnme) also works with 都.

Structure

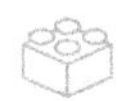 怎么 + Verb + 都 + Predicate

Examples

- 怎么 做 都 可以吗?
  Zěnme zuò dōu kěyǐ ma?
  It's OK if I do it however I want?
- 这些钱你 怎么 花 都 行。
  Zhèxiē qián nǐ zěnme huā dōu xíng.
  You can spend this money however you like.
- 别人 怎么 想 都 不重要。
  Biérén zěnme xiǎng dōu bù zhòngyào.
  It's not important what other people think.

Similar to

- Expressing "everything" with "shenme dou" (A2)
- Expressing "all" with "suoyou" (B1), page 232
- Expressing "some" with question words (B1), page 287

Expressing "how often" (B1)

Asking "how often" is one of those things that seems so simple in English but relatively complicated in Chinese. The way to ask in Chinese is, literally, "how long of a time" (do something) "one time." So you'll need the phrases 多长时间 (duō cháng shíjiān) and 一次 (yī cì).

Asking About Frequency

In English you let the person answering the question decide both the length of time and how many times an action is done within that timeframe. So if you ask "how often," you might get an answer like "twice a week." But in Chinese, the frequency is fixed at "once" as part of the question. That actually won't stop people from answering "twice a week" in Chinese, though; it's just how the question is normally phrased in Chinese.

Structure

> Subj. + 多长时间 + Verb + 一次 (+ Obj.)

Examples

- ✗ 你多长时间踢球一次？
  Nǐ duō cháng shíjiān tīqiú yī cì?
- ✓ 你多长时间踢一次球？
  Nǐ duō cháng shíjiān tī yī cì qiú?
  How often do you play soccer?
- ✗ 你多长时间剪头发一次？
  Nǐ duō cháng shíjiān jiǎn tóufa yī cì?
- ✓ 你多长时间剪一次头发？
  Nǐ duō cháng shíjiān jiǎn yī cì tóufa?
  How often do you cut your hair?
- ✗ 你多长时间刮胡子一次？
  Nǐ duō cháng shíjiān guā húzi yī cì?
- ✓ 你多长时间刮一次胡子？
  Nǐ duō cháng shíjiān guā yī cì húzi?
  How often do you shave?

Talking About Frequency in General

Structure

Subj. + [Length of Time] + Verb + Times (+ Obj.)

Examples

- 我 一周 给妈妈打 两次 电话。
  Wǒ yī zhōu gěi māma dǎ liǎng cì diànhuà.
  I give mom a call twice a week.
- 我们公司 一周 开 一次 会。
  Wǒmen gōngsī yī zhōu kāi yī cì huì.
  Our company holds one meeting per week.
- 我 两个月 剪 一次 头发。
  Wǒ liǎng gè yuè jiǎn yī cì tóufa.
  I cut my hair every two months.
- 我的手机 两天 充 一次 电。
  Wǒ de shǒujī liǎng tiān chōng yī cì diàn.
  I charge my phone every two days.
- 这种药 四个小时 吃 一次 。
  Zhè zhǒng yào sì gè xiǎoshí chī yī cì .
  Take this medicine every four hours.
- 你应该 半年 做 一次 体检。
  Nǐ yīnggāi bàn nián zuò yī cì tǐjiǎn.
  You should have a physical examination every half year.

When NOT to Use This Pattern

The thing about using the pattern above is that it's expected that the activity is done *regularly*, as part of a *habit*. If it's not an activity that's regularly engaged in, it's weird to use the pattern. Consider the following examples:

⚠ 你 多长时间 换 一个 手机?
Nǐ duō cháng shíjiān huàn yī gè shǒujī?
How often do you buy a new cell phone?

⚠ 你 多长时间 加 一次 班?

Nǐ duō cháng shíjiān jiā yī cì bān?

How often do you work overtime?

⚠ 你 多长时间 吃 一次 牛油果?

Nǐ duō cháng shíjiān chī yī cì niúyóuguǒ?

How often do you eat avocado?

In these cases, the speaker is trying to get any idea of how often the other person does something, regardless of how regular or habitual it is. In this case, just use 经常 (or similar) to ask about it.

✔ 你 经常 换手机吗?

Nǐ jīngcháng huàn shǒujī ma?

Do you often buy a new cell phone?

✔ 你 经常 加班吗?

Nǐ jīngcháng jiābān ma?

Do you often work late?

✔ 你 很少 吃牛油果吧?

Nǐ hěnshǎo chī niúyóuguǒ ba?

You rarely eat avocado, right?

Expressing "more and more" with "yuelaiyue" (B1)

越来越 (yuèláiyuè) is used frequently in Chinese to express that some quality or state is increasing with time and is often translated into English as "more and more." This is the simple form of this pattern, which uses 来, but there is also a more complex one (which uses two different adjectives/verbs).

Used with Adjectives

This structure expresses that something is becoming more and more *adjective* over time, with the latter adjective changing with the verb. The most common structure is:

Structure

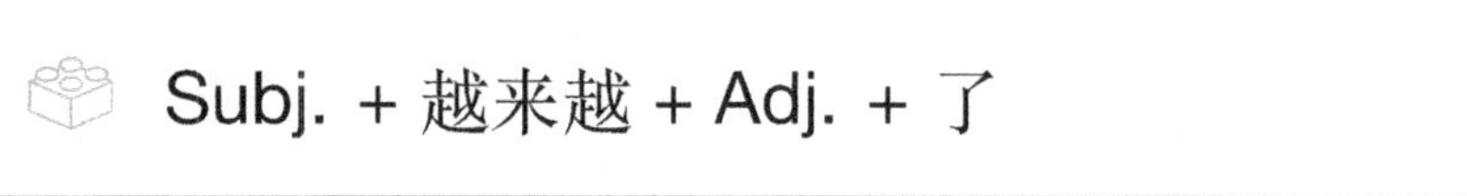

Subj. + 越来越 + Adj. + 了

Examples

- 天气 越来越 冷 了 。
  Tiānqì yuèláiyuè lěng le .
  The weather is getting colder and colder.
- 你女儿 越来越 漂亮 了 。
  Nǐ nǚér yuèláiyuè piàoliang le .
  Your daughter is getting more and more beautiful.
- 你说得 越来越 好 了 。
  Nǐ shuō de yuèláiyuè hǎo le .
  You speak better and better.
- 技术 越来越 发达 了 。
  Jìshù yuèláiyuè fādá le .
  Technology is getting more and more developed.
- 空气污染 越来越 严重 了 。
  Kōngqì wūrǎn yuèláiyuè yánzhòng le .
  The air pollution is getting worse and worse.

Used with Verbs

Structure

 Subj. + 越来越 + Verb + 了

Examples

- 我 越来越 喜欢上海 了 。
  Wǒ yuèláiyuè xǐhuan Shànghǎi le .
  I like Shanghai more and more.
- 你 越来越 了解我 了 。
  Nǐ yuèláiyuè liǎojiě wǒ le .
  You know me better and better.
- 我 越来越 理解我的父母 了 。
  Wǒ yuèláiyuè lǐjiě wǒ de fùmǔ le .
  I understand my parents more and more.

When the verb is negative in Chinese, a translation like "less and less" with a positive verb might be more appropriate in English than sticking with a "more and more" translation. The Chinese pattern doesn't change, though.

- 我 越来越 不 相信他 了 。
  Wǒ yuèláiyuè bù xiāngxìn tā le .
  I believe him less and less.
- 你 越来越 不 懂我 了 。
  Nǐ yuèláiyuè bù dǒng wǒ le .
  You understand me less and less.

Similar to

- Expressing "even more" with "geng" (A2)
- Expressing "along with· · ·" with "suizhe" (B2)
- Expressing "the more… the more…" with "yue· · · yue· · ·" (B2)

Expressing "multiples" with "bei" (B1)

The word 倍 (bèi) is used to express the idea of multiples, as in "3 *times* as many" or "5 *times* more." Its usage can be a little tricky (different from English), so pay close attention to the pattern below.

Directly Expressing Multiples

For this pattern, we're stating *how many times more* amount A is compared to amount B. Pretty straightforward.

Structure

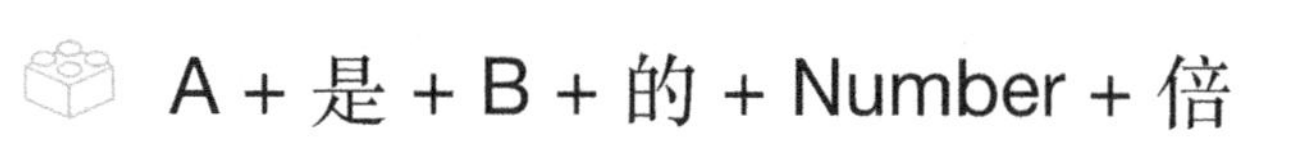

Examples

- 他现在的工资 是 两年前的四 倍 。
  Tā xiànzài de gōngzī shì liǎng nián qián de sì bèi.
  His current salary is four times what it was two years ago.
- 公司现在的规模 是 十年前的五 倍 。
  Gōngsī xiànzài de guīmó shì shí nián qián de wǔ bèi.
  The company's current scope is five times what it was 10 years ago.
- 今年的产量 是 去年的两 倍 。
  Jīnnián de chǎnliàng shì qùnián de liǎng bèi.
  This year's output is twice as much as last year's.

Expressing "More" with Multiples

This pattern involves an adjective, one of the most common being 多 ("many"). You'll see other adjectives related to quantity appearing in this pattern as well, such as 大 ("big"), 贵 ("expensive"), 高 ("tall"), 长 ("long"), etc. In Chinese, it is not common to use the "negative opposite" adjectives in these kinds of comparisons, so you won't normally see the words for "small," "cheap," "short," etc. appearing in this pattern.

Structure

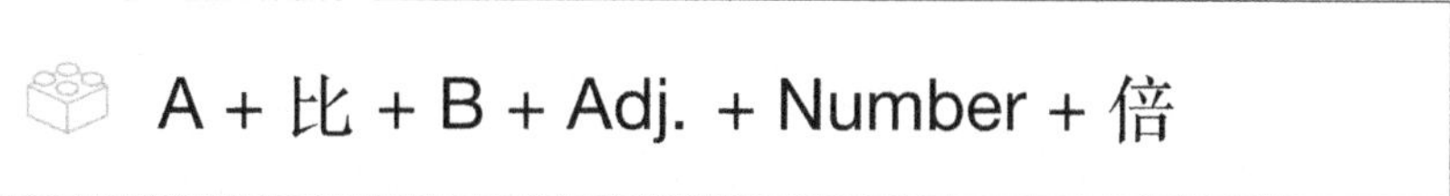

One very important linguistic difference between English and Chinese to note here is that in Chinese, you're typically talking about how many multiples *in addition* to the original amount. So 多一倍 is "x + 1x," in other words "double" the original amount.

Naturally, 多两倍 would be *triple* the original amount (x + 2x). This little detail is sometimes confusing even for native speakers, so if you're talking about multiples and 多 is involved, be sure to use actual numbers to confirm both sides are on the same page!

Examples

- 我家客厅 比 你家客厅 大 一 倍 。
  Wǒ jiā kètīng bǐ nǐ jiā kètīng dà yī bèi.
  My home's living room is double the size of your home's living room.
- 这个 15 岁的男孩 比 一般的孩子 重 一 倍 。
  Zhège shíwǔ suì de nánhái bǐ yībān de háizi zhòng yī bèi.
  This fifteen-year-old kid weighs double what a normal kid at his age should weigh.
- 你的速度 比 我们 快 两 倍 。
  Nǐ de sùdù bǐ wǒmen kuài liǎng bèi.
  Your speed is three times as fast as our speed.
- 他现在的工资 比 两年前 多 了三 倍 。
  Tā xiànzài de gōngzī bǐ liǎng nián qián duō le sān bèi.
  His salary is four times higher now than what it was two years ago.
- 中国人口 比 美国人口 多 四 倍 。
  Zhōngguó rénkǒu bǐ Měiguó rénkǒu duō sì bèi.
  China's population is five times as large as the USA's.
- 他的车 比 你的车 贵 十 倍 。
  Tā de chē bǐ nǐ de chē guì shí bèi.
  His car is 11 times more expensive than your car.

Similar to

- Expressing "compared with" using "gen" (B1), page 296
- Expressing fractions with "fenzhi" (B1), page 118

Expressing "not at all" with "yidianr ye bu" (B1)

Sometimes we may want to say something is "not even the least bit [adjective]." For example, we might say in English: "I am not at all hungry." In Chinese, we can use 一点 (儿) 也不 (yīdiǎnr yě bù) or 一点 (儿) 都不 (yīdiǎnr dōu bù) to express "not at all [adjective]."

Used with Adjectives

The phrases 一点 (儿) 也不 and 一点 (儿) 都不 can both be used to express "not at all."

Structure

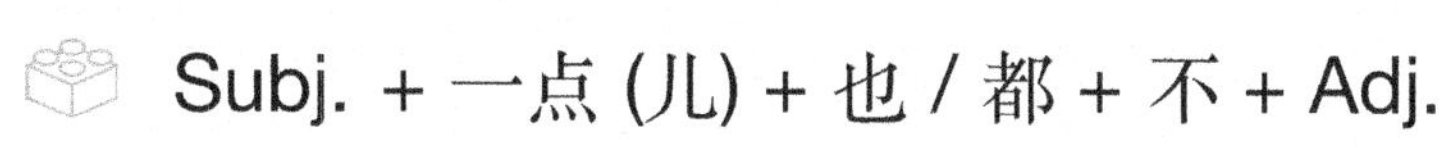

Subj. + 一点 (儿) + 也 / 都 + 不 + Adj.

Examples

- 那个问题 一点儿也不 难。
  Nàge wèntí yīdiǎnr yě bù nán.
  That question isn't difficult at all.
- 这个菜 一点都不 好吃。
  Zhège cài yīdiǎn dōu bù hǎochī.
  This dish isn't tasty at all.
- 我同事 一点都不 幽默。
  Wǒ tóngshì yīdiǎn dōu bù yōumò.
  My colleague is not humorous at all.
- 这个笑话 一点也不 好笑。
  Zhège xiàohua yīdiǎn yě bù hǎoxiào.
  This joke isn't funny at all.

Used with Verbs

This describes the subject as being "not at all *adjective*" or "not even slightly *adjective*." Psychological verbs can also appear in place of the adjective in this structure.

Structure

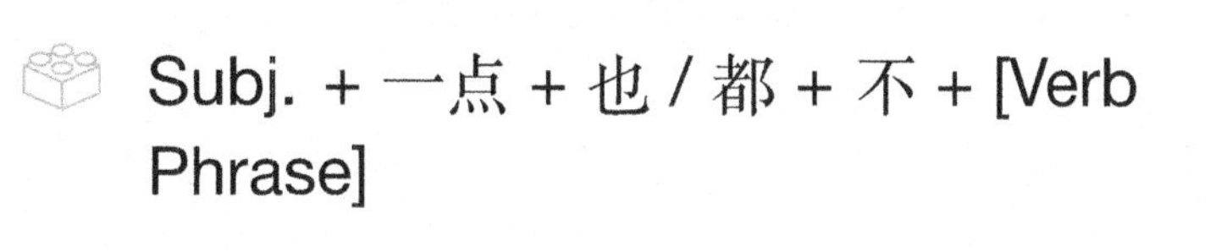

Subj. + 一点 + 也 / 都 + 不 + [Verb Phrase]

If the verb has an object, it sometimes gets moved to the front of the sentence.

Examples

- 我 一点也不 喜欢奶酪。
  Wǒ yīdiǎn yě bù xǐhuan nǎilào.
  I don't like cheese at all.
- 你 一点也不 会说吗?
  Nǐ yīdiǎn yě bù huì shuō ma?
  You can't speak at all?
- 她 一点都不 知道这件事。
  Tā yīdiǎn dōu bù zhīdào zhè jiàn shì.
  She doesn't know about this at all.
- 我儿子 一点都不 爱玩游戏。
  Wǒ érzi yīdiǎn dōu bù ài wán yóuxì.
  My son doesn't like to play games at all.

The phrases "一点也没" and "一点都没" can also be used to express "not at all ." This is used when the statement uses or implies the verb negative form of 有 in the past.

- 我 一点也 没 生气。
  Wǒ yīdiǎn yě méi shēngqì.
  I wasn't angry at all.
- 她 一点都 没 准备。
  Tā yīdiǎn dōu méi zhǔnbèi.
  She didn't prepare at all.
- 作业他 一点都 没 做?
  Zuòyè tā yīdiǎn dōu méi zuò?
  He didn't do his homework at all?
  The object 作业 got moved to the front
- 这个菜你们怎么 一点也 没 吃?
  Zhège cài nǐmen zěnme yīdiǎn yě méi chī?
  Why didn't you eat this dish at all?
  The object 这个菜 got moved to the front

Similar to

- Expressing "everything" with "shenme dou" (A2)
- Comparing "youdian" and "yidian" (B1), page 338
- Expressing "not even one" (B2)

Expressing "some" with question words (B1)

Chinese question words can play a double role. As we know, they are used in questions, but they can also mean "some." The "some" we refer to is the vague, undefined "some," as in "somewhere," "someone," "something," or "sometime."

"Somewhere" with 哪儿

This one is often used with Verb + 过.

Examples:

- 这个人我在 哪儿 见过。
  Zhège rén wǒ zài nǎr jiàn guo.
  I've met this person somewhere before.
- 这首歌我在 哪儿 听过。
  Zhè shǒu gē wǒ zài nǎr tīng guo.
  I've heard this song somewhere.
- 这篇文章我们在 哪儿 看过。
  Zhè piān wénzhāng wǒmen zài nǎr kàn guo.
  I've read this article somewhere before.

"Someone" with 谁

Examples:

- 你让 谁 来帮我一下。
  Nǐ ràng shéi lái bāng wǒ yīxià.
  Ask someone to help me with this.
- 这件事我听 谁 说过。
  Zhè jiàn shì wǒ tīng shéi shuō guo.
  I've heard somebody talk about this before.
- 你找 谁 带你进去吧。
  Nǐ zhǎo shéi dài nǐ jìnqù ba.
  You should find someone to take you inside.

"Something" with 什么

This one is often used with 点 (儿) before the verb.

Examples:

- 我们应该做点儿 什么 。
  Wǒmen yīnggāi zuò diǎnr shénme.
  We should do something.
- 老大，你不说点儿 什么 ？
  Lǎodà, nǐ bù shuō diǎnr shénme?
  Boss, aren't you going to say something?
- 我想喝点儿 什么 。
  Wǒ xiǎng hē diǎnr shénme.
  I want to drink something.

"Sometime" with 什么时候

Careful with this one! If you're not paying attention, you might think that it's a question asking "when," but in reality it might just be polite noise. If the lack of question intonation isn't enough, the 吧 on the end is also a clue that these sentences aren't actually questions.

Examples:

- 什么时候 我们见面谈吧。
  Shénme shíhou wǒmen jiànmiàn tán ba.
  Let's meet and talk about this sometime.
- 什么时候 来我新家玩吧。
  Shénme shíhou lái wǒ xīn jiā wán ba.
  You should come to my new house to hangout sometime.
- 我们 什么时候 去看看他吧。
  Wǒmen shénme shíhou qù kànkan tā ba.
  Let's pay him a visit sometime.

Similar to

- Expressing "every" with question words (B1), page 275

Expressing not knowing how to do something using "hao" (B1)

不知道……好 (bù zhīdào… hǎo) is an expression used to indicate and emphasize that the speaker does not know how to do something or at least does not know how to do something well.

Structure

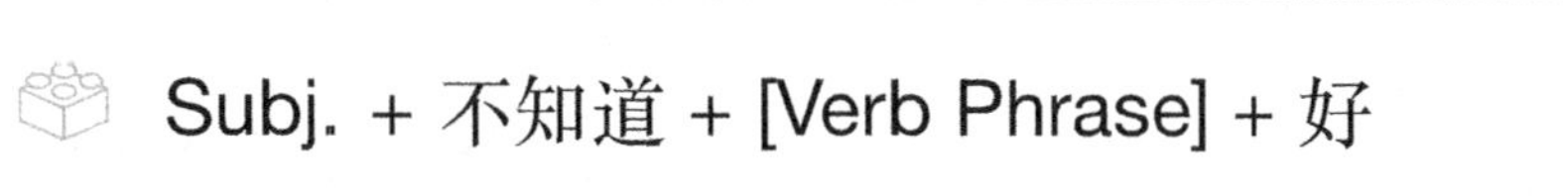

Subj. + 不知道 + [Verb Phrase] + 好

This verb phrase usually includes a question word, like 什么, 谁, 怎么, 哪个, 哪里, 什么时候, etc.

You will sometimes see the adverb 才 preceding the 好, which serves the purpose of emphasis.

Examples

- 我真的不知道怎么办才好。
  Wǒ zhēnde bù zhīdào zěnme bàn cái hǎo.
  I really don't know what to do about this .
- 我们都不知道说什么好。
  Wǒmen dōu bù zhīdào shuō shénme hǎo.
  None of us knew what to say.
- 这件事我不知道跟谁说好。
  Zhè jiàn shì wǒ bù zhīdào gēn shéi shuō hǎo.
  I'm not sure who to talk to about this matter.
- 老板不知道怪谁好。
  Lǎobǎn bù zhīdào guài shéi hǎo.
  The boss wasn't sure who to blame.
- 他的短信我不知道怎么回复好。
  Tā de duǎnxìn wǒ bù zhīdào zěnme huífù hǎo.
  I don't know how to reply to his text.
- 这些钱他不知道放在哪儿才好。
  Zhèxiē qián tā bù zhīdào fàng zài nǎr cái hǎo.
  He doesn't know where to put this money.

- 下雨天我 不知道 带孩子去 哪儿 玩 好 。
  Xiàyǔ tiān wǒ bù zhīdào dài hāizi qù nǎr wán hǎo.
  On rainy days, I don't know where to take my kid to play.
- 都很漂亮，我 不知道 买 哪件 好 。
  Dōu hěn piàoliang, wǒ bù zhīdào mǎi nǎ jiàn hǎo.
  They're all so pretty. I'm not sure which one to buy.
- 好吃的太多了，孩子们 不知道 先吃 哪个 才 好 。
  Hǎochī de tài duō le, háizi men bù zhīdào xiān chī nǎge cái hǎo.
  There was so much delicious food that the children didn't know where to start eating.
- 我想问，可是 不知道 什么时候 问 才 好 。
  Wǒ xiǎng wèn, kěshì bù zhīdào shénme shíhou wèn cái hǎo.
  I want to ask, but I'm not sure when to ask.

Similar to

- Result complements (B1), page 227
- Expressing difficulty with "hao (bu) rongyi" (B2)

Expressing purpose with "weile" (B1)

为了 (wèile) is most often used to indicate the purpose of an action or the person that will benefit from some act of kindness. In the "purpose" sense, it almost exactly corresponds to "in order to" or "for the purpose of" in English.

Basic Usage

When 为了 indicates the purpose of an action, it's usually acting as a preposition. In this role, the *whole* "为了 phrase" should come **before** the verb.

Structure

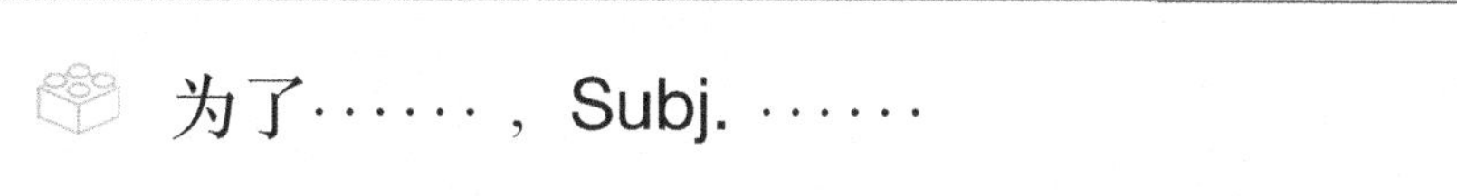

Note also that 为了 is a single word; the 了 here is not serving its role as a particle in this case.

Examples

- 为了 钱，他什么都愿意做。
  Wèile qián, tā shénme dōu yuànyì zuò.
  He's willing to do anything for money.
- 为了 孩子的未来，他决定搬到上海。
  Wèile háizi de wèilái, tā juédìng bāndào Shànghǎi.
  He decided to move to Shanghai for his children's future.
- 为了 这个面试，他买了一套很贵的西服。
  Wèile zhège miànshì, tā mǎi le yī tào hěn guì de xīfú.
  He bought a very expensive suit for this job interview.
- 为了 找灵感，那个作家搬到了农村。
  Wèile zhǎo línggǎn, nàge zuòjiā bān dào le nóngcūn.
  In order to find inspiration, that writer moved to the countryside.
- 五年前，为了 女朋友，他放弃了上海的工作。
  wǔniánqián, Wèile nǚpéngyǒu, tā fàngqì le Shànghǎi de gōngzuò.
  Five years ago he passed up a job in Shanghai for his girlfriend.
- 为了 奖励大家，公司明年带你们去日本旅行。
  Wèile jiǎnglì dàjiā, gōngsī míngnián dài nǐmen qù Rìběn lǚxíng.
  In order to reward everyone, the company will take you all on a trip to Japan next year.

Expressing "the Reason Why"

Sometimes you will see 为了 following 是. In this case, 为了 mean "for." Note that 为了 and 因为 both have the character 为 in them, and they have sort of similar meanings. You will also see 因为 following 是, instead of 为了. It literally means "is because (of)."

Structure

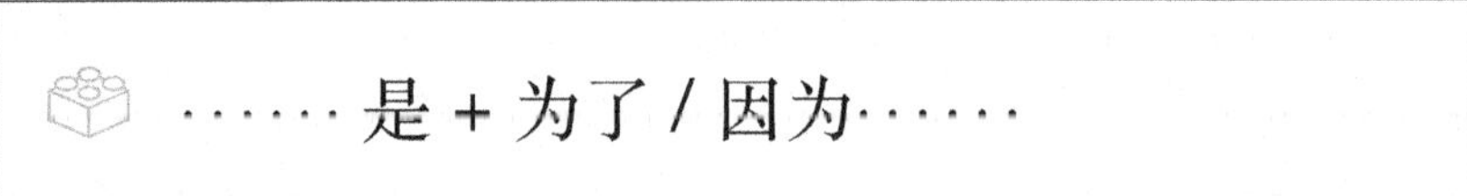

Example

- 我这么做 是为了 帮你。

  Wǒ zhème zuò shì wèile bāng nǐ.

  I did all this to help you.

- 他做兼职 是为了 多赚点钱。

  Tā zuò jiānzhí shì wèile duō zhuàn diǎn qián.

  The reason why he has a part time job is to make a little more money.

- 你学中文 是因为 你的中国女朋友吗?

  Nǐ xué Zhōngwén shì yīnwèi nǐde Zhōngguó nǚpéngyou ma?

  Are you studying Chinese because of your Chinese girlfriend?

- 我们之所以反对 是因为 风险太大。

  Wǒmen zhī suǒyǐ fǎnduì shì yīnwèi fēngxiǎn tài dà.

  The reason why we oppose it is because the risk is too high.

Note that 之所以 is a more difficult pattern, which means "the reason why" in a more formal way.

Similar to

- Expressing "for" with "wei" (B1), page 141
- Expressing "in this way" with "zheyang" (B1), page 59
- Using "lai" to connect two verb phrases (B1), page 107
- Expressing purpose with "hao" (B2)
- Stating the effect before the cause (B2)
- Explaining purpose with "wei… er…" (C1)

Phrases using "laishuo" (B1)

Although the different phrases involving 来说 (láishuō) may seem pretty different, they do share a common structure: a word or short phrase at the beginning of a sentence, followed by 来说, sets the speaker's attitude or point of view before launching into the full comment.

Colloquial Saying 对⋯⋯来说

In English we say "to someone" or "for someone," followed by some information about their particular view or circumstances. In Chinese, the pattern is 对⋯⋯来说 (duì... lái shuō).

Structure

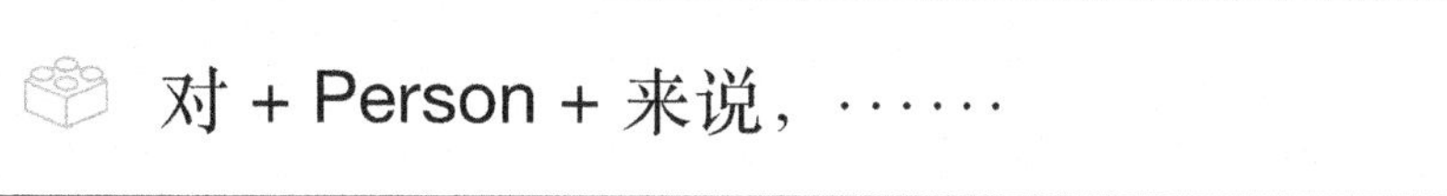

The predicate part of the pattern can be a verb or an adjective.

Examples

- 对 我 来说，中文不容易。
  Duì wǒ lái shuō, Zhōngwén bù róngyì.
  For me, Chinese is not easy.
- 对 你 来说，家庭重要还是工作重要？
  Duì nǐ lái shuō, jiātíng zhòngyào háishì gōngzuò zhòngyào?
  Is family or work more important to you?
- 对 孩子 来说，这个问题太复杂了。
  Duì háizi lái shuō, zhège wèntí tài fùzá le.
  This question is too complicated for kids.

Common Phrases

Structure

These are set phrases that you need to learn individually, but they follow a common pattern. The structure is simply:

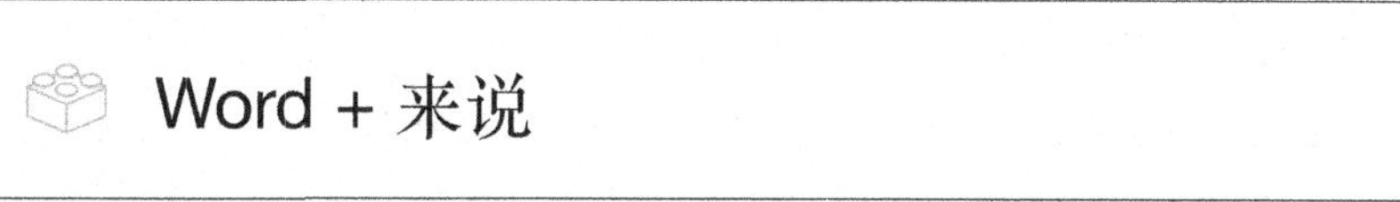

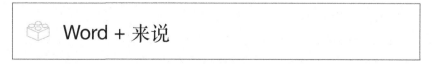

Examples

First, some common phrases:

- 一般来说 (yībān lái shuō) generally speaking, ordinarily
- 总的来说 (zǒngde lái shuō) generally speaking, generally
- 相对来说 (xiāngduì lái shuō) relatively speaking
- 严格来说 (yángé lái shuō) strictly speaking; technically
- 具体来说 (jùtǐ lái shuō) specifically

Now, the sentences:

- 一般来说，私立学校都比较贵。
  Yībān lái shuō, sīlì xuéxiào dōu bǐjiào guì.
  Ordinarily, private schools are more expensive.
- 一般来说，我们只要外国实习生。
  Yībān lái shuō, wǒmen zhǐ yào wàiguó shíxíshēng.
  Generally speaking, we only want foreign interns.
- 一般来说，大城市有更多工作机会。
  Yībān lái shuō, dà chéngshì yǒu gèng duō gōngzuò jīhuì.
  Generally speaking, there are more job opportunities in big cities.
- 总的来说，这次活动很成功。
  Zǒng de lái shuō, zhè cì huódòng hěn chénggōng.
  In general, this event was a success.
- 总的来说，这个情况在改善。
  Zǒng de lái shuō, zhège qíngkuàng zài gǎishàn.
  Generally speaking, this situation has been improving.
- 今天的考试相对来说有点难。
  Jīntiān de kǎoshì xiāngduì lái shuō yǒudiǎn nán.
  Today's test was a little difficult, relatively speaking.
- 相对来说，我更支持我的老板。
  Xiāngduì lái shuō, wǒ gèng zhīchí wǒde lǎobǎn.
  Relatively speaking, I support my boss more.
- 严格来说，他是我负责人，不是我老板。
  Yángé lái shuō, tā shì wǒ fùzérén, bù shì wǒ lǎobǎn.
  Strictly speaking, he's my supervisor, not my boss.

- 严格来说，他是华裔，不是中国人。
  Yángé lái shuō, tā shì huáyì, bù shì Zhōngguó rén.
  Technically, he is ethnically Chinese, not a Chinese citizen.
- 具体来说，这样做有三个好处。
  Jùtǐ lái shuō, zhèyàng zuò yǒu sān gè hǎochù.
  Specifically, there are three benefits in doing it this way.

Expressing "compared with" using "gen" (B1)

If you want to do a straight-up comparison statement, go ahead and use the classic 比 (bǐ) structure. But if you want to lead with a "compared with..." phrase, you'll need a 跟 (gēn) and a slightly different word order.

Used with Two Subjects

This sentence structure is used for comparing one thing *as it relates to* another.

Structure

These patterns are for making a comment about B, *as it relates to* A.

> 跟 + A + 比 (起来)，B……

B can also come at the beginning of the sentence:

> B + 跟 + A + 比 (起来)，……

For both of these structures, you could swap out 跟 (gēn) for 和 (hé) with no real difference, but using 跟 (gēn) is slightly more common.

Examples

- 跟 上海 比，我老家的物价很低。
  Gēn Shànghǎi bǐ, wǒ lǎojiā de wùjià hěn dī.
  Compared to Shanghai, prices in my hometown are very low.
- 跟 东部 比，我更喜欢美国西部。
  Gēn dōngbù bǐ, wǒ gèng xǐhuan Měiguó xībù.
  Compared to the eastern USA, I like the western USA more.
- 跟 他 比，你最大的优势是什么？
  Gēn tā bǐ, nǐ zuì dà de yōushì shì shénme?
  Compared to him, what is your biggest advantage?
- 妹妹 跟 姐姐 比起来 有点害羞。
  Mèimei gēn jiějie bǐ qǐlái yǒudiǎn hàixiū.
  Compared to the older sister, the younger sister is a bit shy.

- 新版本 跟 旧版本 比起来 ，多了一些功能。
  Xīn bǎnběn gēn jiù bǎnběn bǐ qǐlái , duō le yīxiē gōngnéng.
  Compared with the old version, the new version has a few more features.

Used with a Single Subject

比 (bǐ) can also be used for comparing one subject over two different time periods.

Structure

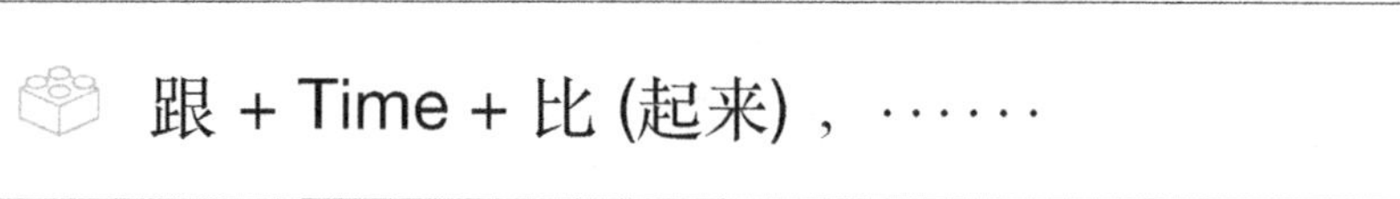
跟 + Time + 比 (起来)， ……

Again, you could use 和 (hé) instead of 跟 (gēn), but using 跟 (gēn) is more common.

Examples

- 跟 去年 比 ，你的中文进步了很多。
  Gēn qùnián bǐ , nǐ de Zhōngwén jìnbù le hěn duō.
  Compared to last year, your Chinese has improved a lot.
- 跟 十年前 比起来 ，中国人的生活水平提高了很多。
  Gēn shí nián qián bǐ qǐlái , Zhōngguó rén de shēnghuó shuǐpíng tígāo le hěn duō.
  Compared to ten years ago, the standard of living for Chinese people has gotten much better.
- 跟 上个月 比 ，这个月的工作很轻松。
  Gēn shàngge yuè bǐ , zhège yuè de gōngzuò hěn qīngsōng.
  Compared with last month, this month our work is a lot more relaxed.
- 跟 前几周 比 ，这个星期的天气舒服多了。
  Gēn qián jǐ zhōu bǐ , zhège xīngqī de tiānqì shūfu duō le.
  Compared to the past few weeks, the weather has been much more comfortable this week.
- 跟 刚毕业的时候 比起来 ，他成熟了很多。
  Gēn gāng bìyè de shíhou bǐ qǐlái , tā chéngshú le hěn duō.
  Compared to when he first graduated, he's much more mature.

Similar to

- Expressing "even more" with "geng" or "hai" (B1), page 298
- Expressing "much more" in comparisons (B1), page 300
- Expressing comparable degree with "you" (B1), page 302

Expressing "even more" with "geng" or "hai" (B1)

When used in a comparison, 更 (gèng) or 还 (hái) can kick up an adjective to an even higher degree. For example, New York City is America's biggest city with a population of around 9 million. Shanghai is China's biggest city, with a population of more than 20 million. So even though NYC's population is big, Shanghai's is even bigger. You'd use 更 or 还 to express this in Chinese.

Structure

Noun 1 + 比 + Noun 2 + 更 / 还 + Adj.

Examples

- 上海 比 纽约人口 更 多。
  Shànghǎi bǐ Niǔyuē rénkǒu gèng duō.
  Shanghai's population is even bigger than New York's.
- 我妹妹 比 我 更 瘦。
  Wǒ mèimei bǐ wǒ gèng shòu.
  My younger sister is even skinnier than me.
- 我的猫 比 我的狗 更 淘气。
  Wǒ de māo bǐ wǒ de gǒu gèng táoqì.
  My cat is even naughtier than my dog.
- 有时候动物 比 人类 更 聪明。
  Yǒushíhou dòngwù bǐ rénlèi gèng cōngming.
  Sometimes animals are even smarter than human beings.
- 大城市的工作机会 比 我老家 更 多。
  Dà chéngshì de gōngzuò jīhuì bǐ wǒ lǎojiā gèng duō.
  There are even more job opportunities in big cities than in my hometown.
- 他 比 姚明 还 高。
  Tā bǐ Yáo Míng hái gāo.
  He is even taller than Yao Ming.
- 昨天 38 度，今天 比 昨天 还 热。
  Zuótiān sānshí-bā dù, jīntiān bǐ zuótiān hái rè.
  It was 38 degrees yesterday, and it's even hotter today.

38 °C = 100 °F

- 这个外国人的汉语说得 比 中国人 还 地道。
  Zhège wàiguó rén de Hànyǔ shuō de bǐ Zhōngguó rén hái dìdao.
  This foreigner speaks even more authentic Chinese than native speakers do.

还 has a more intense tone, and it usually carries a tone of surprise and skepticism. Therefore, using the form of a rhetorical question with 还 can be understood as "how can it be?"

Also note that 更 can be used with 了 in this pattern, indicating change of situation or state, while 还 can't be used in this way.

- ✘ 这个地方 比 以前 还 热闹 了 。
  Zhège dìfang bǐ yǐqián hái rènao le .
- ✔ 这个地方 比 以前 更 热闹 了 。
  Zhège dìfang bǐ yǐqián gèng rènao le .
  This place is even livelier than before.

Similar to

- Expressing "compared with" using "gen" (B1), page 296
- Expressing "much more" in comparisons (B1), page 300
- Expressing comparable degree with "you" (B1), page 302

Expressing "much more" in comparisons (B1)

If you want to up the contrast of your comparisons, you might want to express "much more." You can do this using 多 (duō), but did you know there are actually three different ways to do it?

Structure

As well as expressing that two things differ, you might want to go further and say that they differ **a lot** by adding 很多 (hěn duō), 多了 (duō le), or 得多 (de duō). This is like saying that one thing is *much more Adj.* than another in English.

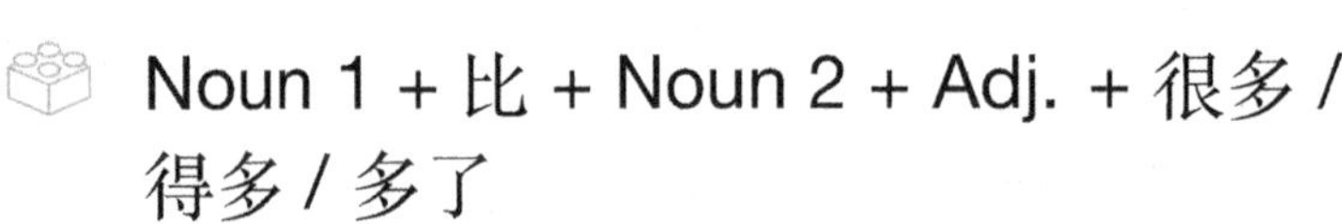

Noun 1 + 比 + Noun 2 + Adj. + 很多 / 得多 / 多了

Examples

- 拼音 比 汉字容易 很多 。
  Pīnyīn bǐ Hànzì róngyì hěn duō .
  Pinyin is much easier than Chinese characters.
- 坐高铁 比 坐飞机方便 很多 。
  Zuò gāotiě bǐ zuò fēijī fāngbiàn hěn duō .
  It's much more convenient to take the high-speed train than the airplane.
- 这个女老师 比 那个男老师严格 得多 。
  Zhège nǚ lǎoshī bǐ nàge nán lǎoshī yángé de duō .
  This female teacher is much stricter than that male teacher.
- 我老婆的工资 比 我高 得多 。
  Wǒ lǎopo de gōngzī bǐ wǒ gāo de duō .
  My wife's salary is much higher than mine.
- 你 比 我有经验 多了 。
  Nǐ bǐ wǒ yǒu jīngyàn duō le .
  You're much more experienced than me.
- 你们 比 我们幸运 多了 。
  Nǐmen bǐ wǒmen xìngyùn duō le .
  You're much luckier than us.

- 他打篮球 比 我厉害 多了 。
  Tā dǎ lánqiú bǐ wǒ lìhai duō le .
  He plays basketball much better than I do.

Short Form with 多了

Given sufficient context, it's possible to use 多了 without the full comparison pattern. 多了 is the only one of the three "much more" phrases introduced in this article which can be used this way.

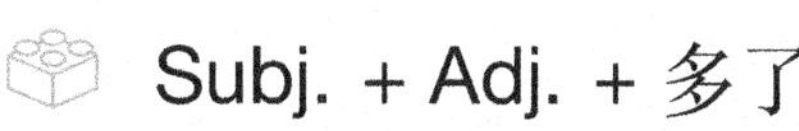

Subj. + Adj. + 多了

A few examples:

- 我的感冒好 多了 。
  Wǒ de gǎnmào hǎo duō le .
  My cold is getting much better.
  We both know I've had this bad cold.
- 最近天气暖和 多了 。
  Zuìjìn tiānqì nuǎnhuo duō le .
  It's been much warmer lately.
  We're both aware of recent weather, obviously.
- 上大学以后，她成熟 多了 。
  Shàng dàxué yǐhòu, tā chéngshú duō le .
  She became much more mature after she went to college.
  We both know how immature she used to be.

Similar to

- Basic comparisons with "bi" (A2)
- Expressing "a little too" with "you dian" (A2)
- Expressing "compared with" using "gen" (B1), page 296
- Expressing "rather" with "bijiao" (B1), page 87
- Basic comparisons with "bu bi" (B2)
- Expressing "a bit too" (B2)

Expressing comparable degree with "you" (B1)

有 (yǒu), besides just meaning "to have," can also be used in comparisons. It's what you use instead of 比 (bǐ) if something is "as [Adj.] as" something else.

Basic Pattern

The structure literally means, "A has B's [Adj.]." The meaning is "A is as [Adj.] as B." This pattern is often used in questions. Think of the jealous girl asking, "is she as pretty as me?" or the insecure weightlifter bro asking, "is he as jacked as me?" Note that for this kind of question, B is usually the one that the speaker prefers.

Structure

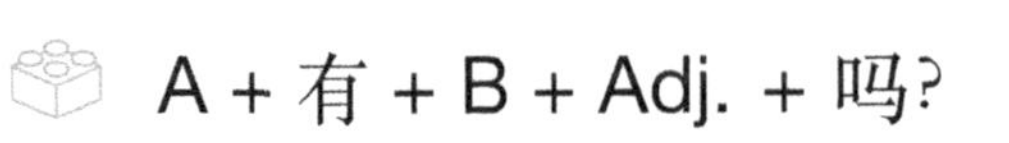

A + 有 + B + Adj. + 吗?

This comparison pattern is generally only used in questions, not statements.

Examples

- 他 有 我帅吗?
  Tā yǒu wǒ shuài ma?
  Is he as handsome as me?
- 你 有 老板忙吗?
  Nǐ yǒu lǎobǎn máng ma?
  Are you as busy as the boss?
- 他 有 姚明高吗?
  Tā yǒu Yáo Míng gāo ma?
  Is he as tall as YaoMing?
- 纽约人口 有 上海人口多吗?
  Niǔyuē rénkǒu yǒu Shànghǎi rénkǒu duō ma?
  Is the population of New York city as big as that of Shanghai?

Pattern Including a Verb

If a verb is included in this pattern to talk about an action, it's probably going to involve a degree complement[1] using this structure below:

1. Degree complement (B1), page 206

Structure

A + 有 + B + Verb + 得 + Adj. + 吗?

Examples

- 他 有 我做 得 好吗?
  Tā yǒu wǒ zuò de hǎo ma?
  Can he do it as well as I do?
- 你 有 Bolt 跑 得 快吗?
  Nǐ yǒu Bolt pǎo de kuài ma?
  Can you run as fast as Bolt does?

Advanced Pattern Using 这么 / 那么

This form is often used with 这么 or 那么, which in this case means "as much." And it indicates that B is already very [Adj.]. When B is absent, 那么 means "so" or "that".

Structure

A + 有 (+ B) + 这么 / 那么 + Adj. + 吗?

Examples

- 她 有 那么 漂亮吗?
  Tā yǒu nàme piàoliang ma?
  Is she really that pretty?
- 这个药 有 这么 神奇吗?
  Zhège yào yǒu zhème shénqí ma?
  Is this medicine really that magical?
- 他 有 姚明 那么 高吗?
  Tā yǒu Yáo Míng nàme gāo ma?
  Is he really as tall as YaoMing?
- 你 有 Bill Gates 那么 有钱吗?
  Nǐ yǒu Bill Gates nàme yǒuqián ma?
  Are you as rich as Bill Gates?

Similar to

- Basic comparisons with “bi” (A2)
- Basic comparisons with “yiyang” (A2)
- Expressing “compared with” using “gen” (B1), page 296
- Expressing “even more” with “geng” or “hai” (B1), page 298
- Expressing “much more” in comparisons (B1), page 300
- Comparisons with “buru” (B2)

Conceding a point with "shi" (B1)

When conceding a point, we often put emphasis on the point we are conceding, and in Chinese, there is a way to do that with 是 (shì).

Structure

This pattern is often used in an argument or debate. It's usually indicating that the speaker is conceding a point, *but* they still have some reservations about the topic at hand. Don't worry, the examples will make this clear.

 Adj. + 是 + Adj. ，但是 / 就是……

Examples

- 工作忙 是 忙，但是 我很开心。
  Gōngzuò máng shì máng, dànshì wǒ hěn kāixīn.
  Work may be busy, but I'm very happy.
- 这件衣服好看 是 好看，但是 不适合我。
  Zhè jiàn yīfu hǎokàn shì hǎokàn, dànshì bù shìhé wǒ.
  This piece of clothing may look nice, but it doesn't suit me.
- 这里的环境好 是 好，但是 交通不太方便。
  Zhèlǐ de huánjìng hǎo shì hǎo, dànshì jiāotōng bù tài fāngbiàn.
  This environment may be nice, but transportation is not very convenient.
- 累 是 累，但是 很值得。
  Lèi shì lèi, dànshì hěn zhídé.
  It may be tiring, but it's really worth it.
- 难 是 难，但是 我相信我能做到。
  Nán shì nán, dànshì wǒ xiāngxìn wǒ néng zuòdào.
  It is difficult, but I believe that I can do it.

When using 但是, the second clause can express positive experiences or something good, as well as negative perspectives. However, when leading with 就是, the second clause needs to express something negative.

- 好吃 是 好吃，就是 不太健康。
  Hǎochī shì hǎochī, jiùshì bù tài jiànkāng.
  It may be tasty, it's just that it's not very healthy.

- 这个东西好 是 好，就是 太贵了。
  Zhège dōngxi hǎo shì hǎo, jiùshì tài guì le.
  This thing may be good, it's just that it's too expensive.
- 这个学生聪明 是 聪明，就是 不太努力。
  Zhège xuéshēng cōngming shì cōngming, jiùshì bù tài nǔlì.
  This student may be smart, it's just that he's not very hard-working.
- 他女朋友漂亮 是 漂亮，就是 有点奇怪。
  Tā nǚpéngyou piàoliang shì piàoliang, jiùshì yǒudiǎn qíguài.
  His girlfriend may be pretty, it's just that she's is a little weird.
- 这个老师教得好 是 好，就是 太严格。
  Zhège lǎoshī jiāo de hǎo shì hǎo, jiùshì tài yángé.
  This teacher may teach well; it's just that she's too strict.

Similar to

- Expressing contrariness with “dao” (B2)

Events in quick succession with "yi... jiu..." (B1)

This pattern tells us that **as soon as** one thing happens, then **another thing happens** immediately afterwards. You mark the two events with 一 (yī) and 就 (jiù).

Used as "As Soon As"

Structure

The pattern involves two different events, the first preceded by "一," and then the second event, which follows in quick succession, preceded by 就.

> 一 + Event 1， 就 + Event 2

The subjects of the two "Events" can be the same, but they don't have to be. If they're the same, then you don't need to repeat the subject for the second one.

Examples

- 饿死了，我 一 下课 就 要去吃午饭。
  È sǐ le, wǒ yī xiàkè jiù yào qù chī wǔfàn.
  I'm starving. I'm going to have lunch as soon as class is over.
- 你能不能 一 下班 就 去接孩子？
  Nǐ néng bu néng yī xiàbān jiù qù jiē háizi?
  Can you go to pick up our kid as soon as you get off work?
- 妈妈 一 到家 就 去做饭了。
  Māma yī dào jiā jiù qù zuòfàn le.
  As soon as mom arrived home, she went off to cook.
- 老师 一 来大家 就 不说话了。
  Lǎoshī yī lái dàjiā jiù bù shuōhuà le.
  As soon as the teacher came , everyone stopped talking.
- 我 一 进门，小狗 就 跑了过来。
  Wǒ yī jìn mén, xiǎogǒu jiù pǎo le guòlái.
  As soon as I walked in the door, the puppy ran over to me.

Used as "Every Time"

Structure

In this case, 一 means "every time," followed by some certain condition, which could be the reason or the cause of what happens after 就. The subjects of the two "Events" are usually the same.

 一 + Reason，就 + Result

Examples

- 我 一 想到这件事 就 不高兴。
  Wǒ yī xiǎngdào zhè jiàn shì jiù bù gāoxìng.
  Every time I think about this, I get upset.
- 她 一 生气 就 脸红。
  Tā yī shēngqì jiù liǎn hóng.
  Every time she gets angry, her face turns red.
- 你怎么 一 吃火锅 就 拉肚子？
  Nǐ zěnme yī chī huǒguō jiù lādùzi?
  How come you get diarrhea every time you eat hotpot?
- 他 一 上英语课 就 想睡觉。
  Tā yī shàng Yīngyǔ kè jiù xiǎng shuìjiào.
  Every time he has English class, he feels like falling asleep.
- 一 说到物理，我 就 头疼。
  Yī shuōdào wùlǐ, wǒ jiù tóuténg.
  Every time we talk about physics, it gives me a headache.

Similar to

- Actions in a row (A2)
- Expressing "every time" with "mei" and "dou" (B1), page 273
- Expressing earliness with "jiu" (B1), page 69
- Expressing "once...then..." with "yidan...jiu..." (B2)

Expressing "although" with "suiran" and "danshi" (B1)

The grammar pattern 虽然……但是……(suīrán... dànshì...) is one of the most commonly used patterns in Chinese, especially in written Chinese. You can think of it as meaning "although," but unlike in English, you still need to follow it up with a "but" word in Chinese.

Structure

虽然……但是……expresses that while the former part of the sentence is true, there is an adverse reaction in the latter part.

Simply put, the pattern means, *although..., but...* In English, you wouldn't normally need the "but" there, but it is required in Chinese. Be aware that 可是 can be used interchangeably with 但是 for the "but" part. Also note that 还是 can be used after 但是 for emphasis, meaning "still."

Examples

- 虽然 外面很冷， 可是 里面很暖和。
  Suīrán wàimiàn hěn lěng, kěshì lǐmiàn hěn nuǎnhuo.
  Although it's cold outside, it's warm inside.
- 这件衣服 虽然 有点贵， 但是 质量很好。
  Zhè jiàn yīfu suīrán yǒudiǎn guì, dànshì zhìliàng hěn hǎo.
  Although this piece of clothing is a little expensive, the quality is good.
- 他 虽然 不想去， 但是 还是 去了。
  Tā suīrán bù xiǎng qù, dànshì háishì qù le.
  Although he didn't want to go, he ended up going.
- 虽然 他家很有钱， 可是 他从来不浪费钱。
  Suīrán tā jiā hěn yǒuqián, kěshì tā cónglái bù làngfèi qián.
  Even though his family is rich, he never wastes money.
- 我妹妹 虽然 很胖， 可是 很灵活。
  Wǒ mèimei suīrán hěn pàng, kěshì hěn línghuó.
  Although my little sister is fat, she is flexible.

- 虽然 她准备得很好，但是 还是 有点紧张。
  Suīrán tā zhǔnbèi de hěn hǎo, dànshì háishì yǒudiǎn jǐnzhāng.
  Although she has prepared very well, she's still a little nervous.
- 你 虽然 学历高，可是 没有工作经验。
  Nǐ suīrán xuélì gāo, kěshì méiyǒu gōngzuò jīngyàn.
  Although you're well-educated, you don't have work experience.
- 奶奶 虽然 八十多岁了，但是 她精神很好。
  Nǎinai suīrán bāshí duō suì le, dànshì tā jīngshén hěn hǎo.
  Although grandma is in her eighties, she is energetic.
- 虽然 你们没有赢，但是 我知道大家尽力了。
  Suīrán nǐmen méiyǒu yíng, dànshì wǒ zhīdao dàjiā jìnlì le.
  Although you didn't win, I know that all of you did your best.
- 虽然 我认识他很长时间了，但是 我 还是 不了解他。
  Suīrán wǒ rènshi tā hěn cháng shíjiān le, dànshì wǒ háishì bù liǎojiě tā.
  Although I've known him for a long time, I still don't know him well.

Similar to

- Two words for "but" (A2)
- A softer "but" with "buguo" (B1), page 95
- Expressing "although" with "jinguan" (B2)

Expressing "either... or..." with "yaome" (B1)

要么 (yàome) is used for offering a pair of choices with a hardline "either/or" feel: *these are the two choices. Choose one.* (It can also be used for more than two choices, but it's usually just two.)

Structure

You can give a series of alternatives by using 要么 (yàome). The structure is pretty versatile, as you can put a wide variety of things after each 要么. It can be used both for commands and non-commands.

 要么 + Option A，要么 + Option B

Examples

- 要么 你去，要么 他去。
  Yàome nǐ qù, yàome tā qù.
  Either you go, or he goes.
- 要么 继续，要么 放弃。
  Yàome jìxù, yàome fàngqì.
  Either keep going or give up.
- 要么 好好做，要么 就别做。
  Yàome hǎohǎo zuò, yàome jiù bié zuò.
  You either do it well or don't do it.
- 要么 现在就买，要么 现在就走。
  Yàome xiànzài jiù mǎi, yàome xiànzài jiù zǒu.
  Either buy it now, or leave now.
- 你 要么 回老家，要么 留在上海。
  Nǐ yàome huí lǎojiā, yàome liúzài Shànghǎi.
  You either go back to your hometown or stay in Shanghai.
- 要么 看书，要么 写作业，不可以出去玩。
  Yàome kànshū, yàome xiě zuòyè, bù kěyǐ chūqù wán.
  Either read or do your homework. No playing outside.
- 你 要么 加入我们队，要么 加入他们队。
  Nǐ yàome jiārù wǒmen duì, yàome jiārù tāmen duì.
  You either join our team or their team.

- 要么 继续找工作，要么 创业，不能什么都不做。
  Yàome jìxù zhǎo gōngzuò, yàome chuàngyè, bù néng shénme dōu bù zuò.
  Either keeping looking for a job or start your own business. You can't do nothing.
- 去年夏天，我每天 要么 去健身房，要么 去图书馆，特别无聊。
  Qùnián xiàtiān, wǒ měi tiān yàome qù jiànshēnfáng, yàome qù túshūguǎn, tèbié wúliáo.
  Last summer I either went to the gym or the library every day. It was super boring.
- 我老公周末 要么 睡觉，要么 打游戏，从来不做家务。
  Wǒ lǎogōng zhōumò yàome shuìjiào, yàome dǎ yóuxì, cónglái bù zuò jiāwù.
  My husband either sleeps or plays video games on weekends. He never does housework.

This "either/or" 要么 pattern is similar to one of the uses of each 要不[1] and 或者.

Similar to

- Expressing "how about" with "yaobu" (B1), page 97

- Expressing the only two possibilities (B2)
- Providing two options with double "huozhe" (B2)

1. Expressing "how about" with "yaobu" (B1), page 97

Expressing "except" and "in addition" with "chule... yiwai" (B1)

Using 除了 (chúle)–often with 以外 (yǐwài)–will help you spruce up your sentences when you want to express the meanings of "except," "besides," or "in addition." You may feel that "except" has a pretty different meaning from the other two. Well, read on!

Used as "Except"

除了······ (以外), 都······ is a pattern used to express "except." Make a special note of the 都 (dōu)!

Structure

除了······ (+ 以外)，Subj. + 都······

以外 can be omitted from the pattern without changing its meaning.

Examples

- 除了他，我们都去过。
  Chúle tā , wǒmen dōu qù guo.
  Except for him, we've all been there.
- 除了白酒，别的酒他都喝。
  Chúle báijiǔ, biéde jiǔ tā dōu hē.
  He drinks all kinds of alcohol except baijiu.
- 除了周末，老板每天都加班。
  Chúle zhōumò, lǎobǎn měi tiān dōu jiābān.
  Except for weekends, the boss works overtime every day.
- 除了价格以外，其他方面我们都很满意。
  Chúle jiàgé yǐwài, qítā fāngmiàn wǒmen dōu hěn mǎnyì.
  We're satisfied with all aspects except for the price.
- 除了政治新闻以外，其他新闻我都看。
  Chúle zhèngzhì xīnwén yǐwài, qítā xīnwén wǒ dōu kàn.
  I read all types of news except for political news.

Used as "in Addition"

除了······ (以外), 也/还······ is used to express "in addition." Make a special note of the 也 or 还!

Structure

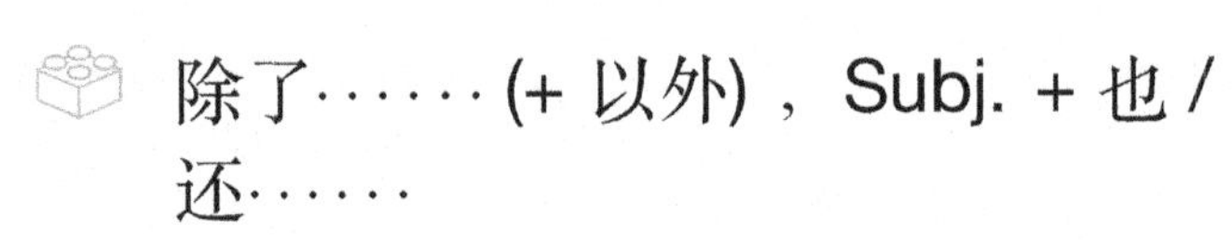

Examples

- 除了 英语，我 也 会说法语和西班牙语。
  Chúle Yīngyǔ, wǒ yě huì shuō Fǎyǔ hé Xībānyáyǔ.
  In addition to English, I can also speak French and Spanish.
- 除了 运动 以外，你 还 有什么爱好？
  Chúle yùndòng yǐwài, nǐ hái yǒu shénme àihào?
  In addition to sports, what other hobbies do you have?
- 除了 猫和狗，我 还 养过兔子。
  Chúle māo hé gǒu, wǒ hái yǎng guo tùzi.
  In addition to a cat and a dog, I also had a rabbit.
- 除了 海鲜，你 还 对什么过敏？
  Chúle hǎixiān, nǐ hái duì shénme guòmǐn?
  In addition to seafood, what else are you allergic to?
- 中国的功夫明星，除了 李小龙和成龙 以外，李连杰 也 很有名。
  Zhōngguó de gōngfu míngxīng, chúle Lǐ Xiǎolóng hé Chéng Lóng yǐwài, Lǐ Liánjié yě hěn yǒumíng.
  In addition to Bruce Lee and Jackie Chan, Jet Li is also a very famous Chinese kung fu star.

Similar to

- Expressing "and also" with "hai" (A2)
- Expressing "in addition" with "haiyou" (B1), page 99
- Expressing "in addition" with "lingwai" (B2), page 101
- Defining scope (B2)

Expressing "if" with "ruguo... dehua" (B1)

如果……的话 (rúguǒ... dehuà) is a pattern commonly used in Chinese to express "if." An easy way to remember the pattern's format is that in the full form, the condition is "sandwiched" between 如果 and 的话.

Fuller Pattern

Structure

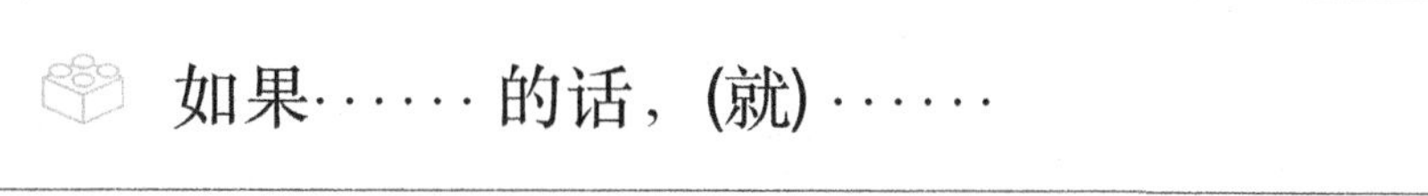

Note that 就 (jiù) is often optional. For more on using 如果 with 就, check out the "if…, then…" two-part pattern with 如果……就……[1].

Examples

- 如果明天下雨的话，我们就不去了。
  Rúguǒ míngtiān xiàyǔ dehuà, wǒmen jiù bù qù le.
  If it rains tomorrow, we won't go.
- 别点那么多菜。如果吃不完的话，就太浪费了。
  Bié diǎn nàme duō cài. Rúguǒ chī bu wán dehuà, jiù tài làngfèi le.
  Don't order so much. It will be a big waste of food if we can't finish it all.
- 如果有人帮他的话，他就不会出事了。
  Rúguǒ yǒu rén bāng tā dehuà, tā jiù bù huì chūshì le.
  If someone had helped him, he would't have had this accident.
- 如果你们不来的话，一定会后悔的。
  Rúguǒ nǐmen bù lái dehuà, yīdìng huì hòuhuǐ de .
  If you don't come, you'll definitely regret it.
- 如果他不同意的话，你怎么办?
  Rúguǒ tā bù tóngyì dehuà, nǐ zěnmebàn?
  What will you do if he doesn't agree?

Simple Pattern

Colloquially, it's also possible to drop the 如果 and just use the 的话 instead to mean "if." 的话 is optional.

1. Expressing "if… then…" with "ruguo… jiu…" (B1), page 317

Structure

Examples

- 不想去 的话 就 别去了。

  Bù xiǎng qù dehuà jiù bié qù le.

  Don't go if you don't feel like going.

- 好吃 的话 ， 就 多吃点。

  Hǎochī dehuà, jiù duō chī diǎn.

  If you think it's tasty, eat some more.

- 喜欢 就 拿走吧。

  Xǐhuan jiù názǒu ba.

  Take it if you like it.

It's even possible to use neither 的话 nor 就, and let the "if" be completely implied.

- 有事给我打电话。

  Yǒu shì gěi wǒ dǎ diànhuà.

  Give me a call if you need anything.

- 有空来我家玩。

  Yǒu kòng lái wǒ jiā wán.

  If you're free, come to my place and hang out.

Note that 如果 can be switched out for the various other terms for "if," including the common 要是 (yàoshi) and the formal 假如 (jiǎrú), among others.

Similar to

- Expressing "if… then…" with "ruguo… jiu…" (B1), page 317

Expressing "if... then..." with "ruguo... jiu..." (B1)

The 如果……，就…… (rúguǒ..., jiù...) two-part structure is very logical and concise, meaning "if... then...."

Standard Pattern

Structure

如果……，就…… is an often-used pattern that is utilized in the same way that "*If…, then…*" is in English. In English we sometimes drop then "then" in the second half of the sentence, and you can do the same in Chinese, dropping the 就.

Examples

- 如果 有困难，就 给我打电话。
  Rúguǒ yǒu kùnnan, jiù gěi wǒ dǎ diànhuà.
  If there is any difficulty, give me a call.
- 如果 你输了，就 给我一百块。
  Rúguǒ nǐ shū le, jiù gěi wǒ yī bǎi kuài.
  If you lose, give me 100 kuai.
- 如果 真的找不回来，就 再买一个吧。
  Rúguǒ zhēnde zhǎo bu huílái, jiù zài mǎi yī gè ba.
  If you can't find it, then buy a new one.
- 如果 他再来，我们 就 报警。
  Rúguǒ tā zài lái, wǒmen jiù bàojǐng.
  If he keeps showing up, we'll call the police.
- 如果 你们已经不相爱了，就 分手吧。
  Rúguǒ nǐmen yǐjīng bù xiāngài le, jiù fēnshǒu ba.
  If you no longer love each other, just break up.

Fuller Pattern

Sometimes 那么 (nàme) is used instead of 就 (jiù), imparting a more relaxed, informal feel to the sentence. Sometimes just 那 (nà) will be used instead of 那么 (nàme).

Structure

 如果……，那么 / 那……

Examples

- 如果 他知道，那 他一定会告诉我。
  Rúguǒ tā zhīdào, nà tā yīdìng huì gàosu wǒ.
  If he knew, he would definitely tell me.
- 如果 大家都不感兴趣，那 我不说了。
  Rúguǒ dàjiā dōu bù gǎn xìngqù, nà wǒ bù shuō le.
  If none of you are interested, I will stop talking.
- 如果 你们真的想合作，那么 我们应该找时间好好谈谈。
  Rúguǒ nǐmen zhēnde xiǎng hézuò, nàme wǒmen yīnggāi zhǎo shíjiān hǎohǎo tántan.
  If you really want to work with us, then we should schedule a day to discuss it.
- 如果 能找到投资，那 下个月就可以开始做了。
  Rúguǒ néng zhǎodào tóuzī, nà xià gè yuè jiù kěyǐ kāishǐ zuò le.
  If we can find the investment, we'll be able to get on it next month.
- 如果 你想申请，那么 现在就要开始准备。
  Rúguǒ nǐ xiǎng shēnqǐng, nàme xiànzài jiù yào kāishǐ zhǔnbèi.
  If you want to apply, you need to start to prepare right away.

Adding in 的话

This article is focused on the two-part "if... then..." pattern 如果……，就……. But it's also possible to take the first half and make it into a "sandwich pattern" using 如果…… 的话.

Expressing "no wonder" (B1)

怪不得 (guàibude) can be used to express that the speaker finds something unsurprising. It can be used alone or in a variety of different structures, as shown below. 难怪 (nánguài) is another way to express the exact same thing.

Emphasis on 怪不得 / 难怪

怪不得 is used to convey the speaker's newfound understanding of a situation, having recently acquired some new information that, in his opinion, explains it.

Structure

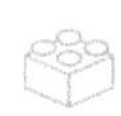

Reason ， 怪不得 / 难怪 + [Observation]

怪不得 can be replaced with 难怪 in the structure without altering its meaning.

Examples

- 小张请假了， 怪不得 今天没有看到他。
  Xiǎo Zhāng qǐngjià le, guàibude jīntiān méiyǒu kàndào tā.
  Little Zhang asked for vacation time, no wonder I haven't seen him today.
- 天天迟到， 怪不得 他被炒鱿鱼了。
  Tiāntiān chídào, guàibude tā bèi chǎoyóuyú le.
  He's late for work every day. No wonder he got fired.
- 她是你妹妹？ 难怪 你们长得这么像。
  Tā shì nǐ mèimei? Nánguài nǐmen cháng de zhème xiàng.
  She's your younger sister? No wonder you two look so much alike.
- 你手机没电了？ 怪不得 我打不通。
  Nǐ shǒujī méi diàn le? Guàibude wǒ dǎ bu tōng.
  Your cell phone is out of power? No wonder my call wouldn't go through.
- 你放了醋？ 难怪 这么难吃！
  Nǐ fàng le cù? Nánguài zhème nánchī!
  You put vinegar in it? No wonder it tastes so bad!

Emphasis on 原来

Structure

 怪不得 / 难怪 + [Observation] ， 原来 (+ 是) + Reason

Examples

- 难怪 学生都不喜欢这个老师， 原来 他的作业太多了。
  Nánguài xuéshēng dōu bù xǐhuan zhège lǎoshī, yuánlái tā de zuòyè tài duō le.
  No wonder the students don't like this teacher. He gives too much homework.
- 怪不得 你们这么高兴， 原来 是要结婚了。
  Guàibude nǐmen zhème gāoxìng, yuánlái shì yào jiéhūn le.
  No wonder you two look so happy. You are getting married.
- 难怪 这里人这么多， 原来 在打折。
  Nánguài zhèlǐ rén zhème duō, yuánlái zài dǎzhé.
  No wonder there are so many people here. There's a sale going on.
- 怪不得 她拉肚子， 原来 她昨天又吃火锅了。
  Guàibude tā lādùzi, yuánlái tā zuótiān yòu chī huǒguō le.
  No wonder she got a diarrhea. She went to eat hotpot again yesterday.
- 怪不得 他没告诉我， 原来 是不想让我担心。
  Guàibude tā méi gàosu wǒ, yuánlái shì bù xiǎng ràng wǒ dānxīn.
  No wonder he hasn't told me. He doesn't want me to worry about this.

The Other Meaning of 难怪

This usage is definitely less common, but sometimes 难怪 is a combination of the 难 + Verb pattern and the verb 怪, meaning "to blame." In this case, the meaning is totally different. Although it's not as common, and you shouldn't need to worry about it too much, we include it here because if you ever run into and think that 难怪 can only ever have one meaning, it can totally throw you for a loop.

A few examples:

- 这也 难怪 他，他这么小。
  Zhè yě nánguài tā, tā zhème xiǎo.
  We can't really blame him. He's so young.

- 这也 难怪 大家，是我们通知晚了。

  Zhè yě nánguài dàjiā, shì wǒmen tōngzhī wǎn le.

  We can't really blame everybody. It was such short notice.

When used in this way it expresses that the speaker assigns no blame in the situation he is describing. Sometimes the specific person undeserving of blame is mentioned directly after 难怪, but not always.

Similar to

- Expressing "all along" with "yuanlai" (B1), page 36

Expressing "not only... but also" (B1)

不但……，而且…… (bùdàn..., érqiě...) is a very commonly used pattern that indicates "not only, ... but also...."

Used with Single Subject

Structure

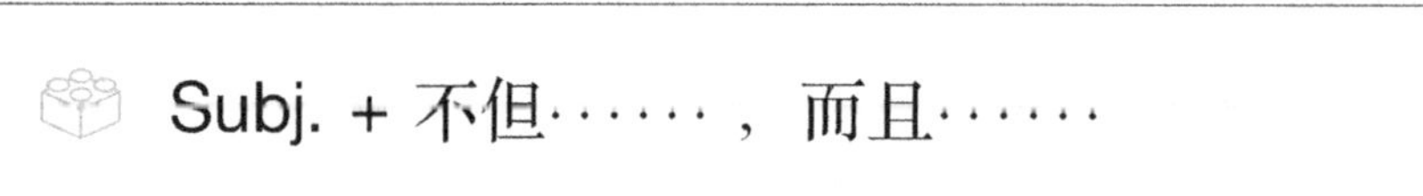

Subj. + 不但……，而且……

The same subject should apply to both the first part and the second part (the part after 而且). The pattern can also be used omitting 而且, and instead using adverbs like 也 and 还 in its place.

Examples

- 这个东西 不但 贵，而且 难买。
  Zhège dōngxi bùdàn guì, érqiě nán mǎi .
  This thing is not only expensive, but also hard to buy.
- 这道菜 不但 好看，也 好吃。
  Zhè dào cài bùdàn hǎokàn, yě hǎochī.
  This dish is not only attractive, but also delicious.
- 她 不但 聪明，而且 很幽默。
  Tā bùdàn cōngming, érqiě hěn yōumò.
  She is not only smart, but also very humorous.
- 她 不但 离开了我，还 拿走了我所有的钱。
  Tā bùdàn líkāi le wǒ, hái názǒu le wǒ suǒyǒu de qián.
  Not only did she leave me, but she also took all my money.
- 他 不但 提前做完了，而且 做得很好。
  Tā bùdàn tíqián zuò wán le, érqiě zuò de hěn hǎo.
  Not only did he finish it in advance, but he did it very well.

Used with Two Subjects

When there is only one subject with 不但…… 而且……, the subject has to come at the beginning of the sentence, before both 不但 and 而且. When using two different subjects, however, you need to put one after 不但 and one after 而且.

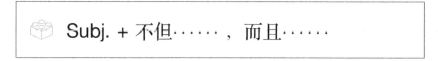

Structure

> 不但 + Subj. 1 ⋯⋯ ，而且 + Subj. 2 + 也⋯⋯

The pattern can also be used omitting 而且, and instead using adverbs like 也 in its place.

Examples

- 不但 大学生找工作难，而且 研究生 也 不容易。
  Bùdàn dàxuéshēng zhǎo gōngzuò nán, érqiě yánjiūshēng yě bù róngyì.
  Not only is it hard to find a job for undergraduates, but it's also hard for graduate students.
- 这个电影 不但 孩子们喜欢，大人 也 很喜欢。
  Zhège diànyǐng bùdàn háizimen xǐhuan, dàren yě hěn xǐhuan.
  Not only do children like this movie, but adults like it too.
- 不但 员工压力大，老板压力 也 很大。
  Bùdàn yuángōng yālì dà, lǎobǎn yālì yě hěn dà.
  Not only are the employees under a lot of pressure, but the boss is under a lot of pressure too.
- 老师发现，不但 学生说谎，而且 家长 也 说谎。
  Lǎoshī fāxiàn, bùdàn xuéshēng shuōhuǎng, érqiě jiāzhǎng yě shuōhuǎng.
  The teacher found that not only did the student lie, but his parents did too.
- 不但 老百姓害怕这些人，而且 警察 也 害怕。
  Bùdàn lǎobǎixìng hàipà zhèxiē rén, érqiě jǐngchá yě hàipà.
  Not only do ordinary folk fear these people, but the police fear them too.

Similar to

- Expressing "and also" with "hai" (A2)
- Expressing "except" and "in addition" with "chule⋯ yiwai" (B1), page 313
- Expressing "in addition" with "haiyou" (B1), page 99
- Expressing "in addition" with "lingwai" (B2), page 101
- Expressing "in addition" with "zaishuo" (B1), page 103
- Using "budan… geng" to express "not only… but also"
- Expressing "not only…, even…" using "budan⋯⋯, shenzhi lian" (B2)

- Expressing “not only· · · but also” with “bujin” (B2)
- Many types of “not only… but also…” (B2)
- Using “er” to explain contrasting ideas (B2)

Expressing "when" with "dengdao" (B1)

The word 等到 (děngdào) can trip up learners, because while it can literally mean "to wait until," it also has the less literal translation meaning "when (the time comes)" or "by the time (something happens)." This is a pattern that appears in complex sentences, with 等到 acting as a conjunction and appearing in the first part as the first word in the sentence.

Used for the Future

When talking about the future, the second part of the sentence uses 就 (jiù) or 再 (zài).

Structure

等 (到) + Time / Event ， Subj. + 再 / 就 + Predicate

The predicate part of the pattern can be a verb or an adjective.

Examples

- 等到 老板知道 就 麻烦了。
  Děngdào lǎobǎn zhīdao jiù máfan le.
  When the boss finds out, we'll be in trouble.
- 等 雨停了我 再 出门。
  Děng yǔ tíng le wǒ zài chūmén.
  When the rain stops, I'll go outside.
- 等到 秋天，这些树叶 就 会变黄。
  Děngdào qiūtiān, zhèxiē shùyè jiù huì biàn huáng.
  When autumn arrives, these leaves will turn yellow.
- 等 做完这个项目，我 就 休假。
  Děng zuò wán zhège xiàngmù, wǒ jiù xiūjià.
  I will take a vacation when I finish this project.
- 等到 老板签了字，我 再 做安排。
  Děngdào lǎobǎn qiān le zì, wǒ zài zuò ānpái.
  I will make arrangements once the boss signs off on it.

Used for the Past

For the past, the second part of the sentence uses 才 (cái). This pattern is very similar to how 直到 (zhídào) is used to mean "all the way until"[1], and also overlaps with the use of 才 to express lateness[2].

Structure

等 (到) + Time / Event， Subj. + 才 + Predicate

Examples

- 等 我回了家， 才 发现手机忘在了出租车上。
  Děng wǒ huí le jiā, cái fāxiàn shǒujī wàng zài le chūzūchē shàng.
  I didn't realize I left my cell phone in the taxi until I got home.
- 等到 孩子上了小学，她 才 开始工作。
  Děngdào háizi shàng le xiǎoxué, tā cái kāishǐ gōngzuò.
  She didn't start working until her children had started elementary school.
- 等 学生都安静了，老师 才 开始上课。
  Děng xuéshēng dōu ānjìng le, lǎoshī cái kāishǐ shàngkè.
  The teacher didn't begin the class until the students all became quiet.
- 等 他有了孩子， 才 知道做父母多么不容易。
  Děng tā yǒu le háizi, cái zhīdào zuò fùmǔ duōme bù róngyì.
  It wasn't until he had had a child that he realized how hard it is to be a parent.
- 等到 他到家了， 才 发现他没有带钥匙。
  Děngdào tā dào jiā le, cái fāxiàn tā méiyǒu dài yàoshi.
  It wasn't until he got home that he found that he didn't have his keys.

Similar to

- Expressing "all the way until" with "zhidao" (B1), page 137
- Expressing "until" with "dao" (B1), page 187
- Expressing lateness with "cai" (B1), page 72

1. Expressing "all the way until" with "zhidao" (B1), page 137
2. Expressing lateness with "cai" (B1), page 72

Expressing good luck with "haihao" (B1)

还好 (háihǎo) can mean "fortunately" or "luckily." Another good translation would be "it's a good thing that…." It is often followed with 不然, which precedes the bad thing that *could have* happened if not for the stroke of luck.

Structure

还好 + [Lucky Incident] ， 不然 + [Bad Outcome]

Examples

- 还好 我们打车来的， 不然 就迟到了。
  Háihǎo wǒmen dǎchē lái de, bùrán jiù chídào le.
  Luckily, we came by taxi. Otherwise we would have been late.
- 还好 我妈没看到， 不然 她肯定要生气。
  Háihǎo wǒ mā méi kàndào, bùrán tā kěndìng yào shēngqì.
  It's a good thing that my mother didn't see it. Otherwise she would definitely be mad.
- 还好 有你在， 不然 我真不知道怎么办。
  Háihǎo yǒu nǐ zài, bùrán wǒ zhēn bù zhīdào zěnme bàn.
  Fortunately you're here. Otherwise I really wouldn't have known what to do.
- 还好 带伞了， 不然 肯定淋湿了。
  Háihǎo dài sǎn le, bùrán kěndìng línshī le.
  It's a good thing I brought the umbrella. Otherwise, I would have definitely gotten soaked.
- 还好 我们买了很多， 不然 肯定不够。
  Háihǎo wǒmen mǎi le hěn duō, bùrán kěndìng bù gòu.
  Luckily, we bought a lot. Otherwise, there wouldn't have been enough.
- 还好 我没听他的话， 不然 就输了。
  Hái hǎo wǒ méi tīng tā de huà, bùrán jiù shū le.
  It's a good thing I didn't listen to him. Otherwise, I would have lost.
- 还好 我保存了， 不然 文件都丢了。
  Háihǎo wǒ bǎocún le, bùrán wénjiàn dōu diū le.
  Luckily, I saved it. Otherwise, I would have lost all of the documents.

- 还好 我没点那么多菜，不然 都浪费了。
  Háihǎo wǒ méi diǎn nàme duō cài, bùrán dōu làngfèi le.
  It's a good thing I didn't order that much food. Otherwise, it would have all been wasted.
- 还好 老板不知道，不然 你肯定被炒鱿鱼。
  Háihǎo lǎobǎn bù zhīdào, bùrán nǐ kěndìng bèi chǎo yóuyú.
  Luckily, the boss doesn't know about it. Otherwise, you would definitely get fired.
- 还好 你提醒我了，不然 我肯定忘了。
  Háihǎo nǐ tíxǐng wǒ le, bùrán wǒ kěndìng wàng le.
  It's a good thing you reminded me. Otherwise, I would have definitely forgotten.

Similar to

- Expressing “thanks to” with “duokui” (B2)

Expressing various aspects with "yi fangmian" (B1)

When talking about various aspects of a situation, 一方面……，(另) 一方面…… (yī fāngmiàn..., (lìng) yī fāngmiàn...) can be used in a way similar to how "on one hand..., on the other hand..." is used in English.

Structure

一方面……，(另) 一方面……

The two aspects in the sentence can both be similar in tone, and they can also be in direct opposition to each other. You will often see the adverb 又, 也 or 还 following 另一方面, which serves the purpose of emphasis.

Examples

- 自己做饭 一方面 健康，一方面 还 能省点钱。
  Zìjǐ zuòfàn yī fāngmiàn jiànkāng, yī fāngmiàn hái néng shěng diǎn qián.
  On one hand, cooking for yourself is healthy; on the other hand, it can also help to save some money.
- 他 一方面 想改变，一方面 又 害怕改变。
  Tā yī fāngmiàn xiǎng gǎibiàn, yī fāngmiàn yòu hàipà gǎibiàn.
  On the one hand, he wants to change; on the other hand, he's afraid of change.
- 我们 一方面 不想这样做，一方面 必须这样做。
  Wǒmen yī fāngmiàn bù xiǎng zhèyàng zuò, yī fāngmiàn bìxū zhèyàng zuò.
  On the one hand, we don't want to do it this way; on the other hand, we must do it this way.
- 抽烟 一方面 对自己有害，一方面 对身边的人 也 有害。
  Chōuyān yī fāngmiàn duì zìjǐ yǒuhài, yī fāngmiàn duì shēnbiān de rén yě yǒuhài
  On one hand, smoking can do harm to the smoker himself; on the other hand, it can also do harm to people around him.
- 用智能手机 一方面 很方便，另一方面 也 很容易浪费时间。
  Yòng zhìnéng shǒujī yī fāngmiàn hěn fāngbiàn, lìng yī fāngmiàn yě hěn róngyì làngfèi shíjiān.
  On the one hand, using smart phones is very convenient; on the other hand, they also make it very easy to waste a lot of time.

- 我们 一方面 要让客户满意，另一方面 也 要控制成本。
  Wǒmen yī fāngmiàn yào ràng kèhù mǎnyì, lìng yī fāngmiàn yě yào kòngzhì chéngběn.
  One the one hand, we need to satisfy our clients, but on the other hand, we also need to control our costs.
- 一方面 他们的服务很专业，另一方面 他们的价格 也 很合理。
  Yī fāngmiàn tāmen de fúwù hěn zhuānyè, lìng yī fāngmiàn tāmen de jiàgé yě hěn hélǐ.
  On one hand, their service is very professional; on the other hand, their price is also reasonable.
- 这样做 一方面 能节省时间，一方面 能提高质量。
  Zhèyàng zuò yī fāngmiàn néng jiéshěng shíjiān, yī fāngmiàn néng tígāo zhìliàng.
  On one hand, we can save time by doing it this way; on the other hand, we can improve the quality.
- 这个项目 一方面 能增加当地人的收入，另一方面 能保护当地的环境。
  Zhège xiàngmù yī fāngmiàn néng zēngjiā dāngdì rén de shōurù, lìng yī fāngmiàn néng bǎohù dāngdì de huánjìng.
  One one hand, this project can increase local people's income; on the other hand, it can protect the local environment.
- 政府 一方面 要发展这些古城，一方面 也 要保护好这些古城。
  Zhèngfǔ yī fāngmiàn yào fāzhǎn zhèxiē gǔchéng, yī fāngmiàn yě yào bǎohù hǎo zhèxiē gǔchéng.
  On the one hand, the government needs to develop these old towns; on the other hand, they need to protect them too.

Similar to

- Idiomatic phrases with “zai” (B1), page 150
- Expressing simultaneous actions with “yimian” (B2)

Comparing “changchang” and “jingchang” (B1)

Both 常常 (chángcháng) and 经常 (jīngcháng) are adverbs expressing the idea of “often,” though their usage differs in some small details.

Used as an Adverb

常常 and 经常 both can be used to express frequency, meaning “often,” and that the time between each instance something happens is very short. In this case, they are interchangeable.

Structure

 常常 / 经常 + Verb

Examples

- 我 常常 收到垃圾短信。
  Wǒ chángcháng shōudào lājī duǎnxìn.
  I often receive spam texts.
- 你们 经常 加班吗?
  Nǐmen jīngcháng jiābān ma?
  Do you guys often work overtime?
- 他们 常常 吵架。
  Tāmen chángcháng chǎojià.
  They often argue.

Neither 常常 nor 经常 can be placed before the subject:

- ✘ 常常 他不吃早饭。
  Chángcháng tā bù chī zǎo fàn.
- ✘ 经常 他不吃早饭。
  Jīngcháng tā bù chī zǎo fàn.
- ✔ 他 经常 不吃早饭。
  Tā jīngcháng bù chī zǎo fàn.
  He often skips breakfast.

Note that 常 (by itself) is used for *future* frequent actions in colloquial Chinese.

- 常 来玩！
  Cháng lái wán!
  Come hang out often!
- 常 联系！
  Cháng liánxì!
  Let's keep in touch!

Used as an Adjective

Although not so commonly used in this way, 经常 can also be used as an adjective referring to things that happens very frequently. 常常 can't be used this way.

A simple example:

- 她忘带钥匙是 经常 的事情。
  Tā wàng dài yàoshi shì jīngcháng de shìqing.
  It's a regular thing for her to forget to bring her keys.

Negative Form

经常 and 常常 can share the same negative form **不常**. You can also simply use 不 to negate both 经常 and 常常, although 不常常 is not super common.

A few examples:

- 他 不常 抽烟。
  Tā bù cháng chōuyān.
  He doesn't smoke very often.
- 我妈妈 不经常 网购。
  Wǒ māma bù jīngcháng wǎng gòu.
  My mother doesn't often shop online.

Similar to

- Comparing "pingshi" and "pingchang" (B2)

Comparing "gang" and "gangcai" (B1)

刚 (gāng) and 刚才 (gāngcái) have similar meanings of "just (now)," but they differ on a few key uses.

刚 as "Just Happened"

刚 is actually an adverb, and it is placed in front of the verb. It emphasizes that the action *just* happened a short time ago. Unsurprisingly, it is similar to the English "just." 刚刚 and 刚 are interchangeable in this case.

The key here is that "a short time ago" is relative and determined by the speaker. For this reason, 刚 can indicate that something "just" happened 1 second ago, 5 minutes ago, 2 hours ago, 3 weeks ago, or even a year ago. The absolute time is flexible, but from the speaker's perspective, it *feels* recent.

刚 Before a Verb

One thing that confuses a lot of learners is that when you use 刚 with a verb, *you normally don't need 了*. Keep that in mind while reading the following examples, and look for the explanation below.

A few examples:

- ✔ 他 刚 到。
  Tā gāng dào.
  He just arrived.

  This gives the impression that not only did he just get here, but he should still be here.
- ✔ 我们昨天 刚 到。
  Wǒmen zuótiān gāng dào.
  We just arrived yesterday.
- ✔ 真不巧，老板 刚 走。
  Zhēn bùqiǎo, lǎobǎn gāng zǒu.
  What bad timing. The boss just left.

It would be wrong to use 刚才 instead:

- ✘ 他 刚才 到。
  Tā gāngcái dào.
- ✘ 我们昨天 刚才 到。
  Wǒmen zuótiān gāngcái dào.

  刚才 should be used for events a lot closer in time than 昨天.
- ✘ 真不巧，老板 刚才 走。
  Zhēn bùqiǎo, lǎobǎn gāngcái zǒu.

And if you mean to say "when I first arrived in Shanghai," use 刚 instead of 刚才:

- 我 刚 到上海的时候，谁都不认识。
  Wǒ gāng dào Shànghǎi de shíhou, shéi dōu bù rènshi.
  I didn't know anyone when I had just arrived in Shanghai.

刚 or 刚刚 before An Adjective

刚, as an adverb, can also be placed in front of a verb, while 刚才 can't be used this way. 刚 can also be used interchangeably with 刚刚.

A few examples:

- 他的感冒 刚刚 好。
  Tā de gǎnmào gānggāng hǎo.
  He just recovered from his cold.
- 天 刚 晴。
  Tiān gāng qíng.
  The sky just became clear.
- 牛肉 刚 熟。
  Niúròu gāng shú.
  The beef just got cooked.

刚才 as "Just Now"

刚才 is a time noun (like 今天 and 现在), and it expresses that the time elapsed is really short, in near-absolute terms. We're talking no more than 1-30 minutes in most situations, and often less than 5 minutes. When used before a verb, 刚才 emphasizes something happened "*just now*."

A few examples:

- 他 刚才 哭 了 。
  Tā gāngcái kū le .
  He was crying just now.
  He was crying a moment ago but he stopped.
- 我 刚才 看到他 了 。
  Wǒ gāngcái kàndào tā le .
  I just now saw him.
  Sounds like he's not here anymore; I just saw him, but don't see him now.
- 现在我感觉比 刚才 好一点 了 。
  Xiànzài wǒ gǎnjué bǐ gāngcái hǎo yīdiǎn le .
  I feel a little better now than just before.

刚才, as a time noun, can directly modify a noun to indicate it is that one from "just now" or "just before," while 刚 can't be used this way.

× 刚 的事情 太让人生气了。

Gāng de shìqing tài ràng rén shēngqì le.

What just happened is really upsetting.

✓ 刚才 的事情 太让人生气了。

Gāngcái de shìqing tài ràng rén shēngqì le.

What just happened is really upsetting.

刚 and 刚才 with 了

You may have noticed that something interesting is going on with regards to 了 in the sentences with 刚 and 刚才. Namely, 了 is not usually required in sentences with 刚, but it is usually required in sentences with 刚才. This is because 刚才 refers to a time in the *recent past*, and you're usually indicated that something *happened just now* (started and finished).

Take these sentences for example:

- 我昨天看了。

  Wǒ zuótiān kàn le.

  I looked at it yesterday.

- 我 刚才 看了。

  Wǒ gāngcái kàn le.

  I looked at it just now.

So these are both simple "subject + verb" sentences. Notice that when they refer to the *past* (including the one with 刚才), the action is completed and you need 了. You don't need 了 for things that haven't happened yet (they're just plans, and nothing is completed). And remember that 刚才 *always refers to the past.*

OK, now what about 刚? *Why does it not need 了?* The key is that you don't need a 了 in a sentence with 刚 if the verb *already indicates a clear result*. So, to use the 看 example from above:

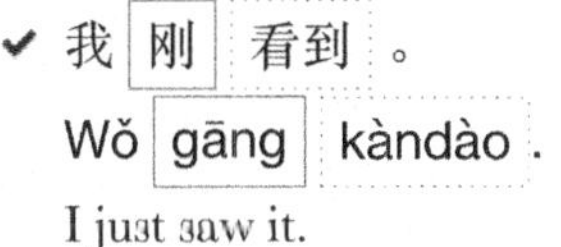

✓ 我 刚 看到 。

Wǒ gāng kàndào .

I just saw it.

Adding a 到 to 看 gives the verb a meaning of the result of "looking at."

× 我 刚 看到 了 。

Wǒ gāng kàndào le .

I just saw it.

了 is not needed here as 看到 includes the result of "looking at."

✓ 我 刚才 看到 了 。

Wǒ gāngcái kàndào le .

I saw it just now.

了 is needed with 刚才 because it feels so recent and unresolved.

A few more examples:

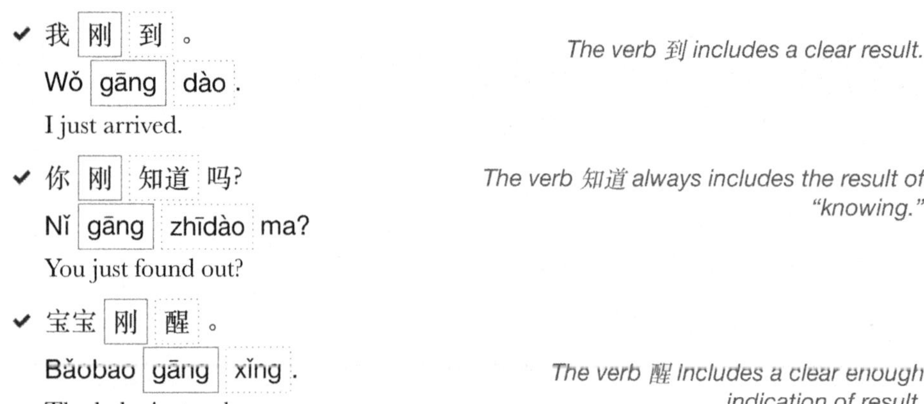

✔ 我 刚 到 。
Wǒ gāng dào .
I just arrived.
The verb 到 includes a clear result.

✔ 你 刚 知道 吗?
Nǐ gāng zhīdào ma?
You just found out?
The verb 知道 always includes the result of "knowing."

✔ 宝宝 刚 醒 。
Bǎobao gāng xǐng .
The baby just woke up.
The verb 醒 includes a clear enough indication of result.

刚 and 刚才 with 没

There's also something going on with 没 in sentences with 刚 and 刚才. The deal here is that you can say something *didn't happen* ***just now*** (刚才), but you can't say that something ***just*** *didn't happen* (刚). [Saying that something "just didn't happen" only works in English if you interpret "just" to mean "simply."]

The takeaway? Just don't use 刚 in sentences where you use 没 to negate the past.

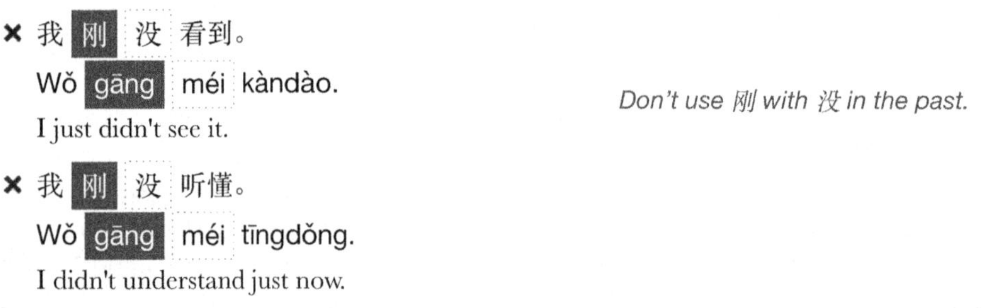

✘ 我 刚 没 看到。
Wǒ gāng méi kàndào.
I just didn't see it.
Don't use 刚 with 没 in the past.

✘ 我 刚 没 听懂。
Wǒ gāng méi tīngdǒng.
I didn't understand just now.

Use 没 with 刚才 (and no 了) to negate the past.

✔ 我 刚才 没 看到。
Wǒ gāngcái méi kàndào.
I didn't see it just now.

✔ 我 刚才 没 听懂。
Wǒ gāngcái méi tīngdǒng.
I didn't understand just now.

Example Dialog

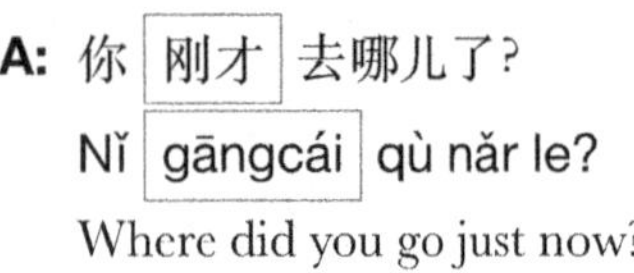

A: 你 刚才 去哪儿了?
Nǐ gāngcái qù nǎr le?
Where did you go just now?

B: 我去上厕所了。刚回来。

Wǒ qù shàng cèsuǒ le. Gāng huílái.

I went to the bathroom. I just got back.

Similar to

- Expressing "just now" with "gangcai" (A2)
- Expressing "just" with "gang" (A2)

Comparing "youdian" and "yidian" (B1)

一点 (yīdiǎn) and 有点 (yǒudiǎn), usually pronounced 一点儿 (yīdiǎnr) and 有点儿 (yǒudiǎnr) in northern China, mean pretty much the same thing on the surface — "a little" or "a bit" — but they have different uses in sentences.

Both Can Be Used for Describing Degree

Usage of 有点

有点 is placed before an adjective, and while used for descriptions, it also expresses a tone of complaint by the speaker, or some other form of negative impression. It doesn't just mean "a bit," but rather "a bit *too*" (for the speaker's liking).

A few examples:

- 今天我 有点 累 。 *This is a complaint.*
  Jīntiān wǒ yǒudiǎn lèi .
  I am a little tired today.
- 这个菜 有点 咸 。 *This is a complaint.*
  Zhège cài yǒudiǎn xián .
  This dish is a bit salty.

Usage of 一点

一点 can't be placed before an adjective. Instead, it is placed *after* adjectives. The adjectives that can be used are particularly limited. 一点 is often used when comparing, requesting, or expressing the speaker's expectation. In this usage, 一点 can also be shortened to just 点。

A few examples:

- 请说 慢 一点 。 *This is a request.*
  Qǐng shuō màn yīdiǎn.
  Please speak a little more slowly.
- 快 点 ，要迟到了。 *This is a request.*
  Kuài diǎn, yào chídào le.
  Hurry up a bit, we're going to be late.
- 老板，便宜 点 吧。 *This is a request.*
  Lǎobǎn, piányi diǎn ba.
  Boss [shop owner], a little cheaper, please.
- 这个比那个 重 一点 。 *This is a comparison.*
  Zhège bǐ nàge zhòng yīdiǎn.
  This one is a bit heavier than that one.

Use 有 (一) 点 for Describing Quantity

一点 can be placed before a noun to mean "small quantity," like 一点水，一点钱 while 有点 can't be used this way. Note that 有点 is also a shortened form of 有一点, which means "there is a little" of something.

A few examples to help you understand:

- 你脸上 有一点 番茄酱 。
  Nǐ liǎn shàng yǒu yī diǎn fānqiéjiàng .
  There's a little ketchup on your face.
- 你碗里还 有点 饭 ，吃完吧。
  Nǐ wǎn lǐ hái yǒu diǎn fàn , chī wán ba.
  There's still a little rice in your bowl. Finish eating it.

Negative Forms

Use 有点 Before Just 不 or 没

After 有点, you can use 不 or 没 before the adjective, however the adjective should have a positive connotation, like 高兴 (gāoxìng), 舒服 (shūfu), 喜欢 (xǐhuan), etc. This makes the overall emotion expressed negative still.

Some examples:

- 孩子们 有点 不 喜欢我们的新家。
  Háizi men yǒudiǎn bù xǐhuan wǒmen de xīn jiā.
  The children don't really like our new home.
- 她 有点 不 舒服。
  Tā yǒudiǎn bù shūfu.
  She doesn't feel very well.
- 我 有点 不 相信那个人。
  Wǒ yǒudiǎn bù xiāngxìn nàge rén.
  I don't really believe that guy.
- 我们 有点 没 听懂。
  Wǒmen yǒudiǎn méi tīngdǒng.
  We didn't really understand what was said.

Use 一点 Before 也不 or 也没

一点 can also be used in the 一点也不 or 一点也没 structure[1] to mean "not at all."

Some examples:

1. Expressing "not at all" with "yidianr ye bu" (B1), page 285

- 这个菜 一点也 不 辣。
  Zhège cài yīdiǎn yě bù là.
  This dish is not spicy at all.
- 作业你 一点也 没 做?
  Zuòyè nǐ yīdiǎn yě méi zuò?
  You didn't do any homework at all?

Common Mistakes

× 今天 一点 热。
Jīntiān yīdiǎn rè.

✓ 今天 有点 热。
Jīntiān yǒudiǎn rè.
It's a little hot today.

This is a complaint.

× 我 一点 饿。
Wǒ yīdiǎn è.

✓ 我 有点 饿。
Wǒ yǒudiǎn è.
I'm a little hungry.

This is a complaint.

Similar to

- Expressing "a little too" with "you dian" (A2)
- Expressing "not at all" with "yidianr ye bu" (B1), page 285
- Expressing "a bit too" (B2)

Comparing "hui," "neng," "keyi" (B1)

The three modal verbs 会 (huì), 能 (néng), and 可以 (kěyǐ) are all often translated as "can" in English. Sometimes they are explained as: 会 means "know how to," 能 means "to be able to," and 可以 means "to have permission to." In reality, their usage does overlap somewhat.

Basic Meanings

The words 会, 能, and 可以 actually overlap a little in meaning. The first step is to understand their basic meanings, though:

- 会 can mean "know how to" and can express an action that you had to *learn* or *be trained in* to do.
- 能 means "to be able to" and expresses having a certain *ability* or having obtained a certain minimum *requirement*.
- 可以 means "may" or "to be allowed to" and expresses having another person's *permission*.

As for overlap, this graphic helps explain nicely:

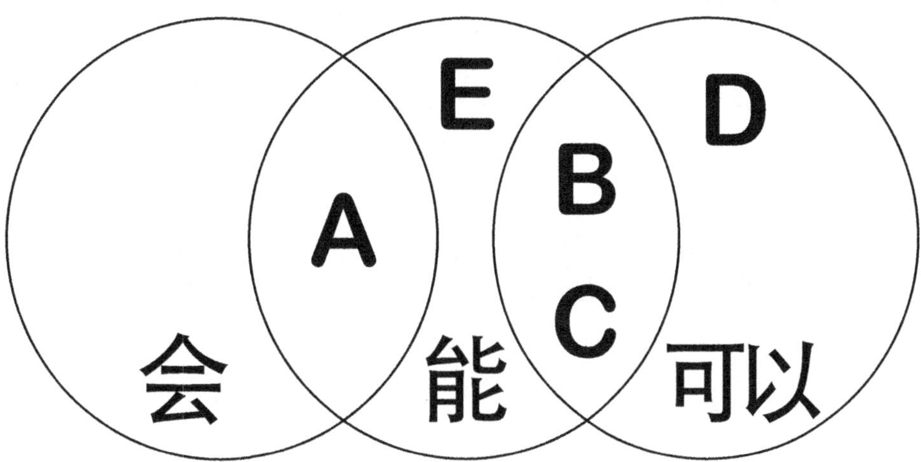

Original diagram by Tian Shou-he, redesign by Sinoplice.com

The regions marked by letters are explained in the sections below:

- A: ability in the sense of "know how to" (会 is more common than 能)
- B: permission/request (use 能 or 可以)
- C: possibility (use 能 or 可以)
- D: permission not granted (use 不可以)
- E: impossibility (use 不能)

Expressing Ability

Both 会 and 能 can be used to express ability in something.

Structure

Examples

- 我们都 会 游泳。
  Wǒmen dōu huì yóuyǒng.
  We all know how to swim.
- 他不 会 修电脑。
  Tā bù huì xiū diànnǎo.
  He doesn't know how to fix computers.

A: 你 会 说中文吗?
Nǐ huì shuō Zhōngwén ma?
Can you speak Chinese?

B: 不好意思，我只 会 说一点。
Bù hǎoyìsi, wǒ zhǐ huì shuō yīdiǎn.
Sorry, I can only speak a little.

A: 你 能 吃三碗米饭吗?
Nǐ néng chī sān wǎn mǐfàn ma?
Are you able to eat three bowls of rice?

B: 不 能 。
Bù néng.
I can't.

Expressing Permission

可以 is used to ask for or give permission. However, 能 can also be used to replace 可以 interchangeably.

Note: When a question is asked using 能 or 可以 it can be answered with 不能 or 不可以, meaning no, and only 可以 meaning yes. Chinese don't really answer with just 能 when it comes to permission.

Structure

可以 / 能 + Verb

Examples

A: 老师，我 可以 早点走吗？
Lǎoshī, wǒ kěyǐ zǎo diǎn zǒu ma?
Teacher, can I leave a little early?

B: 不可以。
Bù kěyǐ.
No, you can't.

A: 我 能 在这里抽烟吗？
Wǒ néng zài zhèlǐ chōuyān ma?
Can I smoke here?

B: 不 能 。
Bù néng.
No, you can't.

Expressing Possibility

能 and 可以 can also be used to express possibility.

Structure

可以 / 能 + Verb

Example

- 明天你 能 早点来吗？
  Míngtiān nǐ néng zǎodiǎn lái ma?
  Is it possible for you to come a little earlier tomorrow?
- 可不可以 换时间？
  Kě bu kěyǐ huàn shíjiān?
  Is it possible to change the time?

A: 外国人 能不能 参加?

Wàiguó rén néng bu néng cānjiā?

Is it possible for foreigners to attend?

B: 不 能 。

Bù néng.

Not possible.

Talking about the Future

Only 会 can be used to mean something is going to happen. It expresses that something in the future will happen and is often used to express trends or possibilities.

Structure

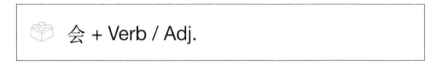

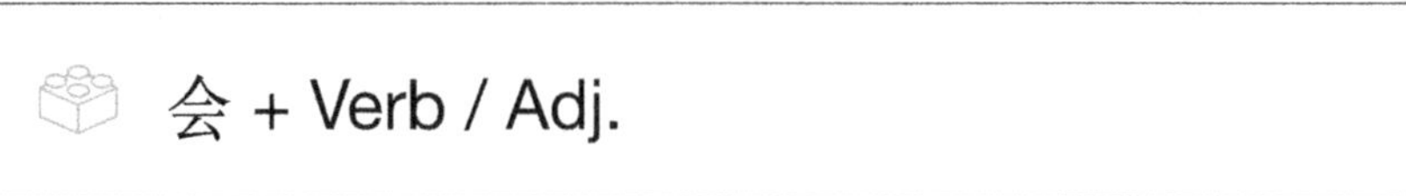

会 + Verb / Adj.

Examples

- 他不 会 跟你结婚。

  Tā bù huì gēn nǐ jiéhūn.

  He's not going to marry you.

- 你 会 生我的气吗?

  Nǐ huì shēng wǒ de qì ma?

  Will you be mad at me?

- 这样穿 会 好看吗?

  Zhèyàng chuān huì hǎokàn ma?

  Will I look good if I dress like this?

A: 今天 会 下雨吗?

Jīntiān huì xiàyǔ ma?

Is it going to rain today?

B: 我看不 会 。

Wǒ kàn bù huì.

I don't think it will.

Using Adverbs to Add Emphasis

By placing 很 (hěn) before 会, it adds emphasis to the level of ability and skill on the action presented. 很会 is commonly used to mean "to be good at" and expresses being very skillful at something, or doing something very well. It can be translated as "really know how to," as in "you really know how to speak Chinese!" Another way to put it is, "You are good at speaking Chinese."

When 很 is placed in front of 能, the meaning takes on a amazed/surprised tone on the action. Although more rarely used, it emphasizes quantity and amount. 很能 is most commonly used with 吃 (chī) to eat, and 睡 (shuì) to sleep. It's like the English equivalent of saying you "can really" do something. For example saying that someone "*can really* sleep" means that they can sleep a lot.

Note: 很可以 is not a phrase, and therefore this pattern does not apply to 可以.

Structure

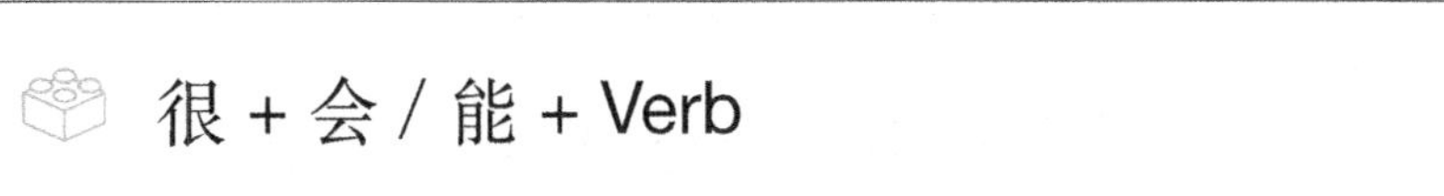

Other degree adverbs like 真 (zhēn), 太 (tài), 这么 (zhème), etc. can also be used in place of 很.

Examples

- 他很能说。
  Tā hěn néng shuō.
  He's quite a talker.
- 我妈妈很会做饭。
  Wǒ māma hěn huì zuòfàn.
  My mother really knows how to cook.
  My mom cooks very well.
- 她才五岁，但是很会说话。
  Tā cái wǔ suì, dànshì hěn huì shuōhuà.
  She's only five but she's a smooth talker.
  The subject has good speaking skills.
- 这个女生很会打扮。
  Zhège nǚshēng hěn huì dǎban.
  This girl knows how to dress up really well.

Note that 很能说 means someone talks *a lot*, 很会说 means they *have a way with words*, but 很可以说 is just bad Chinese.

Examples used with other adverbs:

- 他太能睡了。
  Tā tài néng shuì le.
  He can really sleep.
  The subject can sleep a lot, for many hours.

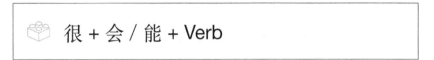

- 你 真 能 吃！
  Nǐ zhēn néng chī!
  Wow, you really can eat!
  The subject can eat a lot.
- 中国人 真 会 吃！
  Zhōngguó rén zhēn huì chī!
  Chinese people can really eat.
  The subject has great knowledge about food and its culture, a true connoisseur.
- 没想到你 这么 能 吃苦。
  Méixiǎngdào nǐ zhème néng chīkǔ.
  I didn't expect you to be able to handle so much hardhsip.

Similar Expression with Different Meanings

- 我的脚好了，现在又 能 跳舞了。
  Wǒ de jiǎo hǎo le, xiànzài yòu néng tiàowǔ le.
  I am able to dance now since my foot is better. (The condition changed)
- 我学了两个月，现在我 会 跳舞了。
  Wǒ xué le liǎng gè yuè, xiànzài wǒ huì tiàowǔ le.
  I studied for two months. I know how to dance now. (It's a learned skill)
- 我爸妈同意了，现在我 可以 跳舞了。
  Wǒ bàmā tóngyì le, xiànzài wǒ kěyǐ tiàowǔ le.
  My parents agreed. I'm allowed to dance now. (Parents gave their permission)

Note that none of the three can be followed by the aspectual particle 过.

Similar to

- The use of Taiwanese Mandarin "hui" (B2)

Comparing "haishi" and "huozhe" (B1)

Both 还是 (háishì) and 或者 (huòzhě) mean "or" and are used to present a choice. However, 还是 is normally used when asking a question, and 或者 is mostly for declarative sentences.

还是 for Providing Choices as a Question

When asking a question, 还是 can be used to provide choices or options.

Structure

Option A + 还是 + Option B ?

Examples

- 你喜欢他 还是 我?
  Nǐ xǐhuan tā háishì wǒ?
  Do you like him or me?
- 你喝茶 还是 喝咖啡?
  Nǐ hē chá háishì hē kāfēi?
  Do you drink tea or coffee?
- 你中午出去吃 还是 叫外卖?
  Nǐ zhōngwǔ chūqù chī háishì jiào wàimài?
  Are you going out for lunch or ordering take-out?

或者 for Giving Options as a Statement

或者 is used in a statement in which options are presented.

Structure

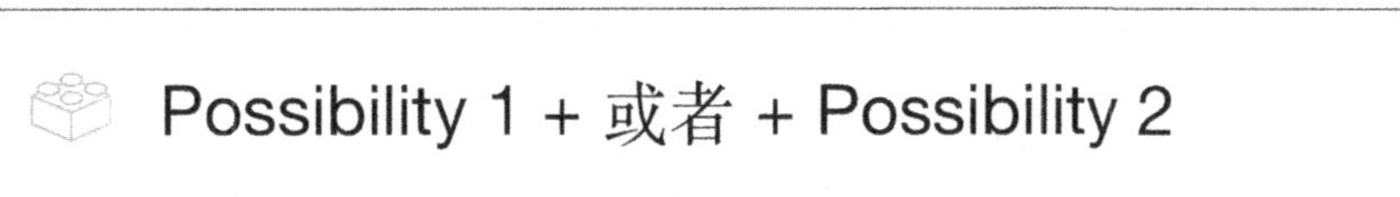
Possibility 1 + 或者 + Possibility 2

The structure for 或者 and 还是 is the same, but the meaning, as well as the context in which 或者 is needed, is different. 或者 drops the "A or B, PICK ONE" attitude in favor of a more open, "maybe A, perhaps B… (or maybe both or neither?)" So it's less exclusive and less demanding of a choice RIGHT NOW.

Examples

- 周末我想在家看书 或者 看电影。
  Zhōumò wǒ xiǎng zài jiā kànshū huòzhě kàn diànyǐng.
  This weekend, I want to stay home and read or watch movies.
- 你可以坐 1 号线 或者 2 号线去人民广场。
  Nǐ kěyǐ zuò yī hào xiàn huòzhě èr hào xiàn qù Rénmín Guǎngchǎng.
  You can take Line 1 or Line 2 to People's Square.
- 我们可以电话 或者 邮件联系。
  Wǒmen kěyǐ diànhuà huòzhě yóujiàn liánxì.
  We can contact each other by phone or email.

还是 for Questions That Are Embedded in Sentences

Deciding whether or not to use 还是 becomes difficult with sentences that contain statements like "I don't know," "I want to know," "I'm not sure," etc. Alone, these statements are not technically questions. However, when used in a sentence that contains choices, these statements imply that a question must be answered. Therefore, you must use 还是.

A few examples:

- 我 不知道 这本书是他的 还是 我的。
  Wǒ bù zhīdào zhè běn shū shì tā de háishì wǒ de.
  I don't know if this book is his or mine.
- 我 想知道 他们是支持 还是 反对。
  Wǒ xiǎng zhīdào tāmen shì zhīchí háishì fǎnduì.
  I want to know if they support or oppose.
- 老板 不确定 是这个周末出差 还是 下个周末出差。
  Lǎobǎn bù quèdìng shì zhège zhōumò chūchāi háishì xià gè zhōumò chūchāi.
  The boss isn't sure if he's going on a business trip this weekend or next weekend.

Incorrect Examples

- ✘ 我们打车 或者 坐地铁?
  Wǒmen dǎchē huòzhě zuò dìtiě?
  Shall we take a taxi or take the metro?
  Since it is a question, it should use 还是
- ✘ 明天 还是 后天都行。
  Míngtiān huòzhě hòutiān dōu xíng.
  Either tomorrow or the day after is fine.
  Since it is a statement, it should use 或者

✘ 我 想知道 那个人是男的 **或者** 女的。 *It's an embedded question, so it should use 还是*

Wǒ xiǎng zhīdào nàge rén shì nánde **huòzhě** nǚde.

I'd like to know if that person is male or female.

Similar to

- Offering choices with "haishi" (A1)
- Expressing "or" in statements (A2)

Comparing "renjia" and "bieren" (B1)

When referring to other people, we can use both the words 人家 (rénjia) and 别人 (biérén). But 人家 has additional grammatical uses which we will explore in this article.

Both can mean "others"

人家 and 别人 both refer to others besides the speaker and the listener. However, 人家 is more colloquial.

人家 and 别人 are interchangeable in these sentences below.

- 我不在乎 人家 怎么说。
  Wǒ bù zàihu rénjia zěnme shuō.
  I don't care about what other people say.
- 别人 怎么想我怎么知道?
  Biérén zěnme xiǎng wǒ zěnme zhīdào?
  How could I know what other people are thinking?
- 那是 人家 的事，你管那么多干嘛?
  Nà shì rénjia de shì, nǐ guǎn nàme duō gàn ma?
  That's other people's business. Why get involved?

Additional Uses of 人家

For these additional uses of 人家, it would be incorrect to use 别人.

人家 as "I" or "me"

人家 can be used to refer to yourself, and it is often used this way by women, giving it a sort of girly, shy, tender feeling.

- 因为 人家 喜欢你啊。
  Yīnwèi rénjia xǐhuan nǐ a.
  Because I like you!
- 讨厌！老是拿 人家 开玩笑。
  Tǎoyàn! Lǎo shì ná rénjia kāiwánxiào.
  You are so annoying! You're always making fun of me.

人家 as "him" or "her"

人家 can also refer to someone previously referred to (in the context of the conversation or body of text) or it can refer to a certain someone that both the speaker and listener know.

- 你快给 人家 道歉。
  Nǐ kuài gěi rénjia dàoqiàn.
  Apologize to them now.
- 你看 人家 多聪明！
  Nǐ kàn rénjia duō cōngming!
  Look how smart he is!

人家 as "residents"

人家 can also refer to households. In this case, it's pronounced as "rénjiā" rather than "rénjia." This use is going to be the least common in everyday spoken Chinese.

- 这个小区有多少 户 人家 ?
  Zhège xiǎoqū yǒu duōshao hù rénjiā ?
  How many households are here in this neighborhood?
- 村子里现在只剩十 户 人家 了。
  Cūnzi lǐ xiànzài zhī shèng shí hù rénjiā le.
  There are only ten households left in this village.

Comparing "zhijian" and "zhongjian" (B1)

When describing spatial relationships, the words 之间 (zhījiān) and 中间 (zhōngjiān) will come in handy to express the concepts of "between" and "among." Both have a few particular uses, though.

Both as "Between… and…"

之间 and 中间 can both refer to a space "in the middle" between two points, as long as we're talking about physical space.

Structure

A + 和 + B + 之间 / 中间

Examples

- 上海在江苏省和浙江省 之间 / 中间 。
  Shànghǎi zài Jiāngsū Shěng hé Zhèjiāng Shěng zhījiān / zhōngjiān.
  Shanghai is between Jiangsu Province and Zhejiang Province.
- 我家客厅和卧室 中间 是洗手间。
  Wǒ jiā kètīng hé wòshì zhōngjiān shì xǐshǒujiān.
  Our bathroom is between the bedroom and the living room.

Grammatically, both 之间 and 中间 are nouns (location nouns, to be precise). One difference between the two, however, is that 中间 can be used all by itself, but 之间 is always used together with other words.

- ✗ 明天早上我有两个考试，之间 有 20 分钟的休息时间。
  Míngtiān zǎoshang wǒ yǒu liǎng gè kǎoshì, zhījiān yǒu èrshí fēnzhōng de xiūxi shíjiān.
- ✓ 明天早上我有两个考试，中间 有 20 分钟的休息时间。
  Míngtiān zǎoshang wǒ yǒu liǎng gè kǎoshì, zhōngjiān yǒu èrshí fēnzhōng de xiūxi shíjiān.
  I have two exams tomorrow morning. There is a 20 minute break in between.

Usages of 中间

中间 as "In the Middle of"

中间 can be used for describing location within an object. This "within" could be "inside" a space, like inside a house, in the middle (center) of a table, or in the middle of the screen. You can't use 之间 in this way.

Structure

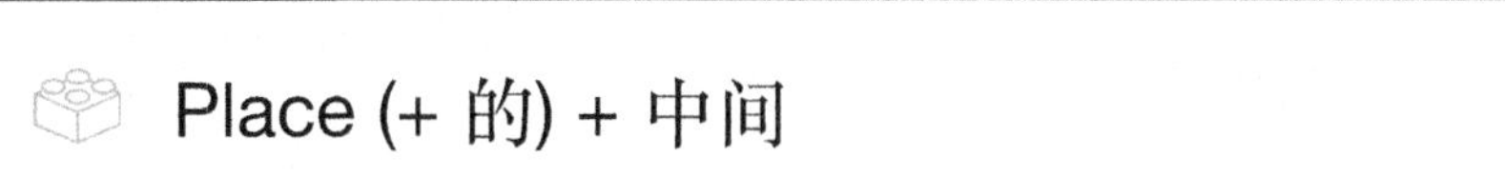

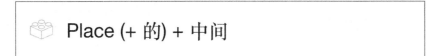

Examples

- 客厅的 中间 有一个沙发。
  Kètīng de zhōngjiān yǒu yī gè shāfā.
  There is a sofa in the middle of the living room.
- 我的座位在 第七排 中间 。
  Wǒ de zuòwèi zài dì-qī pái zhōngjiān.
  My seat is in the middle of Row 7.
- 把花放在 桌子 中间 。
  Bǎ huā fàng zài zhuōzi zhōngjiān.
  Put the flowers in the middle of the table.

Try not to say:

✕ 大厅 之间 有很多人。
Dàtīng zhījiān yǒu hěn duō rén.
There are many people in the middle of the lobby.

中间 as "Among"

中间 is used when referring to one (or more) "among many."

A few examples:

- 你们 中间 有会唱歌的吗?
  Nǐmen zhōngjiān yǒu huì chànggē de ma?
  Can anyone among you sing?
- 这些人 中间 我只认识一个。
  Zhèxiē rén zhōngjiān wǒ zhī rènshi yī gè.
  Among these people, I only know one person.

之间 can't be used to mean "among" like this.

Usages of 之间

之间 as "Ranging from… to…"

This usage refers to examples like "between 8am and 3pm" or "between 20 and 30".

Structure

Examples

- 你可以明天早上八点 到 十点 之间 过来。
  Nǐ kěyǐ míngtiān zǎoshang bā diǎn dào shí diǎn zhījiān guòlái.
  You can come between 8am and 10am tomorrow.
- 45 岁 到 60 岁 之间 的人很容易得这种病。
  Sìshí-wǔ suì dào liùshí suì zhījiān de rén hěn róngyì de zhèzhǒng bìng.
  People aged 45 to 60 years old are susceptible to this disease.

之间 for Describing Relationships

The idea is that the relationship is "between" two or more people, with the abstract "between" part indicated by 之间. This usage of 之间 can also refer to relationships between two (or more) companies, countries, etc., but mostly it's used between people. 中间 can't be used in this way.

A few examples:

- 夫妻 之间 应该多交流。
  Fūqī zhījiān yīnggāi duō jiāoliú.
  There should be plenty of communication between husband and wife.
- 你们 之间 到底发生了什么事情?
  Nǐmen zhījiān dàodǐ fāshēng le shénme shìqing?
  What exactly happened between the two of you?
- 她不太会处理 上下级 之间 的关系。
  Tā bù tài huì chǔlǐ shàng-xià jí zhījiān de guānxi.
  She doesn't really understand how to handle the relationships between superiors and subordinates.

Comparing "li" and "cong" (B1)

Both 离 (lí) and 从 (cóng) can be translated into English as "from." In Chinese, however, their meanings are different. 从 is used in cases where the subject's position relative to a fixed location changes. 离 expresses a "static" distance, or a distance that is unchanging. Both can be used in defining distance or time, however 从 has more meanings than 离.

从 as "from" (Time or Event)

Structure

从 + Time / Event + 开始 / 起

Examples

- 从 下个月 起 ，公司会越来越忙。
  Cóng xiàge yuè qǐ , gōngsī huì yuèláiyuè máng.
  Starting from next month, the company will be busier and busier.
- 从 我上小学 开始 ，就特别喜欢画画。
  Cóng wǒ shàng xiǎoxué kāishǐ , jiù tèbié xǐhuan huà huà.
  I have really liked drawing since starting elementary school.

Colloquial Sayings

从那以后 means "ever since then," while 从今以后 means "from now on."

A few examples:

- 从那 以后 ，我们就没有联系了。
  Cóng nà yǐhòu , wǒmen jiù méiyǒu liánxì le.
  Ever since then, we haven't been in touch.
- 从今 以后 ，我不用再加班了。
  Cóng jīn yǐhòu , wǒ bùyòng zài jiābān le.
  I don't need to work late from now on.

从 as "From" (a Place, Somebody, or Something)

Structure

从 + Place + 上 / 里

Examples

- 你是不是 从 我包里 拿了一百块钱?
  Nǐ shì bu shì cóng wǒ bāo lǐ ná le yī bǎi kuài qián?
  Did you take one hundred RMB from my purse?
- 我 从 他身上 学到了很多东西。
  Wǒ cóng tā shēnshang xuédào le hěn duō dōngxi.
  I learned a lot from him.
- 从 这件事 可以看出你的工作态度。
  Cóng zhè jiàn shì kěyǐ kànchū nǐ de gōngzuò tàidu.
  From this incident, we can see your attitude toward work.

离 as "Distance from"

Structure

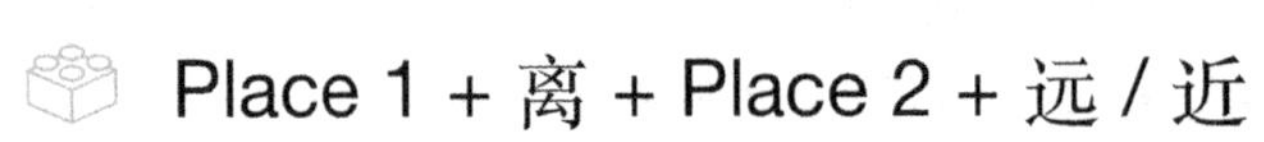

Place 1 + 离 + Place 2 + 远 / 近

Examples

✔ 你家 离 公司 多远 ?
Nǐ jiā lí gōngsī duō yuǎn ?
How far is your home from your company?

✔ 我家 离 公司 很远 。
Wǒ jiā lí gōngsī hěn yuǎn .
My home is far from my office.

Try not to say:

✘ 我家 很远 从 公司。
Wǒ jiā hěn yuǎn cóng gōngsī.

✘ 我家 从 公司 很远 。
Wǒ jiā cóng gōngsī hěn yuǎn .

离 as "From" (a Time or Event)

Structure

 Past Event 1 + 离 + Time + Duration

If you want to say "from now," try this pattern:

 离 + Future Event + 还有 + Duration

Examples

- 上次见面 离 今天快十年了。
  Shàng cì jiànmiàn lí jīntiān kuài shí nián le.
  It's been about 10 years since we met last time.
- 离 我们的婚礼 还有 两个星期。
  Lí wǒmen de hūnlǐ háiyǒu liǎng gè xīngqī.
  We still have two weeks until our wedding.
- 离 毕业 还有 几个月。
  Lí bìyè háiyǒu jǐ gè yuè.
  I am a few months away from graduation.

Colloquial Saying 离…… 还远呢

离…… 还远呢 expresses that something is very far off in terms of time.

- 我们刚刚开始谈恋爱，离 结婚 还远 呢。
  Wǒmen gānggāng kāishǐ tán liàn'ài, lí jiéhūn háiyuǎn ne.
  We've just started our relationship. It's too soon to talk about marriage.

Similar to

- Expressing "from… to…" with "cong… dao…" (A2)
- Expressing distance with "li" (A2)
- Expressing "ever since" with "yilai" (B1), page 111

Comparing "yihou" and "de shihou" (B1)

When talking about when something happens, 以后 (yǐhòu) and 的时候 (de shíhou) are often used. They can both be translated as the English word "when," but their usage in Chinese must be kept straight.

Structure

以后 and 的时候 both appear in the same place in the sentence: after the verb.

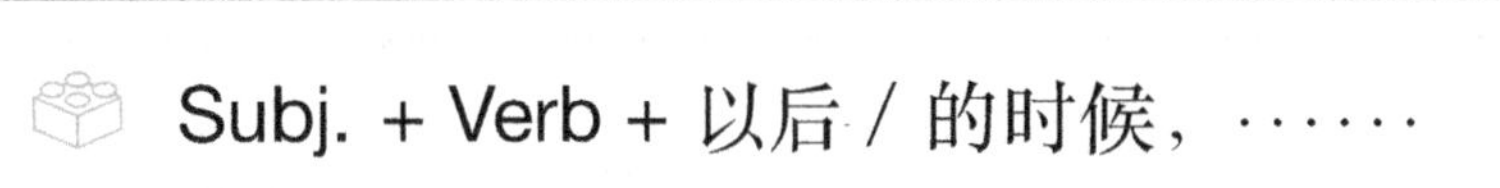

The difference comes in what they actually mean.

Use 以后 for "After"

以后 technically means after, so it is used *after* the action is completed. This can be seen as a way of saying "When you are done (verb)ing." This might seem obvious, but in the following sentences, we could use "when" in English for every single one.

- 下飞机 以后 给我打电话。
  Xià fēijī yǐhòu gěi wǒ dǎ diànhuà
  Give me a call after you get off the plane.
- 来中国 以后 我才发现中国菜那么好吃。
  Lái Zhōngguó yǐhòu wǒ cái fāxiàn Zhōngguó cài nàme hào chī.
  Only when I got to China did I realize how tasty Chinese food is.
- 毕业 以后 我打算去上海工作。
  Bìyè yǐhòu wǒ dǎsuàn qù Shànghǎi gōngzuò.
  I plan to find a job in Shanghai after I graduate.
- 结婚 以后 你想继续工作吗?
  Jiéhūn yǐhòu nǐ xiǎng jìxù gōngzuò ma?
  Do you want to keep working after you get married?

Use 的时候 for "During" or "While"

的时候 means "when" in the sense of during an action. For example, "when you play ball" can be seen as "when you are playing ball." It is this sort of difference that can make 以后 and 的时候 slightly confusing at times.

- 吃饭 的时候 看电视容易长胖。
  Chīfàn de shíhou kàn diànshì róngyì zhǎng pàng.
  It's easy to get fat if you eat while you watch TV.

- 工作 的时候 不要上网聊天。
  Gōngzuò de shíhou bùyào shàngwǎng liáotiān.
  Don't chat online when you're at work.
- 无聊 的时候 可以做些什么？
  Wúliáo de shíhou kěyǐ zuò xiē shénme?
  What can you do when you're bored?

的时候 is also similar to using the 一边 structure. However, 一边 uses two conscious actions that you do, whereas "的时候" can be used for "mindless" activities (like watching TV) or unexpected situations.

Overlapping Usage

There are instances where *both* 以后 and 的时候 could work and still mean the same thing. These are times when there isn't really a duration, it just happens in an instant. For example, "when you see her." This means, "as soon as you see her," as there is only one point where you first see a person. In this case, you can use either one.

- 雨停了 的时候 ，我们就去公园玩。
  Yǔ tíng le de shíhou, wǒmen jiù qù gōngyuán wán.
  When it stops raining, we'll go play in the park.
- 雨停了 以后 ，我们就去公园玩。
  Yǔ tíngle yǐhòu, wǒmen jiù qù gōngyuán wán.
  When it stops raining, we'll go play in the park.
- 商店关门的 时候 ，你再来找我。
  Shāngdiàn guānmén de shíhou, nǐ zàilái zhǎo wǒ.
  Come to find me when the shop is closed.
- 商店关门了 以后 ，你再来找我。
  Shāngdiàn guānmén le yǐhòu, nǐ zàilái zhǎo wǒ.
  Come to find me when the shop is closed.

Similar to

- After a specific time with "yihou" (A2)
- Expressing "when" with "de shihou" (A2)
- Expressing "when" with "shi" (B1), page 114

Glossary

We strive to avoid unnecessarily technical terms on the Chinese Grammar Wiki, but occasionally it's sort of necessary, and sometimes even useful (yes, really!). So to help you out, we've placed all of the grammatical terms related to Mandarin Chinese in one place. Each term has a page on the wiki with a more complete description, and many pages also have lists of grammar points related to the term.

List of Mandarin Grammar Terms

Action verb — *Also known as: 动作动词 (dòngzuò dòngcí) and 行为动词 (xíngwéi dòngcí).* Action verbs describe what a subject did, is doing, or will do, physically.

Adjective — *Also known as: 形容词 (xíngróngcí).* Adjectives are the "describing" words of a language. In Chinese, they have some characteristics that they don't have in English.

Adjectival phrase — *Also known as: 形容词性词组 (xíngróngcí-xìng duǎnyǔ) and adjective phrase.* Adjectival phrases often consist of just an adjective and the adverbs modifying it, but they might also have other structures, such as an adjective and complement.

Adjectival predicate sentence — *Also known as: 形容词谓语句 (xíngróngcí wèiyǔ jù) and 形容词性谓语句 (xíngróngcí-xìng wèiyǔ jù).* A fancy name for a sentence where the predicate consists of an adjective.

Adverb — *Also known as: 副词 (fùcí).* Adverbs are words that modify verbs and adjectives. In Chinese, word order of adverbs is much stricter than in English. Chinese adverbs normally come before the main verb of a sentence, but in some cases come right at the beginning of a sentence.

Adverbial — *Also known as: 状语 (zhuàngyǔ).* An adverbial is a sentence element that functions like an adverb, modifying a verb or adjective.

Adverbial phrase — *Also known as: 副词短语 (fùcí duǎnyǔ) and adverb phrase.* An adverbial phrase is a phrase with two or more words that act like an adverb, modifying a verb or adjective.

Affirmative-negative question — *Also known as: 正反问句 (zhèng-fǎn wènjù) and alternative questions.* A common way to form questions in Chinese is to first use a verb in the positive, then repeat the same verb in its negative form, similar to how in English we can say, "Do you have money or not?" or "Have you or have you not been to the park?" This sentence pattern feels a lot more natural in Chinese than those admittedly awkward English equivalents, however.

Affix — *Also known as: 词缀 (cízhuì).* An affix is a linguistic unit added to the beginning, middle or end of a word to change its meaning (e.g. prefix, infix, suffix).

Aspect — *Also known as: 动作状态 (dòngzuò zhuàngtài).* Chinese does not use the concept of formal tenses. Instead, it employs what is called "grammatical aspect." Rather than conjugating its verbs, Chinese uses particles to indicate how a verb works within a particular timeframe, or how the verb relates to the flow of time. The particles most often used to indicate aspect in Chinese are 了 (le), 过 (guo), and 着 (zhe).

Aspectual particle – *Also known as: 动态助词 (dòngtài zhùcí).* These words are added to verbs to indicate aspect (not the same as tense). The particles most often used to indicate aspect in Chinese are 了 (le), 过 (guo), and 着 (zhe).

Attributive – *Also known as: 定语 (dìngyǔ).* An attributive is the word or phrase that directly precedes the noun it describes. Frequently it is linked to the noun with the structural particle 的 (de).

Auxiliary verb – *Also known as: modal verb, 助动词 (zhùdòngcí), 情态动词 (qíngtài dòngcí) and 能愿动词 (néngyuàn dòngcí).* Auxiliary verbs are "helping" verbs that come before main verbs and help express a tone or mood. (The word "modal" comes from "mood.") In English, auxiliary verbs include words like "should," "will," and "can," which all change something about the situation and the speaker's attitude. Auxiliary verbs express capability, possibility, necessity, obligation or willingness.

Cardinal number – *Also known as: 基数词 (jīshùcí).* Cardinal numbers are numbers such as 1, 2, or 3 used to indicate quantity. They contrast with ordinal numbers.

Causative verb – *Also known as: 使令动词 (shǐlìng dòngcí) and 使役动词 (shǐyì dòngcí).* A causative verb is a kind of verb that is used to indicate that someone or something causes something else to do or be something. In Chinese, 让 (ràng) is a major player in this space.

Complement – *Also known as: 补语 (bǔyǔ) and objective complement.* A complement is a word or phrase following a verb (or sometimes an adjective) that provides additional meaning to the verb phrase. Complements are not the same as objects, and can be as short as one character, or practically as long as a sentence. Complements provide additional information associated with verbs, such as degree, result, direction or possibility, and are extremely common. Complements are not a form of flattery (those are compliments); they're much more versatile than that!

Complex sentence – *Also known as: 复句 (fùjù).* A complex sentence is a sentence with one main clause and one or more subordinate clauses.

Conjunction – *Also known as: 连词 (liáncí).* Conjunctions in Chinese do exactly what they do in English: connect things. They help make the transition between ideas smoother and also show the relationships between those ideas.

Content word – *Also known as: 实词 (shící).* Content words refer to real objects in the real world, whether solid and palpable, or observable in some other way. These words refer to objects, actions, concepts, and even emotions, which exist in some real way as more than just grammatical tools. Words that serve purely grammatical roles are called function words.

Coverb – *Also known as: 副动词 (fùdòngcí) and 伴动词 (bàndòngcí).* A coverb is a verb that modifies the main verb of a sentence when used with its own object.

Degree adverb – *Also known as: 程度副词 (chéngdù fùcí) and adverb of degree.* Degree adverbs intensify or in some other way modify the degree of expression of the adjective (or verb).

Degree complement – *Also known as: 程度补语 (chéngdù bǔyǔ) and complement of degree.* While most complements follow verbs, degree complements can follow both verbs and adjectives. These complements intensify or modify the degree of expression of the verb or adjective.

Demonstrative pronoun — *Also known as: 指示代词 (zhǐshì dàicí).* A demonstrative pronoun is a pronoun used in the place of a noun and specifies what is being referred to.

Dependent clause — *Also known as: 从句 (cóngjù).* A dependent clause is dependent on and modifies an independent clause. Dependent clauses have a subject and verb, but also start with a subordinate conjunction, making it clear that they are not meant to stand on their own.

Direct object — *Also known as: 直接宾语 (zhíjiē bīnyǔ).* A direct object is what is being acted upon, thus receiving the action of a verb. In Chinese grammar, direct objects are often simply referred to as "objects."

Direction complement — *Also known as: 趋向补语 (qūxiàng bǔyǔ), directional complement and complement of direction.* A direction complement is a complement used to describe the direction of a verb. A verb already has some inherent movement implied; adding a direction complement clarifies where, exactly, that action is going.

Directional verb — *Also known as: 趋向动词 (qūxiàng dòngcí).* Directional verbs can be added to other verbs in a direction complement, illustrating which direction the verb is going.

Directional complement — See **direction complement**

Distinguishing word — *Also known as: 区别词 (qūbiécí) and attributive adjective.* "Distinguishing words" are rather foreign to the English speaker. On the surface they may seem like regular adjectives, but distinguishing words cannot have degree, so they cannot be modified by adverbs. Unlike normal adjectives, sentences involving distinguishing words use 是 (shì), and usually 的 (de) as well. Common words include the Chinese words for "male," "female," "real," "fake," and colors.

Existential verb — *Also known as: 存现动词 (cúnxiàn dòngcí).* Existential verbs declare the existence or nonexistence of things.

Function word — *Also known as: 虚词 (xūcí).* Function words do not refer to real objects in the real world; rather they serve purely grammatical roles in sentences, drawing relationships and logical connections between the content words in a sentence. Words that refer to real objects in the real world are called content words.

Judgment verb — *Also known as: 关系动词 (guānxì dòngcí) and 判断动词 (pànduàn dòngcí).* Judgment verbs are verbs used to express the speaker's judgment. This can be as simple as the verb "to be," but also covers a wide range of other verbs.

Indirect object — *Also known as: 间接宾语 (jiànjiē bīnyǔ).* Indirect objects occur when there are two objects in a sentence. The indirect object is for/to whom/what the action of the verb is done and who/what is receiving the direct object. In Chinese grammar, indirect objects are often referred to as second objects.

Independent clause — *Also known as: 主句 (zhǔjù).* An independent clause is a clause that has a subject and a predicate that modifies the subject, allowing it to stand alone as a sentence.

Independent phrase — *Also known as: 独立语 (dúlì yǔ).* An independent phrase has no subject acting out the verb in the sentence.

Interjection — *Also known as: 叹词 (tàncí) and 感叹词 (gǎntàncí).* This type of word is used in exclamations or various kinds of emotional response.

Interrogative pronoun — See **question word**

Intransitive verb — *Also known as: 不及物动词 (bùjíwù dòngcí).* Intransitive verbs are verbs which take no direct object.

Location word — *Also known as: 方位名词 (fāngwèi míngcí), 方位词 (fāngwèi cí) and noun of locality.* Location words are nouns showing direction and location.

Main clause — See **independent clause**

Measure word — *Also known as: 量词 (liàngcí) and classifier.* Measure words are used together with numerals to indicate the quantity of a noun, and sometimes even of an action. The general term for "measure word" in linguistics is "classifier," because measure words involve some kind of classification of the noun (or action) being counted.

Mimetic word — See **onomatopoeia**

Modal adverb — *Also known as: 语气副词 (yǔqì fùcí) and tone adverb.* Modal adverbs express likelihood with adverbs such as probably, possibly, evidently, certainly, etc.

Modal particle — *Also known as: 语气助词 (yǔqì zhùcí), 语气词 (yǔqì cí), Sentence-final particle and Sentential particle.* Modal particles are words used at the end of sentences to indicate mood, or attitude. They tend to be neutral tone and hard to translate, but they add a bit of "flavor" to a sentence. See also particles.

Modal verb — See **auxiliary verb**

Negative adverb — *Also known as: 否定副词 (fǒudìng fùcí).* Negative adverbs negate verbs and adjectives to make a negative statement. The main ones in Chinese are 不 (bù) and 没 (méi).

Noun — *Also known as: 名词 (míngcí).* You may have learned these as "person, place, or thing." Nouns often act as subjects, are modified by adjectives, and can be counted with measure words in Chinese.

Noun measure word — *Also known as: 名量词 (míngliàngcí) and nominal measure word.* As the name suggests, these are measure words that are only used for nouns.

Noun phrase — *Also known as: 名词性短语 (míngcí-xìng duǎnyǔ).* A noun phrase is a phrase with a noun or pronoun as a head word that has any sort of modifier.

Numeral — *Also known as: 数词 (shùcí).* A numeral is a symbol that represents a number.

Nominal predicate sentence — *Also known as: 名词谓语句 (míngcí wèiyǔjù).* Nominal predicate sentences are sentences with a noun phrase that functions as the main predicate of the sentence.

Object — *Also known as: 宾语 (bīnyǔ).* The object is the receiver of the action of the verb.

Onomatopoeia — *Also known as: 象声词 (xiàngshēngcí) and 拟声词 (nǐshēngcí).* Onomatopoeia are words which represent sounds and noises.

Ordinal number — *Also known as: 序数词 (xùshù cí).* Ordinal numbers are numbers used to express rank or sequence. Think "1st," "2nd," etc. Ordinal numbers contrast with cardinal numbers.

Particle — *Also known as: 助词 (zhùcí).* Particles are function words that depend on other words or phrases to impart meaning. They're kind of like prepositions, but more abstract. In Chinese, the key ones are aspectual particles (for indicating aspect), structural particles (for indicating relationships between words), and modal particles (for indicating mood). Chinese particles are also special words because they tend to always take the neutral tone.

Passive voice — *Also known as: 被动结构 (bèidòng jiégòu), 被动句式 (bèidòng jùshì), 被动语态 (bèidòng yǔtài) and the passive.* "Passive voice" is a grammatical term used to refer to sentences in which the "recipient" of an action (often referred to as the "direct object" or simply "object") becomes the subject of the sentence, and the "doer" of the action is demoted to secondary importance or omitted altogether.

Passive structure — See **passive voice**

Personal pronoun — *Also known as: 人称代词 (rénchēng dàicí).* Personal pronouns include 我 (wǒ), 你 (nǐ), 他 (tā), and 她 (tā). To make them plural, all you need to do is add the suffix -们 (-men) to them. There is also a polite second person form 您 (nín), which cannot normally take the -们 (-men) suffix.

Place noun — *Also known as: 处所名词 (chùsuǒ míngcí).* Place nouns are nouns describing the position or place of something.

Place adverb — *Also known as: 处所副词 (chùsuǒ fùcí), location adverb, adverb of place and adverb of location.* Place adverbs modify the location of a verbs or adjective.

Placement verb — See **existential verb**

Phrase — *Also known as: 短语 (duǎnyǔ) and 词组 (cízǔ).* A phrase is a group of words that expresses a concept. It can be focused on fleshing out a particular word, as in a noun phrase or verb phrase. See also clause, which expresses a more complete thought.

Possessive pronoun — *Also known as: 物主代词 (wùzhǔ dàicí).* Possessive pronouns take the place of a noun and show ownership.

Potential complement — Verbs can take potential complements to indicate whether or not an action is possible. Potential complements contain a 的 (de) or a 不 (bu) immediate after the verb being modified, and are quite common in everyday spoken Mandarin.

Predicate — *Also known as: 谓语 (wèiyǔ).* Predicates are the main verb or verb phrase of a sentence, and state something about the subject. Aside from verbs, adjectives and sometimes even nouns can be predicates as well.

Preposition — *Also known as: 介词 (jiècí).* Prepositions are words that indicate location or direction. They are called "pre"-positions because they are positioned *before* the words that they modify.

Prepositional phrase — *Also known as: 介词短语 (jiècí duǎnyǔ).* A prepositional phrase is a phrase beginning with a preposition that precedes the word it modifies and clarifies that word's relationship with another word in the sentence.

Pronoun — *Also known as: 代词 (dàicí).* Pronouns substitute in for regular nouns and proper nouns to avoid unnecessary repetition of the same words over and over again.

Proper noun — *Also known as: 专有名词 (zhuānyǒu míngcí).* A proper noun is specific person, place or thing. Proper nouns are generally capitalized (e.g. Anubis, Asgard, AllSet Learning), both in English and in pinyin.

Psychological verb — *Also known as: 心理动词 (xīnlǐ dòngcí) and psych verb.* A psychological verb is a verb that conveys the speaker's mental state or attitude.

Qualitative adjective — *Also known as: 性质形容词 (xìngzhì xíngróngcí).* Qualitative adjectives describe the quality or nature of something.

Quantitative phrase — *Also known as: 数量短语 (shùliàng duǎnyǔ).* Quantitative phrases express a measurement of amount.

Quantity complement — *Also known as: 数量补语 (shùliàng bǔyǔ), quantitative complement and complement of quantity.* A quantity complement follows a verb and supplies information regarding an amount.

Question pronoun — See **question word**

Question word — *Also known as: 疑问代词 (yíwèn dàicí), question pronoun, interrogative pronoun.* A **question word** refers to a special kind of pronoun used to ask questions. These would include 什么 (shénme), 什么时候 (shénme shíhou), 谁 (shéi), 哪儿 (nǎr) / 哪里 (nǎlǐ), 哪个 (nǎge), 为什么 (wèishénme), 怎么 (zěnme). Beginners should pay attention to the placement of question words.

Reduplication — It is one of the great ironies of linguistics that the term for repeating a word is overly repetitive itself. You'd think that the word "duplication" would work just fine, but the linguistic term really is reduplication. In Chinese, verbs and adjectives are often reduplicated.

Relational verb — See **judgment verb**

Result complement — *Also known as: 结果补语 (jiéguǒ bǔyǔ), complement of result, resultative complement and result compound.* Result complements are a kind of verbal complement that appears very frequently in Chinese. Surprisingly enough, they're used to describe the result of a verb.

Scope adverb — *Also known as: 范围副词 (fànwéi fùcí).* Scope adverbs modify and expand a verb or adjective.

Sentence with a nominal predicate — See **nominal predicate sentence**

Sentence with a verbal predicate — *Also known as: 动词谓语句 (dòngcí wèiyǔ jù).* A sentence with a verb as the main element of its predicate is called a sentence with a verbal predicate. This type of sentence is extremely common.

Sentence with an adjectival predicate — See **adjectival predicate sentence**

Sentence with a subject-predicate structure as predicate — *Also known as: 主谓谓语句 (zhǔ-wèi wèiyǔ jù).*

Sentence-final particle — See **modal particle**

Sentential particle — See **modal particle**

Separable verb — *Also known as: 离合词 (líhécí) and verb-object phrase.* "Separable verbs" get their name from their ability to "separate" into two parts (a verb part and an object part), with other words in between. In fact, you could also simply call separable verbs "verb-object phrases."

Subject — *Also known as: 主语 (zhǔyǔ).* A subject is a noun or pronoun that the sentence centers around. It is the actor of the verb and is what something is said about.

Subject-predicate construction — *Also known as: 主谓结构 (zhǔ-wèi jiégòu).* The subject-predicate construction consists of a subject and a predicate, and may be part of a larger sentence, or may serve as a sentence on its own.

Subject-predicate sentence — *Also known as: 主谓句 (zhǔ-wèi jù).* A sentence composed of a subject and a predicate. The vast majority of sentences fit this description.

Subordinate clause — See **dependent clause**

State complement — *Also known as: 状态补语 (zhuàngtài bǔyǔ), 情态补语 (qíngtài bǔyǔ) and complement of state.* State complements describe an achieved state of an action. State complements are usually adjective phrases (adverb + adjective) but can take the form of verb phrases, subject-predicate phrases, or other complements. State complements that are adjective phrases often look the same as degree complements and thus are often lumped together with degree complements in textbooks.

Stative adjective — *Also known as: 状态形容词 (zhuàngtài xíngróngcí).* A stative adjective is an adjective describing a relatively unchanging or permanent condition/state.

Stative verb — *Also known as: 状态动词 (zhuàngtài dòngcí), 静态动词 (jìngtài dòngcí), state verb and static verb.* A stative verb is a verb describing a relatively unchanging or permanent condition/state. Stative verbs in Mandarin are usually translated as adjectives in English.

Structural particle — *Also known as: 结构助词 (jiégòu zhùcí).* A structural particle is a function word that denotes the structural/grammatical relationship between elements of a sentence.

Time adverb — *Also known as: 时间副词 (shíjiān fùcí).* Adverbs of time express the when, how long, or how often of a verb.

Time phrase — *Also known as: 时间短语 (shíjiān duǎnyǔ).* A time phrase occurs before the verb phrase and indicates the when, how long, or how often of a situation.

Time noun — *Also known as: 时间名词 (shíjiān míngcí), 时间词 (shíjiāncí), time nominal and temporal noun.* Time nouns are nouns that indicate a point in time.

Time-measure complement — *Also known as: 时量补语 (shí-liàng bǔyǔ).* Time-measure complements show the state or duration of an action.

Tone adverb — See **modal adverb**

Topic-comment structure — *Also known as: 主题句 (zhǔtí-jù), 主题结构 (zhǔtí jiégòu), 主题评论结构 (zhǔtí-pínglùn jiégòu), 主题述题结构 (zhǔtí-shùtí jiégòu) and 主题评述结构 (zhǔtí-píngshù jiégòu).* A topic-comment structure is an alternative to the typical subject-predicate sentence structure, whereby a topic (or theme) is followed by the speaker's comment on that topic. The topic is not the "doer" (subject) of the sentence, but rather sets the scope of the comments (some thoughts related to the topic).

Transitive verb — *Also known as: 及物动词 (jíwù dòngcí).* A transitive verb is an verb which takes a direct object.

Verb — *Also known as: 动词 (dòngcí).* Verbs are the "action" words which make up the predicates of most sentences, but may also simply indicate relationships, changes, or mental activity rather than physical actions. Verbs may take objects, and can also be reduplicated in Chinese. They can be negated, as well as modified by particles.

Verb measure word — *Also known as: 动量词 (dòng liàngcí), verbal measure word and verbal classifier.* A verb measure word accompanies the number of times a verb occurred to count the frequency or re-occurrence of an action. See: Measure words for verbs

Verb phrase — *Also known as: 动词性短语 (dòngcí-xìng duǎnyǔ) and verbal phrase.* A verb phrase is a phrase with a verb as a head word that has any sort of modifier. It commonly includes modal verbs before it and objects after it.

Verbal measure word — *Also known as: 动量补语 (dòng-liàng bǔyǔ), verb measure word, verbal classifier and action-measure complement.* This type of measure word is not used to count nouns. Rather, it is placed after verbs to show the frequency of an action.

Verbal predicate sentence — See **sentence with a verbal predicate**

Acknowledgments

The Chinese Grammar Wiki may have been pioneered by AllSet Learning, but it would not be possible without the hard work of many selfless individuals, including AllSet Learning interns, students, teachers, and regular users. Thank you!

AllSet Interns

· Donna Yee · Lucas Simons · Hugh Grigg · Greg McAndrews · Jonathan Pope · Pavel Dvorak · Parry Cadwallader · Jack Overstreet · Dan Emery · Erick Garcia · Moi Tong · Ben Slye · Brandon Sanchez · Logan Pauley · Ashlyn Weber · Michelle Birkenfeldt · Zach Herzog · Jazlyn Akaka · Salomé Vergne · Natalie Kuan · Jack Du · Erick Garcia · Cai Qingyang · Michael Moore · Liza Fowler · Mike Blood · Jacob Rodgers · Dominic Pote · Amani Core · Michelle Guerra · Amanda Gilbride · Callan Mossman · Jenna Salisbury · Audrey Brady · Jocelyn Kwong · Natalia Tun · Jake Liu ·

Special thanks to intern Jake Liu for all the excruciating pinyin and typo checking, as well as the structural refinements he helped with leading up to the publication of the B1 book.

Volunteer Editors

Some of these editors did tons of work on their own, while others emailed in issues they found. We thank them all for the hard work and valuable contributions!

· Nicholas Fiorentini · Noémi Németh · Betsy · HuaWei · Kryby · Jay · Luolimao · Trackpick · Morris · Philip Harding · Gintaras Valentukonis · Benedikt Rauh ·

Benedikt Rauh in particular was a huge help, sending in feedback and corrections for B1 and B2 grammar points as he found them. He saved our editors a lot of time, and we are indebted to him.

AllSet Teachers and Staff

· 马丽华 (Mǎ Lìhuá) · 李炯 (Lǐ Jiǒng) · 陈世霜 (Chén Shìshuāng) · 刘倖倖 (Liú Xìngxìng) · 赵以华 (Zhào Yǐhuá) · 于翠 (Yú Cuì) · 杨仁君 (Yáng Rénjùn) · 毛思平 (Máo Sīpíng) · 吴蒙蒙 (Wú Méngméng) · 贾贝茜 (Jiǎ Bèixī) · Parry Cadwallader · Michael Moore · John Pasden ·

Although many AllSet Learning employees have worked on the wiki over the years, both part-time and full-time staff, a special shout-out goes to 陈世霜 (Chén Shìshuāng), who has toiled tirelessly on the wiki behind the scenes for years without complaining. Big props also go to full-time staff 李炯 (Lǐ Jiǒng) and 马丽华 (Mǎ Lìhuá) for their unflinching dedication to repeated proofreading tasks as we completed the final checks of the print book.

Sincere thanks to Parry Cadwallader for making both the original wiki itself as well as the ebook version of the Chinese Grammar Wiki possible technically, with very little extra production work needed from the academic team. A big thank you also to Adam Abrams for all the layout work that went into creating the print version.

Other Credits

Our awesome book cover was designed by Anneke Garcia, someone we would never had met had her husband Erick not interned at AllSet Learning in Shanghai, once upon a time. Thanks so much for contributing your artistic touch to our products, Anneke!

The Chinese Grammar Wiki website and ebook both make use of the **Silk** icon set **FamFamFam.com**. The Chinese Grammar Wiki BOOK (print edition) uses a "structure" icon from **Pixeden.com**, as well as several icons from **Icomoon.io**.

References

This page is a bibliography for the Chinese Grammar Wiki. It lists all sources referenced extensively when researching the content of the Chinese Grammar Wiki grammar points.

- Chen, Ru 陈如, and Xiaoya Zhu 朱晓亚. *Hanyu Changyong Geshi 330 Li 汉语常用格式 330 例 [Common Chinese Patterns 330]*. Beijing: Beijing Foreign Languages Printing House, 2010. Print.
- Fang, Yuqing 房玉清. *Shiyong Hanyu Yufa 实用汉语语法 [A Practical Chinese Grammar]*. Beijing: Beijing Yuyan Daxue Chubanshe, 2008. Print.
- Herzberg, Qin Xue, and Larry Herzberg. *Basic Patterns of Chinese Grammar: A Student's Guide to Correct Structures and Common Errors*. Berkeley, CA: Stone Bridge, 2011. Print.
- Ho, Yong. *Intermediate Chinese*. New York: Hippocrene, 2004. Print.
- Li, Charles N., and Sandra A. Thompson. *Mandarin Chinese: A Functional Reference Grammar*. Berkeley: U of California, 1981. Print.
- Li, Dejin 李德津, and Meizhen Cheng 程美珍, eds. *Waiguoren Shiyong Hanyu Yufa 外国人实用汉语语法 [A Practical Chinese Grammar for Foreigners]*. Beijing: Beijing Yuyan Daxue Chubanshe, 1998. Print.
- Li, Luxing 李禄兴, Ling Zhang 张玲, and Juan Zhang 张娟. *Hanyu Yufa Baixiang Jianglian: Chuzhongji 汉语语法百项讲练：初中级 [Chinese Grammar–Broken Down Into 100 Items]*. Beijing: Beijing Language and Culture UP, 2011. Print.
- Li, Xiaoqi 李晓琪, ed. *Xiandai Hanyu Xuci Shouce 现代汉语虚词手册 [Modern Chinese Function Words Handbook]: A Guide to Function Words in Modern Chinese*. Beijing: Beijing Daxue Chubanshe, 2003. Print.
- Liu, Delian 刘德联, and Xiaoyu Liu 刘晓雨. *Hanyu Kouyu Changyong Jushi Lijie 汉语口语常用句式例解 [Exemplification of Common Sentence Patterns in Spoken Chinese]*. Ed. Liwen Song 宋立文. Beijing: Beijing Daxue Chubanshe, 2005. Print.
- Liu, Xun 刘珣, ed. *Xin Shiyong Hanyu Keben 新实用汉语课本 [New Practical Chinese Reader Textbook 1]*. Beijing: Beijing Language and Culture UP, 2002. Print.
- Liu, Xun 刘珣. *Xin Shiyong Hanyu Keben 新实用汉语课本 [New Practical Chinese Reader Textbook 2]*. Beijing: Beijing Language and Culture UP, 2002. Print.
- Liu, Xun 刘珣. *Xin Shiyong Hanyu Keben 新实用汉语课本 [New Practical Chinese Reader Textbook 3]*. Beijing: Beijing Language and Culture UP, 2003. Print.
- Liu, Yuehua 刘月华, Wenyu Pan 潘文娱, and Wei Gu 故桦. *Shiyong Xiandai Hanyu Yufa 实用现代汉语语法 [Practical Modern Chinese Grammar]*. Beijing: Shangwu Yinshuguan Chuban, 2001. Print.
- Liu, Yuehua, and Tao-chung Yao. *Zhongwen Tingshuo Duxie 中文听说读写 [Integrated Chinese Textbook Simplified Characters Level 1 Part 2]*. 3rd ed. Boston: Cheng & Tsui, 2009. Print.

- Liu, Yuehua, and Tao-chung Yao. *Zhongwen Tingshuo Duxie 中文听说读写 [Integrated Chinese Textbook Simplified Characters Level 2 Part 2]*. 3rd ed. Boston: Cheng & Tsui, 2009. Print.
- Liu, Yuehua, and Tao-chung Yao. *Zhongwen Tingshuo Duxie 中文听说读写 [Integrated Chinese Textbook Simplified Characters Level 1 Part 1]*. 3rd ed. Boston: Cheng & Tsui, 2009. Print.
- Liu, Yuehua, and Tao-chung Yao. *Zhongwen Tingshuo Duxie 中文听说读写 [Integrated Chinese Textbook Simplified Characters Level 2 Part 1]*. 3rd ed. Boston: Cheng & Tsui, 2009. Print.
- Lü, Shuxiang 吕叔湘, comp. *Xiandai Hanyu Babai Ci 现代汉语八百词 [800 Modern Chinese Words]*. Beijing: Shangwu Yinshuguan, 1980. Print.
- Ma, Jing-heng Sheng, and Claudia Ross. *Modern Mandarin Chinese Grammar: A Practical Guide*. London: Routledge, 2006. Print.
- Mu, Ling, Rongzhen Li, and Peisong Xu. *Chinese Usage Dictionary*. Center for Language Study, Yale University, 2004. Web.
- "Qingwen." Podcast audio content. *ChinesePod*. Web.
- Ross, Claudia. *Schaum's Outline of Chinese Grammar*. New York: McGraw-Hill, 2004. Print.
- Teng, Wen-Hua. *Yufa!: A Practical Guide to Mandarin Chinese Grammar*. London: Hodder Education, 2011. Print.
- *Xiandai Hanyu Xuci Lishi 现代汉语虚词例释 [Modern Chinese Function Words Examples and Explanations]*. Beijing: Shangwu Yinshuguan, 1957. Print.
- Yip, Po-ching, and Don Rimmington. *Chinese: An Essential Grammar*. London: Routledge, 1997. Print.
- Yip, Po-ching, Don Rimmington, Xiaoming Zhang, and Rachel Henson. *Basic Chinese: A Grammar and Workbook*. London: Routledge, 1998. Print.
- Zhang, Jing 张婧, ed. *Yufa Jingjiang Jinglian 语法精讲精练 [Practicing HSK Grammar]*. 1st ed. Beijing: Sinolingua, 2008. Print.
- Zhu, Xiaoxing 朱晓星, ed. *Jianming Hanyu Yufa Xuexi Shouce 简明汉语语法学习手册 [Simple Chinese Grammar Study Handbook]: Chinese Grammar without Tears*. Beijing: Beijing Daxue Chubanshe, 2002. Print.

Made in the USA
Columbia, SC
10 January 2021

30647432R00213